Hercules

SCOTT BATEMAN MBE

MICHAEL JOSEPH

PENGUIN MICHAEL JOSEPH

UK | USA | Canada | Ireland | Australia
India | New Zealand | South Africa

Penguin Michael Joseph is part of the Penguin Random House group of companies
whose addresses can be found at global.penguinrandomhouse.com

First published by Penguin Michael Joseph, 2024
002

Set in 13.5/16pt Garamond MT Std
Typeset by Jouve (UK), Milton Keynes
Printed and bound in Great Britain by Clays Ltd, Elcograf S.p.A.

The authorized representative in the EEA is Penguin Random House Ireland,
Morrison Chambers, 32 Nassau Street, Dublin D02 YH68

A CIP catalogue record for this book is available from the British Library

HARDBACK ISBN: 978–0–241–65558–0
TRADE PAPERBACK ISBN: 978–0–241–65559–7

www.greenpenguin.co.uk

This book is dedicated to the crews of Star Trek 3 and Hilton 22, who lost their lives doing what they loved, flying the Hercules at low level. Although the Hercules has flown off into the sunset, their sacrifice will never be forgotten.

Sans Peur

Contents

CONTENTS

Author's Note

Over an eighteen-year military career, I have been fortunate to be part of the Hercules family, and, as a member of the fabled 47 Squadron, to have filled three of the crew positions on the aircraft: air loadmaster, co-pilot and captain. While I have gathered all the stories you are about to read, and blended them with a couple of my own, I am by no means a gifted pilot or crew member. Many whose stories are to be found in this book are. Aviators operating at the pinnacle of tactical air transport. I am truly standing on the shoulders of giants.

Due to the sensitive nature of operations and tactics, some of the stories within these pages have had to be anonymized, and, in a few cases, slightly altered. This won't, I hope, detract from your reading enjoyment.

Welcome to *Hercules*. Pull up a sandbag and let's begin.

Scottie Bateman
May 2024

							UNLESS OTHERWISE SPECIFIED DIMENSIONS ARE IN INCHES	CONTRACT NO. IRAD	CODE C	LOCKHEED MARTIN AERONAUTICS COMPANY · MARIETTA, GEORGIA

TOLERANCES ON:
FRAC-TIONS ±1/16 | DECIMALS .X ±.1 .XX ±.03 .XXX ±.010 | ANGLES ±2°
INTERPRET DRAWING PER DS5025

ENGR A.MAURO 141007
CHKR J.MCKINNON 150112
STRESS E.MICKUS 150113
SUPV A.CLEMMER 150119

GENERAL ARRANGEMENT C-130J (MODEL 382J)

	3366830	382J-02G			
REGULATED ASSEMBLY NUMBER	DASH NO.	NEXT ASSEMBLY	USED ON	NEXT ASSY	USED ON
		APPLICATION		QTY REQD	

FABRICATE ITEMS ONLY WITH APPROVED MATERIALS IAW LMA-D0006 ENGINEERING PURCHASING SPECIFICATIONS

THIRD ANGLE PROJECTION

SIZE K | CAGE CODE 98897 | DWG NO. 3367526
SCALE 1/30 | SHEET 1 OF 1

LOADING CONDITION	STATIC STRUCT EXT NOSE	MAIN	WEIGHT-LB	C.G. LOCATION % M.A.C. APPROX	A	B	C
MAX TAKE-OFF GROSS WT.	4.8	2.4	155,000	25.0	42.9	40.7	455.2
OPERATING WT.	6.7	7.3	75,000	16.9	45.8	48.7	466.1

AIRFOIL SECTIONS AND DATA

WING NACA 64A318-ROOT
NACA 64A412-TIP
MAC 164.5
WING INCIDENCE – ROOT +3°
WING INCIDENCE – TIP 0°

HORIZONTAL STABILIZER
NACA 23012 (MODIFIED)

VERTICAL STABILIZER
NACA 64A015

TOTAL SURFACE AREAS AND ANGULAR MOVEMENTS

	SQ. FT.	
WING AREA	1745.5	(ASPECT RATIO 10.09)
AILERON AREA (2)	100	+15°-25°
AILERON TAB AREA (2)	5.8	+20°-20°
FLAP AREA (4)	342	+36°
HORIZONTAL TAIL	545	(ASPECT RATIO 5.02)
ELEVATOR (2)	155	+15°-40°
ELEVATOR TAB (2)	.19.9	+25°-6°
VERTICAL TAIL	300	(ASPECT RATIO 1.81)
RUDDER	75	35°L 35°R
RUDDER TAB	5	25°L 25°R

NOTE – DENOTES UPWARD MOVEMENT
+ DENOTES DOWNWARD MOVEMENT

⑤ MAIN TIRE PRESSURE, AS REQUIRED TO GIVE 33% TIRE DEFLECTION FOR EACH LOADING CONDITION OR 60 PSIG, WHICHEVER IS GREATER

④ EXTENSION WILL HAVE SUFFIX E STATIONS

③ NOSE TIRE PRESSURE IS 60 PSIG AT ALL GROSS WEIGHTS

② SUBJECT TO AIRFRAME LIMITATION OF 19,600 IN-LB INDICATED TORQUE

① MAX TAKE-OFF GROSS WT

NOTE:

ENGINES

④ ALLISON AE2100D3 TURBOPROP
② T.O. ESHP 4,591 MAXIMUM CONTINUOUS ESHP 4,591
POWER TURBINE RPM NORMAL 14,267
POWER TURBINE RPM LOW GROUND IDLE 10,329
GEAR RATIO 13.977:1

PROPELLERS

(4) DOWTY AEROSPACE R391 PROPELLERS
6 BLADE, COUNTERWEIGHTED, ELECTRO HYDRAULIC CONTROLLED
FULL FEATHERING-REVERSIBLE-CONSTANT SPEED

WEIGHT DATA (FOR DESIGN)

	MAX PAYLOAD MISSION (2.5G)
WEIGHT EMPTY	77,388
OPERATING EQPT & CREW	2,114
OPERATING WEIGHT	79,502
CARGO & TIEDOWN EQPT	37,850
ZERO FUEL WEIGHT	117,352
FUEL	37,648
TAKE-OFF GROSS WEIGHT	155,000

REFERENCE DRAWINGS

337003 BASIC DIMENSIONS – OUTER WING
337004 BASIC DIMENSIONS – WING CENTER SECTION
344478 DIAGRAM-CARGO DOOR & RAMP HOOK LOCATIONS
3305005 BASIC DIMENSIONS – FUSELAGE
3365268 EMPENNAGE INSTL
370500 WING JOINT – BASIC DIMENSIONS
3305028 JOINT DIAGRAM – 100 INCH FWD EXTENSION
3303503 BASIC DIMENSIONS – LANDING GEARS
3319207 JOINT DIAGRAM – 80 INCH AFT EXTENSION

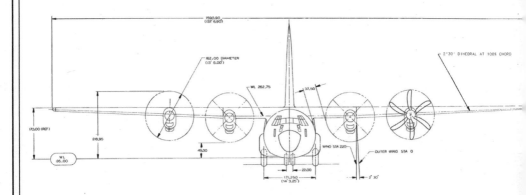

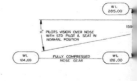

LOCKHEED MARTIN

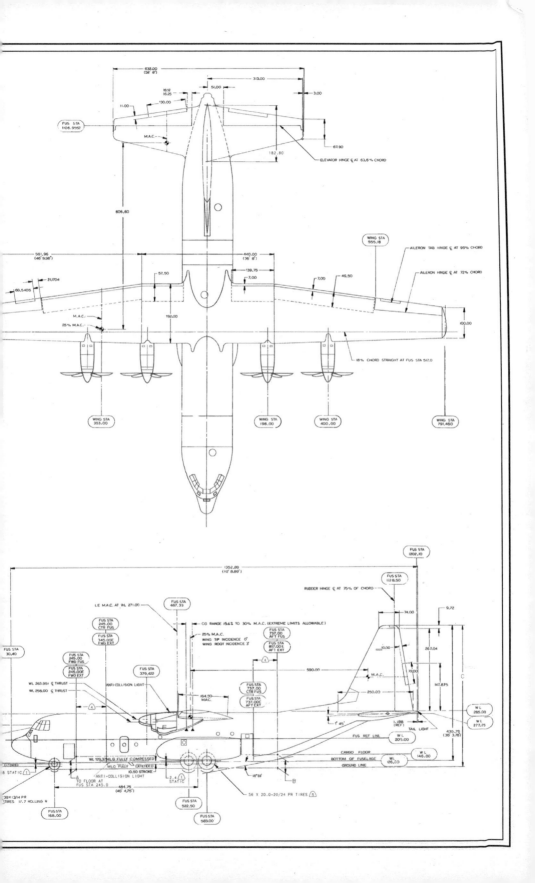

Sans Peur

Without Fear

1. Playing *HALO*

Hercules (/ˈhɜːrkjʊˌliːz/, US: /-kjə-/) is the Roman
equivalent of the Greek divine hero Heracles,
son of Jupiter and the mortal Alcmena. In classical
mythology, Hercules is famous for his strength
and for his numerous far-ranging adventures.

Wikipedia

Basra, Iraq, Early 2000s

Dawn is just breaking over the arid desert landscape, fingers of sunlight giving form to the undulating dunes, their tips swept by the downwash of a fleet of menacing-looking AV-14 Attack VTOLs, whose engines are making the very air vibrate. The atmosphere is becoming thick with clouds of spiralling dust and the noxious smell of jet fuel prickles in our nostrils. This is a perilous situation and none of us are confident of success.

From our elevated position, we can see a vast military bunker far below us. Rockets from the VTOL attack are now arcing skywards, before plunging into their targets with a reassuring crump. With the entire airfield complex wreathed in leaping dayglo-orange flames, personnel are scattering, like so many rats fleeing a burning nest.

We're tooled up, expecting trouble, and the tension is palpable as we slam our technical into gear and career towards the remote desert airstrip.

I raise my weapon to begin engaging targets ahead of us, but then – 'Boom!' – the windscreen explodes. My driver's been hit.

I shake my head in exasperation and turn to *Coolpilot54*. 'Fuck's sake, bro!' I berate him. 'Will you stop getting killed!'

We're three weeks into our five-week detachment in Basra, and definitely establishing a routine. There is lots of flying, of course, but we also have downtime to fill. So we watch endless DVDs, do the whole 'eat, sleep, fly, repeat' thing, and spend a great deal of time in the rudimentary gym. Though our favourite activity by far, we all agree, is to engage in combat of the 'first-person shooter' variety: challenging the other Herc crews to games of *HALO* on our Xboxes, having managed to hook them up between our tents. Nothing like a bit of a busman's holiday.

On the way back from dinner one evening, as I've done many times before, I mosey past the ops room to see what's planned for us the following day. I look at the board and see that next to my name there is no destination. Just a single, intriguing word, 'Spec'. Since our experience of this conflict so far is more *Groundhog Day* than *HALO*, this news is met by the team with a frisson of excitement.

Arriving at the operations facility early the next morning, I'm met by an old friend who has been recently promoted.

'Your special mission,' he informs me, 'is to take some "special" people into Baghdad. It is vitally important,' he adds, 'that they get there.'

I'm disappointed. So not one requiring any superior aviation skills, after all. In fact, all a bit mundane. Just a routine flying task, with secret passengers.

Or at least that's my thought until I read the TAF (weather forecast) for Baghdad. This day looks like it is going to be anything but routine; the forecast visibility is shockingly little in the shamal around Baghdad (the shamal being the desert equivalent of the mistral, with lots of added sand). Given the severity of the sandstorm, it's obvious that any attempt to land there will be way outside our peacetime norms.

'Have you seen the TAF?' I ask my new boss. 'This clearly isn't going to happen.' Only a mad person would contemplate such a rash act, I think but don't say.

At this point, I am politely taken aside and the command position is made a bit clearer. I must do it, so I *will* do it. I just have to find a way *to* do it. A rather one-sided Mexican stand-off then ensues. This task must be bloody important.

The compromise we agree on is that, as a qualified instructor, I will fly from Basra to Kuwait with an aircraft filled to the gunwales with fuel, and on the way we will carry out some 'continuation training approaches' to 'go around' at Baghdad, with 'no actual intention of landing there' – unless the opportunity presents itself, that is, in a gap in the appalling weather.

We both understand now what I have *really* been asked to do, without, of course, anyone saying so out loud. Backed into a corner, all I can think is that I am about to become that very mad person.

We arrive at the aircraft to find our passengers are

3

already settling in. I have no idea who they are, but they're definitely not your normal troops. For one thing, they all have rather splendid black beards; for another, rather than military garb, they are wearing clothes from the North Face summer catalogue collection.

'We need to get to Baghdad urgently,' their leader tells me, 'so we can get helicopters into the Green Zone, so we can carry out a job.'

Forty minutes later, on being handed over to the Baghdad controller we announce that we, Surf 28, request to carry out some practice approaches to the airfield before proceeding on to Kuwait.

'Not possible,' the controller informs us. Then, to no one's surprise, adds, 'The aerodrome is closed due to severe weather.'

I leave a short pause, then ask if we can hold in the vicinity instead, till the weather improves. Which, with a quick glance below us revealing a maelstrom of sand engulfing Baghdad, it obviously shows no sign of doing.

'How long are you willing to hold for?' they ask.

'Sixteen hours,' we reply. Which is obviously bonkers.

'No,' they respond, not unreasonably.

I then inform them that we will be taking up the hold anyway, and get a grudging, 'Roger.' And when it becomes obvious that, incredibly, we don't appear to be bluffing, an American voice can be heard on the radio, clearing us for a training approach, as requested. I suspect they must have at least an inkling of what's *really* happening because who does training approaches in the middle of a war zone?

Not us. We have every intention of landing. Others

wouldn't. The vast majority of others wouldn't. Now we're playing *HALO* for real. (Be careful what you wish for.)

Luckily, the Hercules C-130J is an amazing aircraft. And the tempo of operational flying – we are doing this seven days a week, day and night – means that it feels like a second home. It's so responsive that it's like an extension of your body, so much so that you can make it do almost anything you want with complete confidence. Today, though, we are going to need a little tech help to get us where we want to go (i.e. down), and that means radar.

The weather radar in the C-130J is the same as is fitted to the F-16 fighter jet for target mapping, and, when offset slightly from what you want to map, it's great for extremely accurate ground mapping. Before leaving Basra, therefore, we'd already decided that we would carry out a slightly offset approach and then use the radar to identify the runway and surrounding features. We've played with it during good weather, on several occasions, so why not use it now in anger? It at least gives us a Plan A, if not a Plan B.

'Surf 28,' says the Arab-sounding air traffic controller, 'you are cleared for your practice approach and go-round.'

Here goes nothing then. We duly start our descent, which takes us straight down into the very middle of the sandstorm, and it gets very dark very, very quickly; so dark, in fact, that it feels as if the Herc has been enveloped by a sheet of red-tinted paper, and the symbology in the head up display starts getting brighter.

I call to the loadie on the intercom. 'Can you come up and watch the instruments for us?' We need an extra set of eyes now, because the co-pilot and I don't have enough – all our focus needs to be on what's going on outside, and then some.

'Shout out anything that looks out of place,' I tell him once he's joined us. 'Especially if you think we're going to kill you.'

I'm only half joking. Somehow we have to find the runway in all this.

The first sweep of the radar and we are more than surprised; despite the interference of many tons of swirling airborne sand, our electronic eye can see it, even if our real ones cannot. The Master Chief is obviously looking out for us. No need to respawn today.

'Fifty . . .'

'Thirty . . .'

'Twenty . . .'

'I've got it!' I announce, as the edge of the runway finally comes into view. There is an audible exhalation of our collective breath.

We arrive with a thump. It's not pretty, but at least we are down. Today, at least, it's not going to be Game Over. I select reverse and brake hard; barrelling through a sandstorm is generally never recommended, especially in a fifty-ton aeroplane. Though air traffic control are now becoming a bit anxious; since we're on the ground, they obviously haven't heard us fly overhead on the go-around. 'Surf 28,' they keep asking, 'what is your position?'

My co-pilot answers with commendable calm. 'Due to a technical emergency on approach,' he lies, 'we have had to continue to land. We are now on the runway, stopped on the ground, and are requesting taxi instructions.'

The tower controller, who has only cleared us for a

training approach to go around, is, understandably, fucking furious. 'I cannot *see* the ground!' they shout back.

Once they've calmed down enough to give us instructions, it takes us longer to taxi to the northwest military ramp – some forty-five minutes – than it has for the flight here from Basra.

On arrival at the ramp, we are met by an RAF movements officer, who, under a head-to-toe covering of fine desert sand, is dressed like a character from *Star Wars*.

'Where have you come from?' he asks me, and I can tell from his expression that by 'where' he means 'Which part of this airfield?'

'Basra,' I tell him. He gapes at me in shock. 'I have a special team on board,' I add, 'in need of an urgent helicopter transfer to the Green Zone, to do a "job".'

He is aghast. 'The helicopter crews stacked for the day hours ago,' he informs me. Because nobody, but nobody, would be mad enough to go flying in this appalling weather.

He is wrong, of course.

A few of us are . . .

2. The Twelve Labours

I am standing in a bar, the small space tightly packed with people; as chat buzzes around the room in competition with the blaring music, the smell of beer is heavy on the air. It could be any bar across the country in the run-up to Christmas, but this one is different: almost everyone is wearing combat uniform or flying suits. For this is something special. An event called Guinness and Mince Pies, a Christmas party held annually by 47 Squadron – *my* squadron – to thank those who have supported them throughout the year. It is also a chance for old hands and veterans to return and, at least for a short period, to feel young again, as we swap our stories of derring-do.

This year's celebration, however, feels poignant. The squadron is due to disband in 2023, so it's the last of these gatherings we'll be attending for a while. It's the close of a big chapter in all our lives, so, despite the high spirits and buoyant festive mood, there is a tinge of sadness and emotion to our reminiscences. But this gathering doesn't just mark the ending of 47 Squadron. It's also about the ending of another, arguably even more historic, era. That of our beloved 'Fat Albert'.

For over fifty years, the Royal Air Force has had a constant. In every single conflict, skirmish, or major overseas operation the UK has been part of – and in some that it hasn't, at least officially – it has had the Lockheed Martin

C-130 Hercules, the lump of aluminium that binds all of us together. As the RAF sunsets this capability, it is only fair that we celebrate the engineering and innovation that has served us so well for over five decades. We have had fun times and dangerous times, and also some very sad times, as our own personal Hercules stories have been written.

And, for every one of us, it's been quite a ride.

The first labour of Hercules was to slay the Nemean Lion, who was causing havoc to the farms and farmers of Nemea. My own labours, on the way to becoming a Hercules pilot, were naturally a little less life or death. It's worth noting, however, that, as a boy growing up in Scotland, becoming a Hercules pilot couldn't have been further from my thoughts. Yes, I wanted to become a pilot, but a very different kind of pilot. After all, what was remotely heroic about flying what I regarded as an airborne removals van?

For as long as I can remember, I have always had a passion for all things aviation and, in particular, the RAF. My first memory of flying was as a seven-year-old driving from Dundee down to Gatwick – an adventure in itself – to board a Boeing 720 bound for Malta, where we were headed on a family holiday. I was so excited I was literally bouncing in my plane seat, driving everyone mad for almost the entire flight. In fact, my main memory of the holiday was that for much of it all I could think about was the excitement of the journey home.

A few years later, my early fascination was cemented when my dad took me by train to RAF Leuchars, near

Dundee, to visit their 'Battle of Britain at Home' day. The opportunity to sit in a Lightning sealed the deal. I was hooked, and though I had no idea how to go about it, I knew my future: I was going to be a fighter pilot.

My dad, who worked in oil refining and loved what he did, was thrilled that I too had found a passion and a focus, and to get me on the right track he went on to spend a small fortune on limited-edition posters and squadron prints. Mum thought it an extravagance, but it helped keep the flame alive and, in 1984, at the age of thirteen years and three months (the youngest you were allowed to), I joined the Air Cadets in Dundee.

As well as our twice-weekly meetings, where we learned aviation-related academic subjects, the Air Cadets gave me the opportunity to participate in some amazing annual camps, one of which was at RAF Lossiemouth, on the northeast coast of Scotland, where they had a Sea King rescue helicopter and several ancient Avro Shackletons, as well as Buccaneers.

I was fortunate to be picked to spend a day with one of the rescue crews and, back then, that meant flying in the helicopter. Many who know me now will be surprised at this, as these days I have a pathological and not at all irrational fear of helicopters. But as a teenager, with typical teenage bravado, I was beyond excited to be on board this yellow-painted paraffin-fuelled canary (as these rescue helicopters were affectionately known), just as I suspect our new Prince of Wales might have felt when he first tried them.

During the day with the crew, we flew the Sea King at low level, and did some practice winching with a trawler, lowering a winchman down to the deck and then picking him up again a few minutes later. We even landed in someone's back garden at one point, so the winch operator could drop a parcel off to his wife. We didn't know (and obviously didn't dare ask) what was in it, but given that it was a plain brown jiffy bag and no one offered to enlighten us, speculation was rife.

This, to me, felt like the coolest job ever, and all my thoughts of flying a fast jet were now consigned to the bin; it was now rescue helicopters all the way. It felt perfect, combining my love of flying with hillwalking, something I was into in a big way, loving the fresh air, the dramatic scenery and, most of all, the solitude; the freedom to think my important teenage thoughts.

Later in the camp, I was given the opportunity to fly in one of the Shackletons. A direct descendant of the Lancaster, the Shackleton was an aircraft that was truly from the World War II era, with four big propeller engines, and, being a 'taildragger', I thought it looked like a Lancaster. I was plonked in a seat with a view at the front of the aircraft and, with the exception of a pee break, stayed in place for some five hours as the crew flew around Scotland at about 5,000 feet, doing whatever they were doing, which was never really made clear. The views were spectacular but, compared to the excitement of being on the paraffin canary, the job itself seemed very dull to me. I vowed that day that I would never want to fly a multi-engine aircraft because it was so mundane. Oh, how wrong I would turn out to be.

The Harris Academy – my then high school – was a fine educational institution and provided me with all the tools to be successful. So said the brochure, and I know it to be true. It was just that, at the time, I lacked both the wisdom to appreciate it and the emotional maturity to make use of it. Despite having managed to pass a respectable eight O grades, the distractions of my teens (mostly beer, girls and showing off in my dad's 'champagne'-coloured Austin Ambassador) meant that I had no passes at Highers.

That university was off the table was no issue, however, because RAF officer training only required five O grades; so, as soon as I could, I applied to become a pilot and awaited my interviews at the careers office in Dundee. Though I had by now added 'realist' to my modest skill set. Knowing full well that few ever made it as pilots, I took the lead from several of my air cadet friends and applied to the police service as well.

On the day of the RAF interview, I was the most nervous I had ever been in my young life. There was a dream at stake, after all, and I had done everything in my power to ensure I had the best chance of getting through to RAF Biggin Hill and the Officer and Aircrew Selection Centre (OASC), including reading my bodyweight in textbooks and scouring broadsheet newspapers, plus practising every question I thought might conceivably come up.

I was met by a sergeant, who ushered me into a room with an officer, where I was asked some questions about myself and my career aspirations. They also asked, as they would, if I'd considered any other roles, and I answered with a resounding 'no'. It was aircrew or nothing for me. I wanted to fly. And I wanted them to know just how much.

My confidence when Dad picked me up wasn't entirely misplaced, either. In just over a week, I received my invite to Biggin Hill and to a selection process that was days long, and also pretty complex. Bring it on, I thought airily. I can do this.

That said, I was still a little wet behind the ears. Leaving Scotland on my own was a bit daunting. These were different times, and I had never really travelled without my family, or as part of a group like the Air Cadets. Just venturing into London and then out the other side was a pretty big deal for me. So it was with a sense of satisfaction that I negotiated Bromley South Station, and finally made it to RAF Biggin Hill.

Once installed in the accommodation, and having said hello to my cohort of selectees, I settled in for a night of serious study, to ensure I was prepped for the morning. And I was right to be conscientious, because the following day I was subjected to a barrage of exams and computer-based tests, and measured and poked by medics for what felt like hours. In between these various tests, we returned to a central reception area where, every so often, the receptionist, an RAF airman, would call a name and direct its owner to the second door on the left.

This, I learned early on, was definitely not a good thing. Unlike a modern airliner, where turning left means first class, that door meant the opposite – you were not going forward to the next stage. So once 5 p.m. came around and I hadn't been directed through it, my relief was intense. Boom! I'd survived to fight another day!

Just before I'd set off, my dad had slipped me a £20 note: a substantial sum of money back in those days. 'For emergencies,' he'd told me. 'In case you need to buy yourself some snacks or are in the bar and want to buy someone a beer.' And there was indeed a bar area, near the candidate's cornered-off area of the airmen's dining room. However, determined not to squander any opportunity to study by hanging around in a bar drinking, I scurried back to my room and my books. Little did I know – and would only find out on the train on the way home – that the socializing was also a part of the selection process; seeing the candidates in a social environment was just as important as any test they put us through during the day. Thankfully, they didn't hold it against me.

Day two was dominated by what are still colloquially known as 'shark-infested custard problems', a mix of reasonably complex team-building conundrums that we were each required in turn to try and resolve as a leader, working with a team of other candidates. They were an opportunity to show leadership, followership and emotional intelligence, after which we faced desktop versions of the same type of problems, both as an individual and as a team.

To my delight, I had avoided the 'door of doom' once again, and, at the end of this day, we were all given a letter explaining what would come next, including the fact that, whether positive or negative, our results would take a while to arrive. I then returned home, and on the train back, just as we were passing Alnwick, I saw an RAF Sea King flying up the coast. I let myself dream, just a little. One day that could be *me*.

I returned to good news: the police had accepted me. Assuming my RAF dream turned out to be short-lived, I at least had employment; I was to start training at the Scottish Police College in five weeks. Which would mean a big decision, but I still had a few weeks' grace. I wasn't ready to give up on the RAF just yet.

The clock continued to tick, however, and with three weeks already passed, I knew it would be wrong of me to procrastinate further. So I decided, with just a little family pressure, to do the sensible thing and accept the police job. After all, as things stood, I had no viable alternative and I needed to stand on my own two feet. But just a week later, and with my flying dream on indefinite hold now, Dad called me in from the garden to take a call from 'some RAF chap'.

The chap in question was a wing commander from OASC, and he wanted to know, if I wasn't selected for pilot, whether I would consider any other role, such as airman aircrew. It was obvious that I hadn't made the grade, and though I knew I should feel grateful that they were considering me for something else, I was gutted. So I told the wing commander that it was pilot or bust for me, and resigned myself to heading off to police college.

Then came the letter, in an 'On Her Majesty's Service' brown envelope. I assumed, given our conversation, it would be bad news. Yet I opened it to find that they had offered me a post anyway – not as a pilot, but as sergeant aircrew air loadmaster.

It's amazing how a young mind can change in an instant. For all my 'pilot or bust' nonsense, I felt nothing but elated; I could still be on rescue helicopters, not as a pilot but as a winchman, and suddenly that didn't seem so bad after all. In fact, it made me realize just how badly I wanted to be in blue – not police blue, but RAF blue.

I started my six weeks of initial training at RAF Swinderby on 12 June 1990. Because of my years in the Air

Cadets, which had been exactly like this, I had a huge advantage, and sailed through recruit training. I also somehow managed to be awarded the trophy for best recruit.

None of that, however, was on my mind – far from it – when I arrived at RAF Finningley for the Airman Aircrew Initial Training Course. This was a whole different level. Where I'd coasted initially, now I struggled to keep up. The basic problem was not only that I lacked sufficient maturity, but that I also lacked the maturity to accept my deficiencies: in short, that I was neither mentally or physically equipped for this course. No wonder my distress when, having done the entire course, I was told I didn't meet the standard, and would be recoursed back to the beginning.

The blow was huge. I was lost. Was the RAF really for me, after all?

I had a week until the start of the next (same) course and sought the counsel of Jack Daniels on several occasions, in the Ritzy nightclub and an eclectic bar called Camelots, in Doncaster. It was there, one night, that I fell in with the medical staff who support the AAITC on their outdoor activities, and one of the nurses offered me a shoulder to air my woes. I owe her: she gave me advice that allowed me to pick myself up and keep moving forward in the face of what seemed a life-changing catastrophe. It wasn't an earth-shattering revelation, but it was such sound and wise counsel that I still use it as my mantra today. It was, in brief, that nothing is ever as bad as you think it is, nobody else probably cares, and nothing will change unless you change it yourself.

I stopped moping and vacillating and swallowed my pride, and two days later I started again. This time, my wounds licked and important lessons learned, I passed the AAITC eight weeks later. To this day, I have never done anything so mentally and physically demanding. It taught me a lot about myself and also made me realize that OASC had been correct: I was not equipped to be a pilot at eighteen.

Now a sergeant, I started my training as an air load-master but, on day one at the school, it was bad news. The first Gulf War was a couple of months in and seeing huge demand being put on the Chinook fleet; we were all told that we would be doing a short rotary course to be streamed to the Chinook as helicopter crewmen.

Once again, I was despondent. I had always wanted to be a search and rescue guy. I wanted to help people stranded in the mountains, have adventures, be heroic – not be crew on a lumbering support helicopter. But at least we were off to war, which was obviously what we'd trained for; so, putting aside my disappointment, I started in earnest that morning to become a helicopter crewman.

The bad news, however, did not stop there. On day three of the course, we were told that, 'due to competing demands', there were going to be some further changes. And they were big ones: two of us wouldn't even end up as helicopter crew. No, we'd be going to the Hercules.

This was my worst nightmare. Not just a lumbering support helicopter, potentially a lumbering support *plane*. Me, who had vowed, after my brain-numbing experience on that Shackleton, that I would never, *ever*, become a fixed-wing guy. I hoped some other young airmen, who didn't care as much as I did, would be the ones whose names were called out that day.

But of course they weren't. It was me and one other equally unhappy guy selected for the Herc, and duly fast-tracked to meet a training slot in just a few weeks' time, on the ponderously named Hercules Operational Conversion Unit.

I could not have felt more miserable. While the 'heroes' were going to fly the search and rescue and support choppers, what were we going to be? The delivery guys. And even worse, we were all 'fast-tracked' together, to grasp the fundamentals before transferring to our respective aircraft-specific conversion units, so I was reminded of this fact every day. While others were learning exciting stuff, such as how to undersling loads beneath their helicopters, we were learning . . . the principles of food hygiene.

And didn't everyone know it. I quickly discovered that we were referred to as the 'tea and coffee queens'. Trainee helicopter crewmen would come into the school crew room and never miss the chance to let us know they'd like two sugars, please.

I put a brave face on it, because you had to, but I was gutted. My dream of being a search and rescue helicopter winchman was dissolving faster than the sugar in that bloody tea. I felt more disappointed than I'd ever been in my young life, and even questioned whether an air force that had so cruelly denied me my dream was the right place for me.

Little did I know that I was, in fact, joining the ranks of some of the most incredible, heroic people I would ever encounter. Still less did I realize that I had just begun what would become a lifelong love affair. With the most iconic military aircraft ever built.

3. An Icon Is Born

'Smile. We're going to build a thousand of these.'

Stanley Beltz, 1911–1955
Lockheed Martin test pilot

Untroubled by the fact that, some thirty-six years in the future, a misguided young RAF airman would dismiss it so rudely, the first C-130 Hercules rolled off the production line in 1954, an aircraft that would go on to become one of the most important in aviation history.

A little under five years after the end of World War II, the USA was entering the Korean War, and found its trusty C-47 Skytrain – one of Eisenhower's five World War II-winning weapons – was now falling short. As things stood, the US Air Force had to use their C-47s in combination with their much larger C-124 aircraft based in Japan, in a two-step 'spoke and hub' model, whereas the ideal would be a single aircraft-type with the capability to airlift combat troops over medium distances and also deliver them to small, rough airfields.

Some new thinking was clearly needed and several big aviation firms, including Lockheed, Boeing, Douglas and Fairchild, all set to work. Each factory had the same specifications, issued by the USAF, for a new, currently only theoretical, 'Swiss army knife' of tactical airlifters. At that point, the specifications given were so challenging that the Lockheed Martin engineers honestly didn't think they could get anywhere near them, either in terms of performance or manoeuvrability. They tried, though, putting together a proposal using all the latest technologies, including new turboprop engines. This complicated and relatively new jet technology was challenging to incorporate on a large transport propeller aircraft, but would turn out to be the key to their success.

The turboprop is a jet engine that powers a propeller, a big change from the piston engines that powered the DC-3, its military C-47 variant and other early transport aircraft. Turboprops work at a constant speed, but the props can be twisted at their root in order to provide more or less power, as required by the pilot. Crucially, the blades can also be turned right around in order to provide reverse thrust – something which would give the C-130 such an advantage over any of its predecessors. A new era in tactical air transport was born.

In July 1951, the aerospace giant that was Lockheed had by now seen off the competition, and was given the green light to build and fly two of its experimental transport aircraft, which it would later name Hercules in homage to the Roman god known for his strength and many adventures. Then, on 23 August 1954, test pilots Stanley Beltz and Roy Wimmer started up the first one and tentatively taxied it from the terminal at Burbank Airport, California.

For its time – for *any* time – the Hercules was an arresting, slightly odd-looking aircraft, but then it was never intended to be a show pony. Its looks were a reflection of its capabilities. Its enormous nose housed an astonishing twenty-three cockpit windows, allowing the crew maximum visibility even in steep and sticky situations, and the wings were set high (in line with the top rather than the midline of the fuselage) to allow the Herc to operate from even the roughest airfields. It wasn't slick, it wasn't sleek, and it certainly wasn't pretty, but it was fast (it could reach speeds of 360 miles per hour) and, with its low centre of gravity, it could outperform any comparable machine that had come before it. With those four engines, moreover, it also had sufficient surplus power to pressurize the enormous 40,000-pound freight bay — something that would enable it to operate efficiently at high altitudes.

The noise those engines made, everyone recalled, was incredible: a low hum that has since become the signature of the Hercules. But on that day, all that the assembled mechanics and engineers could do was look on and pray that it was as good as it sounded; that they had got it right, and it would live up to their faith in it.

As the aircraft turned and taxied onto the runway, the noise began building, then it leapt forward, much faster than anyone was expecting. The ugly duckling of the Lockheed stable was moving! Those on the ground thought that Stanley was bringing the nose up way too early, but then the aircraft lifted off, and roared magnificently past everyone standing on the flight line.

Mouths dropped open in shock. The first C-130 Hercules had taken off, and it had only taken 855 feet for it to become airborne! (For comparison, that was less than a fifth of the distance normally required by aircraft of similar size.)

Beltz probably had an inkling about the calibre of air-craft he was taking up for its maiden flight. He's quoted as having said afterwards that 'she's a real flying machine. I could land it crossways on the runway if I had to.'

Hercules was clearly going to be a bigger game-changer than anyone had thought – a military aircraft that could land and take off almost anywhere. An aircraft that, at least in theory, was so strong and powerful that it could even land on one engine in a crisis. An aircraft that would go on to prove its worth for seven decades.

Beltz reckoned they'd sell a thousand. In fact, they went on to sell over 2,500.

Rather older than the aircraft that would come to be so associated with it, 47 Squadron was the only one in the RAF to be entirely equipped with the C-130 Hercules, since being allocated its first ones back in 1969.

The squadron itself is far older. Formed in Beverley, Yorkshire, in 1916, as a reconnaissance squadron, the unit also holds the unique accolade of being the only RAF squadron ever to have fought under its own flag, a tricolour which now adorns the shoulder of those who serve on it.

The squadron has a rich history, which spans almost the entire life of the Royal Air Force. One of the only excep-tions was during the Russian Civil War in 1919–20, when the squadron was hastily, and temporarily, disbanded, and redesignated 'A Flight'.

British involvement in a civil war on foreign territory was obviously politically sensitive, so this 'rebrand', which happened not long after the squadron was deployed to support the White Army, was – in what would turn out to be a sign of things to come – all part of a covert operation. All personnel were personally recruited and conveyed to Russia by Squadron Leader (later Air Vice-Marshal) Ray Collishaw, and since all were volunteers (so technically not RAF crew) and no longer flying under a British flag, it was possible for it to be truthfully announced in the House of Commons that 'no RAF squadron is involved in a foreign civil war'.

The participation of British troops in the Russian Civil War was, in fact, extensive. In the early stages, Collishaw was, incredibly, even appointed temporary governor of Crimea, and A Flight formed the sole aviation support for one million soldiers, organized into three armies. Historically, it also achieved a couple of air firsts. It sank nineteen out of twenty-three armed Red Army gunboats, and, having comprehensively decimated the opposing ground forces, killed off the use of a cavalry as a viable weapon. It was also the only RAF squadron in recorded history to conduct a campaign without any whisky – but, unsurprisingly, not without vodka.

After mounting political pressure in the UK, A Flight was recalled in early 1920, so it avoided the final showdown of the Russian Civil War, but its red, white and blue tricolour lives on. Though with the white having darkened to yellow in the harsh Russian climate, a new colour scheme of red, blue and yellow was adopted from then on.

The squadron was re-formed in 1920 and spent much of the period between World Wars I and II in East Africa and the Mediterranean. This included Egypt and Sudan, where it was mostly engaged in reconnaissance, and where the squadron's official and unofficial emblems have their roots.

While 47 Squadron is unique within the RAF in having its own flag, like all squadrons it also has its own official crest and standard. 'Squadron standards' were introduced in 1943, and to be eligible squadrons had to have twenty-five years' standing, or the monarch's appreciation for outstanding operations. This is the squadron's official flag, and is what was laid up in the rotunda of RAF College Cranwell, in September 2023, after 47 disbanded. It will remain there until a new role is found for the squadron and the new team comes to collect it.

The official crest shows a demoiselle crane on a background of white and blue water, which represents the White and Blue Nile rivers, whose confluence is at the city of Khartoum. The Latin legend, 'The name of the Nile will be an omen of your strength', adorns it. The unofficial badge, which predates the official one, shows a sun rising over a pyramid with the legend *Sans Peur*, meaning 'Not Afraid' or 'Without Fear'. It also has the word *Khartoum* underneath.

After spending World War II based in East Africa, in 1946 the squadron left behind its legacy of flying fighter bombers and reconnaissance aircraft and was equipped as a transport squadron instead. Returning to the UK, it first flew converted Halifax bombers, before switching to the more modern Hastings, which were rushed into service to allow the unit to support the Berlin Airlift in 1948. The aircraft mainly carried coal into the city, delivering 22,000 tons across the air bridge, in 3,000 sorties.

In 1956, 47 Squadron was the first in the RAF to equip with the new Blackburn Beverley transport aircraft, perhaps a nod to its roots in the Yorkshire town. This aircraft served the country until late 1967, when it and, as a result, the squadron were both disbanded.

A few months later, in early 1968, 47 Squadron re-formed in its new home of RAF Fairford, in order to embark on what would become a fifty-four-year relationship with the Lockheed Martin C-130 Hercules. The squadron moved to RAF Lyneham in September 1971, a few months after my birth, and some twenty years later I walked through the door of that very unit to start my first operational tour.

Since I have left the RAF and the Hercules fleet, RAF Lyneham has closed, and the fleet has significantly reduced in number and is now focused on its delivery of niche capabilities in support of demanding operations in theatres such as Afghanistan and Syria. This has naturally changed the structure of the squadron. And while the current balance is classified, it is likely the bias is leaning towards crews having the training and ability to support esoteric capabilities; all a bit more James Bond these days, rather than Pickfords removals van.

Everyone who has been part of any RAF Squadron always feels an affinity with the first one they ever served on. It feels like your original RAF family and your spiritual home. 47 Squadron is more than that to me, though. It is a truly special place; one with a camaraderie that I have never seen anywhere else. It is globally recognized; it has the unique flag that unifies everyone connected to it, and, with that, a joint identity they are proud to represent.

I was hugely privileged to serve in three roles on the squadron and work with and for some amazing people. Like me, these are people who truly love the Hercules.

Who see it not just as an aircraft, but as if it is a living, breathing part of the squadron family and, it goes without saying, one as equally cherished. It's hard to really understand the depth of this bond until you leave the fold and find yourself on the outside looking in – no longer part of the current collective, but still a member of the wider 47 Squadron family who appear occasionally, to touch base and reminisce about the past.

Probably anyone in any military squadron anywhere has felt much the same about their situation, but it's my belief that the unique chemistry between a certain extraordinary squadron and a certain extraordinary plane created a marriage made in heaven.

But I would say that, wouldn't I?

4. International Rescue

Anyone who has ever seen the iconic 60s children's TV puppet show *Thunderbirds* will know that Thunderbird 2, piloted by the most steely nerved of the Tracy brothers, Virgil, bears more than a passing resemblance to a Hercules. Though apparently never based on any specific real-world aircraft, the supersonic jet had lots of nods to the C-130, from the nose cone, and the styling, to the cavernous freight bay. In one key design feature, however, Gerry and Sylvia Anderson's creation differed. In order to operate out of Tracy Island, with its minuscule landing strip, Thunderbird 2 was fitted with the vertical take-off and landing technology (VTOL) that had been developed for military use in the 1950s and would go on to be first seen in reality in 1967, in the iconic Harrier jump jet.

Back in the real world, the Hercules wasn't endowed with such futuristic bolt-ons, but the aircraft that was designed for the Korean War, and would dominate in the Vietnam one, was soon performing astonishing feats. The footage of Lieutenant James H. Flatley III landing a KC-130F on the carrier USS *Forrestal* in November 1963 has been viewed tens of thousands of times for good reason; it was, arguably, the Hercules' most astonishing exploit yet.

Flatley's landing is the stuff of aviation legend, not least because he didn't perform this feat just once; in order to demonstrate the Herc's suitability to deliver heavy and/or outsized loads to ships at sea, he did it successfully a full *twenty-one* times, testing weights up to fifty-five tons. And though it was ultimately decided that it was impractical to roll this capability out – mostly due to space constraints on the carrier deck – Lieutenant Flatley still entered the aviation record books, as landing the largest and heaviest aircraft on a carrier – a record that still stands today.

He also made it look easy. Which it isn't.

Pilots are regularly tested and challenged in the simulator building, with every scenario you can think of, as well as some you probably can't. Unlike our civilian counterparts, who are normally tested on their key skills every six months to a year, RAF pilots see themselves in the simulator sometimes three or four times a month, honing both their skills and their breadth of knowledge about the aircraft they fly, as well as its limitations, and their own. From having a fire on board that necessitates ditching in the ocean, to complex battle damage that has knocked out hydraulic systems, they are always expected to work as a team to come up with a solution that would be largely survivable. But there is usually time allotted to try and push pilots' boundaries, and one of the scenarios that everyone always wants to try is to replicate Flatley's record-breaking carrier-landing feat. It was, after all, the stuff of any teenaged air cadet's dreams, mine included.

Fast-forward to 2005, and, by this time having done many natural-strip landings in the C-130, I felt rather more confident in my abilities. I was an experienced driver now. How hard could it be?

My plan for successfully landing on the carrier was to

use the same technique we preferred for these short-field operations; so, once the simulator instructor had positioned me ten miles from the carrier, I reduced the thrust and, as the electronic engine noise in the simulator diminished, watched the airspeed indicator like a hawk.

Slowing through 180 knots, it was time for some flaps to be deployed.

'Flaps 50,' I announced, and as the co-pilot moved the lever I felt the aircraft pitch and climb a little, as the high lift of the extra angle took effect.

The speed now falling through 165 knots, I asked for 'gear down'. There was a clunk, and the gear indicators switched, to show the wheels were now moving. So far, so good. That was until we got a little closer to the carrier.

As we approached 150 knots I increased the power, to stabilize the aircraft at that speed. All this time, I had, of course, been looking out of the window. And it was only now apparent that what I'd thought was some sort of mark on the glass was, in fact, the aircraft carrier I was aiming for. *My god*, I thought. *It's like a postage stamp!* A postage stamp floating above a grey and uninviting sea.

At about four miles from the carrier, the true scale of the task now becoming even more apparent, I let the speed trickle back through 145 knots.

'100 flap,' I asked, and the aircraft duly pitched forward, but, with back pressure on the column and a little more power, I arrested the aircraft's temptation to descend until we reached 130 knots, at which point we were committed – towards putting our arses on the postage stamp.

By this time I had gone uncharacteristically quiet. So the flight engineer, having realized just how hard I was working to try and land on the right place on the carrier, started reading out the aircraft's speed periodically, while the navigator called out height against distance to go. Meanwhile, still transfixed on the miniature-sized carrier, I began to realize that this might not work after all.

The C-130 has two sets of speeds for take-off and landing: a normal set that conform to the safety regimes of something called 'performance A', which is used by airliners for certification purposes all over the world and gives reasonable safety margins during these critical phases of flight. The second are referred to as the 'tactical speeds', and significantly lessen these margins for take-off and landing in a military scenario. A normal take-off speed at a mid-weight (fifty-seven tons) would be around 106 knots, with the tactical speed being maybe ninety-eight knots. This would greatly reduce the ground roll required, but would not take into consideration an engine failure, which means it comes with significant risk.

In terms of landing the aircraft, at typical weights (fifty-four tons) the landing speed would be around 121 knots, with a tactical speed of ninety-eight knots. The lower speed relies on using full flap with power on, so that the props blow more air over the wing, and thus provide more lift, which results in a slightly flatter approach. This means the aircraft can't be conventionally landed – i.e. powered off – instead, it is flown *with* power, right to touch down, which often results in a firm arrival at the destination.

The advantage of this is probably obvious. The lower touchdown speed would reduce the landing ground roll considerably, enabling us to stop before we went swimming – even if, in my case, it would only be a virtual dip. Despite having all of this knowledge in my head to reassure me, less reassuring was that although the carrier deck was getting very close, it was not getting as big as I had hoped. Though this was the sim, I was now really sweating, realizing I might have bitten off a little more than I could chew, and that the results of my misplaced over-confidence were surely about to come home to roost.

Nothing for it but to press on and attempt it, however, and, at less than a mile, and with everything at least looking relatively stable, I decided to start to let the speed begin to reduce towards the ninety-eight knots I was targeting at touchdown. Tiny movements on the throttle and the column were the order of the day now if I was to keep the rate of descent the same, with the speed decaying.

'Half a mile,' the nav called. With any remaining bravado having completely gone AWOL, I was totally focused on the end of the carrier's deck, determined not to waste a foot of it by landing long. My eyes were now constantly flicking between the speed and the deck, the speed and the deck, as the engineer started counting down the radar altimeter heights.

'150, 125, 100, 80, 70 . . .'

Watch that speed! I began shouting in my head.

'. . . 60, 50 . . .'

Then, to my astonishment, having forgotten the carrier sat fifty feet above sea level, there was a bang – quite a big one – and we were down. I slammed all four engines into reverse and stomped on the brakes so hard that I actually lifted myself out of the seat.

Stop! the voice in my head was yelling now. *Stop! For fuck's sake, STOP!*

33

And eventually we did, with just twenty feet to spare.

'Piece of cake,' I announced. Because that's what you do.

It was, of course, anything but. If there was one thing I was 100 per cent sure of in that moment, it was that I would NEVER have attempted anything so bonkers for real.

We had, however, landed on the carrier at forty-four tons, and into a headwind of fifty knots down the deck. This meant that the aircraft was actually doing a ground speed of about forty-four knots on landing, or about fifty miles per hour.

What Flatley had done was a whole different ball game. He had landed his *fifty-five-ton* Hercules in *real life*, and with almost no headwind to help him. Not once, but an incredible *twenty-one* times – not to mention the twenty-nine times he touched the deck too late and had to keep going.

The C-130's numbers were themselves impressive: the shortest landing at fifty-five tons on the carrier was 460 feet – compared to the 315 feet for an F-18 to stop using arrestor wires – and the plane used 745 feet at take-off. But what Flatley did as a pilot was nothing short of exceptional. I left that simulator as wet with sweat as I would have been with sea water had we plunged off the end of that carrier and into the ocean – and, if it were possible, with even greater respect for him.

Flatley's 1963 achievement was one of several at this time that must have had the RAF and UK government drooling at the prospect of getting hold of some of these amazing aircraft for themselves. And in 1965 they duly did, ordering sixty-six, and accepting them into RAF service in the late 1960s, direct from Marshall of Cambridge, who painted them in RAF colours, before being processed through the maintenance unit at RAF Colerne.

At one point, the RAF was accepting one aircraft a week and, after training at the USAF's Seward Air Force Base in Tennessee, crews would ferry the Hercs back to the UK. The entire training and delivery process involved twenty-six crews in total, and took just over a year.

The UK and RAF had a bold aspiration: to have every C-130 in service in just over a year, with enough crews to deliver the operational output of five squadrons. These Hercules were to be replacing the British-built stalwarts, the Hastings and the Beverley, and, in contrast to the buzz of excitement as newly trained crew members got to grips with their incredible new bit of kit, this replacement wasn't politically popular. Each aircraft was to cost the RAF £900,000, the equivalent of about £7 million today. (Which actually seems a bargain: you can't even buy a small business jet for that price today.) But the real challenge was that the government had chosen an American aircraft over the homebuilt Hawker Siddeley 681 STOL then in development. This led to the cancellation of that project, and many job losses too; but it made fiscal sense to buy a proven platform and get it into service quickly, to allow the UK to project its global presence.

It wasn't long before the Hercules started proving its worth within the RAF too. Within a matter of months, in November 1967, it was pressed into service in Aden, to transport British forces out of the country following the collapse of the federal government and its replacement by a communist regime.

One of those based at Muharraq, Bahrain, to oversee the withdrawal of British troops was Navigator Chris Mead, who had previously crewed Beverleys. He wasn't alone in being astounded by the difference in the respective aircrafts' performance. Where the Beverley cruised at 130 knots, the Hercules almost tripled that, managing 330. Similarly, the Hercules' range of 3,000 nautical miles dwarfed the Beverley's 1,200. And even though it would go on to excel at extreme low-level flying, the Herc, being pressurized, could also cruise at 30,000 feet, as opposed to the Beverley's normal operating altitude of just 10,000. Indeed, the Herc could actually cruise climb with a theoretical maximum of 40,000 feet, but cruise climbing was banned fairly quickly, as it was conflicting with the much faster jet aircraft that cruised at similar altitudes. The Herc was already punching well above its weight.

In the minds of the UK public, however, perhaps the first operation to really put the C-130 on the map was in 1972, when it was deployed to drop four bomb-disposal experts onto a threatened cruise liner midway through a voyage across the Atlantic Ocean. It would also prove to be an early example of the close bond that would develop between 47 Squadron and the UK's elite forces.

For Hercules flight engineer Patrick Quaid, the day began with a call from Lyneham Ops, who had received notification from the MoD of a bomb threat they considered valid. He lived on the base at the time, and was in the middle of having lunch when he was ordered to report urgently to flight operations. Once there, and with the remains of his ham sandwich left behind uneaten, he was told to prepare an aircraft for a flight to the mid-Atlantic.

While Patrick set to work, still unaware where they were going or why, the bomb-disposal experts had already been briefed on the finer details. The perpetrators of the threat, which had been received via a phone call to the ship's captain on 17 May, had claimed that they had planted six bombs in suitcases aboard the liner, then on its return journey from New York to Southampton. There were also apparently two accomplices hidden among the passengers, and the devices were set to explode on the 18th, if the $350,000 ransom was not paid.

With a crew of 906 and a full complement of almost 1,500 passengers at risk on the ship, HM government decided to take action. While the government stalled the paying of the ransom with some ruses, early in the morning of 18 May a senior Royal Marines captain was ordered to plan a mission to deliver two specialists into the cold waters of the North Atlantic. With no specific location forthcoming at this point, the officer opted to go on the mission himself, taking a young corporal as his number two.

The men flew by helicopter to RAF Lyneham to meet the rest of their team: an army captain, who was an ammunition technical officer; and an IED specialist, Staff Sergeant Clifford Oliver.

As the ATO had never jumped into the sea before, he was given a crash course in doing so by the RAF Parachute Training School, who met them at the aircraft side, and within the hour all four were aboard the 47 Squadron Hercules, where the scope of their mission was revealed to them: to rendezvous with the ship and parachute in, then to locate and defuse the bombs apparently hidden among the luggage – by now only hours from being detonated.

The promised clement weather was anything but. In fact, it was atrocious, with squally winds buffeting the aircraft relentlessly. The ATO was violently sick for the entire four-hour journey but, despite that, the Royal Marine captain continued to instruct him in how to parachute, to augment the necessarily scant training he had so far received. It was also decided that the corporal would be dropped into the sea first with Oliver, along with the bulk of their equipment, leaving the two officers to then go consecutively. 'To ensure you don't drown when you hit the water,' the marines captain offered as reassurance to the still green-looking ATO.

The weather, meanwhile, continued to work against them, with the cloud base as low as only 400–600 feet. They could not see the ship, and with a twenty-knot wind, there were also five-foot waves to contend with; conditions so poor that in normal circumstances the drop would not even have been attempted.

With so many lives at stake, however, these were far from normal circumstances. So, on the flight deck, a decision was made by the pilot: he was approaching the ship at only 300 feet above sea level, but as soon as he saw the liner he would immediately apply full power, in order to 'pop up' to the minimum dropping height of 800 feet. This was tricky at the best of times, and this was definitely not the best of times; but with the clock ticking, literally, there was very little choice. The four-man team, including the ATO, who was now weak from constant vomiting, would have to jump blind into the turbulent water.

On the first run in, with the port side-door open, the fully kitted-up team clung on to the aircraft as it was buffeted at around 100 feet above the angry, churning sea. At any moment the pilot would 'pop' the Herc's nose up, and then climb like hell – the green light for them to go only coming on when they passed 800 feet, giving them enough time, should anything go wrong, to open their reserve parachutes.

Watching all this from the deck of the liner, the passengers must have been very bemused, especially when the Herc, having popped out at the base of the clouds, immediately shot back up into them. It must have seemed as if it had come from nowhere, and disappeared again just as dramatically. No wonder the whole side of the ship was alight with camera flashes, as those on deck, blissfully oblivious to the seriousness of the situation they were in, looked up in awe at the spectacle that was playing out above their heads.

Up on board the Herc, however, it was a slightly different story as, once the pilot initiated the sudden level-off, the entire team and crew went into negative G. The parachutists were weightless now, floating in the back of the aircraft, clinging tightly to the airframe to avoid toppling out, before the green light finally illuminated – GO! GO! GO!

Staff Sergeant Oliver went out first, with the young corporal immediately behind him; on the second run, the captain pushed the ATO out ahead of him, to ensure his best chance of surviving the drop. They hit the water hard and fast, going some way under before bobbing up again, and they feared for all the vital kit, but thankfully their flotation devices still worked. Though what with the vomiting, the maiden jump into the sea and – the final insult – the ingestion of about a gallon of salt water (obviously just the ticket when you can't stop being sick), the poor ATO was not exactly in fine fettle. But he was still alive – which, under the circumstances, was a win in itself, even if it didn't feel like it at the time.

Quickly picked up by the highly efficient crew from the liner, the four men went straight into action. While the ship's captain, William Law, announced the bomb threat to the astonished passengers, the team kicked into gear and took charge. The ship's crew had already located three suspicious suitcases, ones that hadn't been claimed by any passengers, and while the bomb and ammunitions specialist set about examining them, the marine captain and corporal went to search all the cars down below – several being on board while their owners flew back.

With the cars searched, and two of the three cases having been found bomb-free, only eighteen minutes till detonation time remained. The decision was therefore made to conduct a controlled explosion on the final suitcase. After blowing the case's lock, they were relieved to discover it contained nothing more menacing than the crackle of cellophane packaging; it was full of new clothes, not even opened, let alone worn.

Only then were they confident that all on board were, in fact, safe. They had been victims of an elaborate hoax.

Having completed their own mission, Quaid and the rest of the Herc crew were already on their way back to Lyneham, which left the bomb-disposal team now, quite literally, at sea. Needless to say, though, they were very well looked after. After a short period of rest, they were coaxed out of their makeshift quarters by the grateful passengers, and continued on to Southampton as the heroes of the hour, not least for what they'd done to put British forces on the map and, with their heroics splashed across all the media in words and pictures, for doing such wonders for military recruitment.

All went on to be awarded the Queen's Commendation for Brave Conduct, and their efforts were further celebrated and immortalized on the silver screen, in the 1974 thriller movie *Juggernaut*.

As well as proving itself the incredible military asset the RAF had envisaged, the C-130 also quickly proved itself as a humanitarian relief tool. Now already a stalwart of 24 and 47 Squadrons, it was sent in 1973 to the remote famine-stricken villages of west Nepal as part of Operation Khana Cascade. During just one month, the Hercules airdropped just over 2,000 tons of grain, maize and rice to the starving villagers in the RAF's biggest airlift since the one in Berlin twenty-five years earlier. It was the Herc's first big test and it literally delivered everything that the government had envisaged – including, apparently, a rumoured kitchen sink.

At a time of relative peace, however, much attention was given to training. During the Cold War, the Lyneham Wing of RAF Hercules trained endlessly for the airborne assault that would be needed in a post-apocalyptic nuclear world, as well as making constant resupplies to standing forces in Germany that were directly facing the spectre of destruction from the USSR.

This training for the war that everyone hoped would never come didn't prevent the Hercules from delivering on a few more evacuation missions, though. In 1974, following the Turkish invasion of Northern Cyprus, RAF

Hercules aircraft evacuated service families from the air-base at Akrotiri back to the safety of the UK. They also managed to rescue British nationals from Tehran during the Iranian Revolution in 1979, something that now seems insane, given the politics of that region.

When it came to airlifting humans to safety, however, the Herc still had more tricks up its sleeve. The Vietnam War was one of the USA's most intractable and bloody conflicts. Since the direct involvement of US troops in the 1960s, the Hercules had become a stalwart of US Air Force operations there. But in an increasingly complex and fraught situation, the US military's involvement in supporting its South Vietnamese allies was no longer tenable. By early 1975, North Vietnam forces were set to capture Saigon; realizing that any further fighting would be futile, the US began evacuating its many thousands of troops.

On 29 April 1975, the day before Saigon fell, North Vietnamese forces had destroyed all but one of the air-craft at Tan Son Nhut Airbase. The last aircraft standing, amid the burning wreckage of almost 100 destroyed planes, was a USAF C-130A.

Major Phuong, a South Vietnamese instructor pilot, was determined to make use of it; after all, it was his own crew's final ticket to safety. He was also determined that they would take as many people as possible. Word spread quickly, and hundreds of panicked refugees rushed to the airfield, running through the choking smoke, hoping to board the aircraft and get to safety.

A C-130 was only designed for – or, indeed, had room for – ninety-eight combat troops. But realizing that to leave anyone behind was akin to signing their death warrant, Phuong – who was by now about to start the aircraft – ordered the loadmasters to start boarding everyone who was waiting to get on, and to pack in as many as they could. They duly began doing so, throwing out anything that wasn't needed, including seats, military kit and the hastily thrown-together possessions that the desperate evacuees had managed to grab before they fled. They then began squeezing people into every conceivable space.

The aircraft was soon completely rammed with people, and when one of the loadmasters attempted to close the rear door, the sheer volume of souls inside made it impossible. He relayed this to Phuong, on the flight deck, who was by now ready to depart, anxious about the aircraft being shot at or shelled. Phuong thought for a moment. It was unthinkable to leave anyone. Then a solution, in theory at least, dawned.

'Lift the ramp, and hold on,' he responded to the loadmaster, before taxiing the aircraft forward a short distance and then slamming on the brakes. Everyone in the aircraft was immediately thrown forward, allowing the loadmaster to close the ramp. They were off.

At the end of the runway, Phuong pushed the power levers forward, let the brakes off and prayed. He had no idea of the number of people aboard the aircraft but was fairly sure their combined weight must be substantially over the official maximum, meaning there was a high chance they would run out of runway.

What Phuong *did* have, however, was faith in the aircraft. There were many lives at stake and he knew the Herc would not let them down. The acceleration was slow and, at the very moment they had run out of road, he pulled back on the column, hoping to lift the lumbering aircraft into the air. It was struggling to get speed, so he kept the nose very low, prioritizing acceleration over climbing away from the ground. After what seemed an age, they eventually reached the normal take-off speed and, to his great relief, Phuong felt the Herc start to climb. He could breathe out at last. They were airborne.

They were, however, not out of danger. The plan was to fly to the safety of Utapao Airbase in Thailand, around ninety minutes away, but Phuong was now lost over the Gulf of Siam, circling and almost out of options. All seemed hopeless, till a map was found and given to Phuong, who managed to identify sufficient terrain features that they were able to navigate to Utapao. After what turned out to be a three and a half hour flight, to finally land was a great relief. Given the number of people packed in, had they been forced to fly for longer, it would almost certainly have led to loss of life. As it was, 452 people were airlifted to safety, thirty-two of them on a flight deck that was designed to take five.

The saving of those lives, and the repatriation of that last C-130, was yet another example of the almost symbiotic relationship between human and Hercules; of human courage and ingenuity being reciprocated in kind by an aircraft that would always punch well above its already not inconsiderable weight.

The aircraft is still proudly on display at Little Rock Air Force Base, Arkansas, and the feat achieved – Phuong managed to get it airborne some *10,000 pounds* overweight – was yet another feather in Lockheed's engineering department's cap. Was there any challenge you couldn't throw at the Hercules?

The next big test for the RAF C-130s was in the UK's peacekeeping role during the turbulent period in the late 1970s and early 80s when a deal was struck between the UK Foreign Office and Ian's Smith's Rhodesian government to give the former colony its independence. A world away from all the ongoing Cold War and tactical training, playing a key part in ensuring a peaceful transfer of power to Joshua Nkomo and Robert Mugabe gave the experienced Hercules crews a chance to really test their mettle in conditions that would present them with a number of challenges, in terms of both military threat and the natural hazards they would encounter. Just as had been the case for the US Air Force's crews during the Vietnam War, it would enable them to find out precisely what their C-130s were capable of.

Op Agila, which began in December 1979, involved several Commonwealth countries providing a monitoring force to Rhodesia to oversee elections and the move to independence. Three Hercules and their crews were deployed from 47 Squadron, their first priority being to get all the monitoring teams into the bush before 1 January 1980, when a ceasefire was to come into force, and the rebels would be moving into the nominated assembly areas and holding camps.

At about three times the size of England, however, Rhodesia was a very large theatre of operation, and the crews were warned that the flying would be demanding and potentially dangerous, due to the threat from surface-to-air missiles (SAMs), radar-laid anti-aircraft artillery, regular anti-aircraft guns, small arms fire and, on the unpaved landing strips they would be using, possibly landmines as well. As the only self-protection 'systems' the aircraft had were white crosses that had been hastily painted on with household emulsion, this was sobering news.

The allocated Hercules crews were pre-positioned in Cyprus in readiness, but were unable to cross Africa before negotiations in London were completed and the subsequent agreement signed. As a result, there was an urgent requirement to get crews and aircraft into theatre to assess the situation. Back home at RAF Lyneham, Squadron Leader Tony Webb was given just two hours notice to find a crew and to set off for the Rhodesian capital, Salisbury, via the Azores and Ascension Island.

Aged thirty-six, and having been the instructor and examiner on a small unit embedded within 47 Squadron since it was set up in 1973, Tony was well qualified to assess the situation and advise on tactics. He and his crew landed in Salisbury shortly after midnight, following two days and twenty-seven flying hours. It was only at the top of descent that they had received a radio message confirming that they were to stay in theatre.

Having found their accommodation, Tony and his crew soon collapsed into an exhaustion-inspired sleep. The next day, they managed to discover that an air commander and an air adviser were already installed on the staff of the interim governor, Sir Christopher Soames. They met up, and found that their task was to distribute the Commonwealth Monitoring Force to sixteen assembly areas around the country. Unfortunately, the rebel Patriotic Front fighters were accustomed to seeing South African Hercules operating in support of the Rhodesian armed forces, and there was no reliable method of informing them that the RAF aircraft were working for peaceful purposes. Tony therefore had to assume that they would be treated as hostile and urgently needed to know the extent of the potential threat. Because they had left Lyneham at such short notice, and had no inkling of what they were going to be involved in, they had little or no intelligence to draw on – only some outdated maps that happened to be in the station map store. Most of what they knew came from what they had read in the newspapers or heard on the news.

They decided that their best bet was to ask the Rhodesian Air Force's Dakota squadron, based in Salisbury, if they would be prepared to help. Thankfully, the squadron commander was very cooperative and gave the crew access to much of what they knew; they also provided some more up-to-date maps. Based on this information, they now had to decide on tactics.

Rhodesia/Zimbabwe divides into three areas: the low veldt, middle veldt and high veldt. The high veldt is between 3,000 and 5,000 feet, with the highest point at about 8,000 feet. The country's population at the time was about 7 million, so the population density was very low. In December and January, summer in that part of the world, the weather was generally fine but subject to occasional days of rain and low cloud. On the other hand, the crew was completely unfamiliar with the geography and terrain and unused to a hostile environment.

SAM-7s were effective up to a height of 14,000 feet, so

in the interests of speed of transit it seemed reasonable to spiral up above that altitude and down again over the relatively safe centres of population. The best tactic thereafter would be to fly as fast and as low as possible. However, crews routinely trained at 250 feet above ground level and at 210 knots, which would be too high and too slow. So what could they do to minimize the threat?

Five days after arriving, Tony and his crew were able to fly a trial sortie, spiralling up over Salisbury and down over Bulawayo. They would then see how fast and how low was maintainable. This turned out to be 300 knots and sixty feet; in an aircraft with a 133-foot wingspan, it required a great deal of concentration. As time went on, they found that alternating the two pilots every fifteen minutes was a sensible option. There were other oddities with this tactic too. For instance, a strip arrival would also be at sixty feet, with no visual circuit to orientate oneself. A pre-determined speed reduction point was calculated in order to arrive at the strip in the right landing configuration at the right speed. Strange though this felt, it was perfectly achievable.

Another of the unforeseeable problems was the degree of familiarity that the intensity conferred. Over time, flying three sorties each day, one became so accustomed to sitting in the aircraft that, instead of increasing alertness, you had to resist relaxing; it became the normal environment, where you felt most at home. A further syndrome was what might be called 'motorway tiredness'. The task was exhausting, and the concentration so fierce, that there was a terrifying inclination to doze off – not a good idea when driving along a motorway, and considerably sillier when flying at great speed a few feet above the ground. The crew soon became adept at watching each other for signs of sleep.

Following the trial trip and the lessons that it taught, Tony was in a position to brief the other crews when they arrived a few days later. One of those crews was led by young Hercules captain Flight Lieutenant Harry Burgoyne, and, after they had received their briefing from Tony, he was soon strategizing about how best to deal with the various threats.

At the age of twenty-eight, Harry had joined the small unit within 47 Squadron as captain only earlier that year. He had always wanted to be a pilot, however; his father had been an RAF aircraft mechanic, and his late second cousin a Lancaster pilot (he was sadly shot down and killed in 1944). Keen to start his career, Harry had joined the Air Cadets straight from school in 1969, and was especially proud, having being accepted at the prestigious RAF College Cranwell, to be the first in his family to go on to higher education.

In fact, every moment of Harry's time so far in the RAF had been an education, and as he pondered this new deployment and the RhAF officer's grim prediction about their chances, he was pretty sure there was still much to be learned. All they had to do now was survive . . .

Happily, however, everyone seemed to agree that Tony Webb's suggested strategy – to fly fast and low – was the best one. Though clearly demanding, it would make any enemy's job of hitting them a bit more tricky.

'They'll have to take us like a low-flying grouse!' one of the pilots quipped.

'And a low-flying grouse with a useful target on it,' one

of the engineers pointed out, echoing Tony Webb's fears that the painted-on white crosses that had been designed to protect them might end up doing the reverse.

There were still, of course, all the non-military hazards to navigate, but for Harry and his crew it was also highly exhilarating as they began testing their C-130's capabilities to the limit on their first trip in-country, on Boxing Day 1979.

They were first tasked to fly to Bulawayo to offload troops and equipment, then fly at low level to Wankie airfield in the Wankie National Park for a further offload, and finally return to Salisbury via Bulawayo. It was a beautiful day as they took off from Bulawayo, and Harry settled the aircraft at about 100 feet before accelerating to 300 knots. It was both the lowest he had ever flown over land and the fastest he'd ever flown in a Hercules, some thirty knots above its peacetime maximum.

He had also prudently positioned his ground engineer, Bill Brown, in the window beside his seat as an extra pair of eyes to watch for the aerial electrical wires they had been warned were randomly strung around the landscape. The nav, Paul 'Ollie' Shepherd, who stood behind the co-pilot, Chris Mann, shared the navigation and provided lookout, and Flight Engineer Ted Lecount, who looked after the aircraft systems, contributed a fifth pair of eyes from his seat in the middle. If there *were* wires, surely one of them would spot them? Meanwhile, the air loadmaster, Clive Moate, remained on the back to reassure the passengers as the hot-air currents bumped them around.

It took about fifteen minutes for Harry to settle into the exhilarating and demanding flying this hazardous and novel environment required. Everything seemed to be happening much quicker than he was used to; the thin air at 5,000 feet above sea level meant that turns were much wider, causing the aircraft to slide and skid through the sky. All eyes were peeled not only for wires but also for possible threat action; even so, it was hard to believe they were in a war zone as the verdant countryside sped past below them at almost 400 miles per hour.

They reached the strip at Wankie, slowed down and carried out a standard tactical landing, about fifteen knots slower than normal to reduce the runway-length required. The offload of the troops and equipment took ten minutes, while the aircraft engines were kept running, and they were soon en route back, with the prospect of cold beers ahead. Everyone felt confident, and all were agreed: they had both the tactics and the aircraft to achieve what they had been asked to do.

The following day, they were tasked for a further six flights to and from strips at Grand Reef, in the east, and Rutenga and Lupane, both northwest of Bulawayo, in what would be their first exposure to Rhodesia's natural-surface strips. Of them, Rutenga was going to be particularly challenging, as it was fairly short and surrounded by tall trees. This meant it would be difficult to spot on the approach at low level, and the aircraft would have to be 'dropped' into the strip only once clear of the trees. There was only about fifty feet of clearance for the wings on either side, and there was no turn-round area at the end. The aircraft therefore had to be reverse-taxied back up the strip prior to take-off and there was a possibility they might overheat the engines. But as they walked out into the sunshine of another hot Rhodesian morning, they were looking forward to the day ahead and said cheerful hellos to the captain and navigator of an RAF Puma they passed, also about to start their own day of operations.

They took off towards Grand Reef and, feeling more familiar flying at low level now, Harry gradually eased down until they were steady at around sixty to eighty feet above the ground. Though navigational markers were few and far between, requiring intense and focused map-reading, their first trip went to schedule and without incident.

On the second trip, they transited at high level to Bula-wayo and carried out the second and third landings. Once again, all went well and the crew were even gifted the sight of some local wildlife, spotting elephants, giraffes and a large herd of buffalo – all of which were delightful. But with equally plentiful birdlife, they were ever aware of the dangers of birdstrike – and especially mindful that, given the multiple threats, taking avoiding action (the usual tactic being to fly up and over flocks) might put them in even greater jeopardy.

Sixteen hours later, they returned to Salisbury feeling buoyant, only to be greeted by the news that, tragically, an RAF Puma had apparently hit some unmapped wires and crashed, killing all three aboard, including the pilot and nav they'd met only that morning. It was a stark reminder that the threat from wires was very real.

It wasn't the only sobering news they received that even-ing. One of their own small fleet of Hercules, XV176, had been hit by small arms fire. The bullet had entered the air-craft, narrowly missing the (thankfully empty) liquid oxygen tank, before ricocheting off support beams and ending up embedded in the back of the co-pilot's instrument panel, pointing straight at him. All on board were safe, but it did focus everyone's minds.

On 28 December, Harry and his crew were tasked to operate to three strips: Binga in the north, and Gwanda and Rutenga (again) in the south. The trip to Binga was uneventful but, on return to Salisbury, they were informed that the weather in the south was very poor, with low cloud, and reduced visibility due to drizzle and fog. With only four more days remaining to complete the deployment phase of the op, however, they elected to press ahead and do what they could.

They transited to Bulawayo as usual but had to make an instrument approach to get visual below the cloud base of 500 feet. They then set off at low level towards Rutenga, but with the weather deteriorating; clouds were about 200 feet and visibility was soon reduced to about a mile.

Harry slowed the aircraft to 140 knots, but eventually the weather closed in and they had to climb out to about 2,000 feet to gain the clear air above the extensive stratus cloud.

Chris and Ollie, poring over maps, soon came up with a plan. It seemed a railway line ran close to the strip, and they were reasonably confident that if they could find a hole in the cloud, descend through it and get back visual below, they could find it and follow it to Rutenga strip.

This would be working on the very edge of the safety envelope, Harry knew, but with little choice in the matter, and every confidence in his crew and aircraft, he found a very small hole, and, with about sixty degrees of bank and pulling 2G to keep within it, he duly spiralled down through. To his relief, he popped out below cloud and in the clear. (Well, clearish; the cloud base was still around 300 feet and visibility was no more than one mile.) They duly set off again, at 140 knots, with the landing gear and flaps set for landing, because Harry knew that if they *did* find the strip it would be a very late spot, with little time for configuring the aircraft and running pre-landing checks.

Very impressively, within a minute Chris and Ollie had fixed their position, and soon, coming across the railway, they began following it towards the strip. The cloud base was now at around 250 feet and Chris warned Harry that the ground was rising slowly. 'Don't worry, though,' Chris was quick to reassure him. 'The railway track cuts through a narrow valley about two miles ahead. We'll be descending towards the strip then, and hopefully into better weather.'

About a mile later, Harry spotted the gap in the hills and, though he was confident they would get through it, to avoid going into cloud he would have to fly the aircraft even lower. In effect, they would have to fly through a 'letterbox' of land and cloud, with valley sides disappearing into the clouds just 100 feet above them. As they approached the gap, there was just enough visual to see through it and, confident now that there were no wires or other obstructions, Harry pressed on and flew through the tiny opening, only to experience the shock of his life. A steam train, billowing its own clouds, suddenly emerged from the mist and was thundering at some speed towards them! Harry's eyes were bulging as the aircraft flew straight into its smoke trail, only to emerge several heart-thumping seconds later back into the clear. He took a very deep, thankful breath; there had been no more than thirty feet of altitude between them, and he could only guess at the blood pressure of the engine driver and his fireman on seeing a massive Hercules thundering so close above them. It was likely an encounter they would not forget.

Ditto the crew in the cockpit, who had all been rendered speechless, and now, with mere moments left to do so, had to focus for their imminent arrival at Rutenga strip. The cloud base was now about 300 feet and visibility had at least improved slightly, to about 1.5 miles. There was rain, though, so Harry quickly turned on the windscreen wipers, and as Chris and Ollie talked him from the railway to the landing site he spotted it with only a mile left to go.

Harry called for 100 per cent flap, slowed the aircraft to landing speed of about 100 knots and carefully guided the aircraft towards the strip. His heart still pounding, he reduced the power as they cleared the trees and sank towards the landing zone. Unfortunately, however, he forgot all about the thin air, and was late in reapplying the power to arrest the rate of descent.

Unsurprisingly, perhaps, they hit the ground for the hardest landing of Harry's life – so hard, in fact, that the Herc bounced straight back up into the air. Between them, however, Harry and Chris wrestled the aircraft back under control, and landed and stopped about halfway down the strip.

There was a moment of silence as everyone contemplated their last, hectic few minutes. 'Before we do anything further,' Harry announced, 'we're going to sit and collect our thoughts. And I'm going to have a fucking cigarette!'

Flight Engineer Ted had his own preoccupations. 'I know there's a form for a birdstrike,' he noted. 'But I'm not sure there's one for a bloody train-strike! Or for a giraffe-strike, for that matter,' he continued. 'So it's lucky we didn't meet any of those either!'

The day continued to throw up complications. Though the second trip was largely without incident, on arrival at Gwanda for their next unload of personnel and equipment it was to find that the strip was completely waterlogged and very muddy. After landing, Air Loadmaster Clive Moate went outside to supervise the offload but quickly reported that the aircraft was sinking into the mud, with potentially highly dangerous connotations. To avoid this perilous situation, there was no choice but to complete the offload while taxiing. It was only when they'd finished and were turning around for take-off that Harry noticed the huge ruts left in the ground by the aircraft's wheels, necessitating an offset – and extremely hairy – take-off.

'I know we're from Wiltshire,' he quipped as they finally climbed away, 'but I didn't think we'd be ploughing bloody fields in Rhodesia!'

Though the weather continued to worsen, the operation continued, and by 30 December some 10,000 rebels had reported to the assembly areas – far more than had been expected. Food and shelter now became the main priority. With several of these sites being some distance from a strip, and with ground transport in short supply, the decision was taken to provide tents, equipment and food by airdrop.

Harry and his crew were now tasked with free-dropping

very large and heavy tents, and parachuting harness packs of the associated tent poles and one-ton containers of food and equipment. The one-tons were dropped from 400 feet, the harness packs from 250 feet and the tents, without parachutes, from twenty-five feet; they were simply rolled off the ramp and would bounce and skitter to a stop, usually none the worse for wear.

They duly found the drop zone, and all went according to plan until it came to the free-dropped tents. Clive Moate was at the rear, supervising the 47 Air Despatch Squadron army personnel, who, as Harry flew along the drop zone at 125 knots, were rolling the tents off the back of the ramp.

Harry was concentrating hard on maintaining the correct height and speed when he heard Clive suddenly bellowing at him. 'One of the tents has hit a cow!' he yelled. 'It's now airborne and, bloody hell, it's chasing after us!' he added – not a sentence most people expect to hear in their lifetimes. Luckily, the flying cow fell short, but it was yet another timely reminder that the hazards in the Rhodesian bush really could come from anywhere.

Still, for some at least, the episode was not without a silver lining. As they left the landing zone, a very laid-back New Zealand Army DZ safety officer came on the radio. 'Thanks very much for your help today, mate,' he drawled. 'And thanks for the pre-tenderized steaks we'll be having for dinner!'

Though a tense and challenging time, Op Agila proved a fertile C-130 testing ground, with every crew member receiving on-the-job advanced training on how to fly and handle their magnificent machines. And to fix them, as well, necessity having proved very much the mother of invention, particularly when it came to patching up their aircraft after regular and often multiple birdstrikes.

It wasn't just the heroic sorties that became the stuff of Hercules legend, however. For one aviator, a momentary lapse in concentration in 1981 would be chuckled over for many years to come.

Squadron Leader Max Roberts was by this time a Hercules veteran. He'd been among the first crews to train for and bring back the original fleet of aircraft, and by now he'd been a Hercules qualified flying instructor and examiner for quite a few years.

One of the duties of that role, when on a squadron and not flying in the right-hand seat, was screening or examining qualified crews – standing behind them, except during take-off and landing. This would be mainly for route flying, such as screening new pilots into difficult airfields – old Kai Tak in Hong Kong, say, or Gibraltar. It could also be checking crews out on day or night, low-level or cross-country flying, and on any of the various types of loads the Hercules could drop, from 250-pound harness packs to eight-ton medium stressed platforms, and, of course, paratroopers.

The flight in question involved Max, along with an experienced navigator, screening a fairly new crew on a day low-level flight through Wales and Scotland before dropping a one-ton container at Keevil, with the intention, as was traditional, of getting back in time for tea and medals.

A simple enough task, at least in theory; it was a clear summer's day, with unlimited visibility and only lightish winds from the west. And sure enough, it was such a lovely flight, in fact, that Max found himself wishing he could pilot the aircraft himself.

He was also pleased that the young crew were doing so well. They were reaching their turning points exactly on time, with the captain in training flying smoothly and accurately at the regulation 250 feet above ground level.

The bucolic peace, however, was soon to be broken. They were twisting and turning through the impressive Cairngorms, when a red light on the engineer's panel suddenly came on. Quite an important one too, so Max allowed himself to be distracted by it for a few seconds; a few seconds in which he heard something along the lines of, 'Navigator captain, turn right now up this valley heading 030.' He looked up and out to get his situational awareness and saw an unfamiliar valley ahead. Had they taken a wrong turn? He glanced over at the navigator to check, but very quickly realized he didn't need to. Was that the village of Ballater? Uh-oh . . . And that castle . . . that lovely castle with the colourful flag flying from its tower? The penny dropped. Hard. Double uh-oh!

'Pull up, pull up!' Max yelled, and the startled pilot duly did. But not before accidentally flying over Balmoral Castle. And with the Herc still at no more than 2,000 feet, they were low enough to see the Royal Standard proudly fluttering above it. Which of course meant Her Majesty was in residence.

This was, to put it mildly, very serious. Not only had they flown over a royal residence, and royal residences always have protected airspace around them, but they'd done so with the Queen actually *in* residence, which was unforgivable. Unthinkable. Perhaps even treasonous. The repercussions would be severe indeed.

During a tense flight back, Max had already begun composing his report to the squadron commander in his head, with the recommendation that they might as well skip the formalities and head straight to the shot at dawn part. Because he knew, without doubt, that he was in what was technically referred to as deep shit.

After landing, Max slunk into the crew room to prepare for the worst, but two policemen from the RAF's special investigation branch were already in there. His heart sank – feeling the pain of a promising career cut short. The SIB men asked for his verbal report, their faces solemn. Max gave it. The senior policeman then asked him, 'Is that all, sir?'

Max nodded, still fearing the worst.

'Well,' said the policeman, with a strange look in his eye. 'Her Majesty wishes for me to convey to you that she enjoyed the fly-past immensely!' He then nodded at Max's squadron commander, who was now hovering nearby.

'No further action,' the policeman then quipped. 'I think we'll leave it at that, sir.'

At the time, Max had no idea how he'd escaped with his job, let alone with no further action being taken. He genuinely could not believe his good fortune. Though legend has it that when the low-flying Herc thundered over Balmoral, Her Majesty was coincidentally in a meeting with the Chief of the Air Staff, and both saw the aircraft thunder over them.

'Oh,' she's reported to have said. 'That pilot looks like he's in trouble.'

To which the Chief of Air Staff replied, 'He is now!'

It might be true, it might not. But it's heart-warming to think a royal pardon might just have saved the day – and that well-placed comment to the Chief, Max's job. In any event, thank you, boss. RIP.

The Hercules' first decade in RAF service saw it prove its worth time after time as an airlift platform, so it was no wonder that it was always seen as a transport aircraft rather than at the tip of the spear. This, however, was all about to change. In 1976, the C-130 would have perhaps its greatest chance yet to shine, when its true capabilities were pushed to their absolute limits and ears began to prick up across the globe.

The event was a daring rescue carried out by the Israel Defence Forces.

The location was Entebbe.

5. Entebbe

The 'office' gives us some amazing views. It's a cool spring evening in 2004 and we are flying at 15,000 feet over Wiltshire. The lights of London are twinkling off to the east. They are orange and white, web-like and, as with every big city, have their own sprawling signature, while the vehicle lights snaking on the M4 motorway below us form familiar red and white strings. To this day, I never tire of looking out of the window and wondering if there is anyone gazing up at us.

Tonight, however, things are very soon going to look a little different. We have few external lights on, so we'll be difficult to spot (hopefully), and the flight deck is bathed in a sea of green hues from lighting that needs to be compatible with night vision goggles. This is a training flight and tonight we aren't looking to land on a brightly lit airfield, but on one that has no lighting at all.

As soon as we pull down our NVGs, the night sky, normally black, and with just a smattering of stars, is completely transformed. There are myriad stars now, trillions of them, ones not normally visible to the naked eye. It's a privilege to witness, and a wonder to behold; though as it's going to be my first time doing this kind of landing, focusing on the job in hand definitely takes precedence, especially with my instructor, Merky Baines – technically the captain – sitting, eagle-eyed, to my right.

The first thing that strikes you about NVGs – other than that they resemble a pair of high-tech toilet-roll tubes – is the weight. They put a huge strain on your neck, which can only be countered by putting some additional weight on the back to balance it all out. If you're lucky, this takes the form of a purpose-built weight that's moulded to fit and attached using velcro, but sometimes, particularly in the early days of the technology, it could be as simple as a tin of beans taped to the back of the helmet.

We configure our aircraft for landing and commence a predetermined racetrack pattern (an elliptical shape with two long straights and two corners) which sees the aircraft start a six-degree descent rate, using idle power. That's double the rate of a normal airliner – more akin to the short, steep approach to an airport like London City – causing the aircraft to feel uncannily tilted forward, with the windscreen full of more ground than air. We hold this until about two miles from the landing runway, where power is added to arrest the rate of descent and make the final approach feel more like the norm.

The racetrack has a purpose: it is designed to keep you within the protected (and hopefully therefore safe) area of the airfield footprint, and can be done from the cruise at a maximum of 26,000 feet. The idle power serves to cool the engines, reducing both the thermal signature and the noise. All of which are good in a hostile environment. The drag from the full flap and landing gear allows a higher rate of descent than normal; the steep angle also points the hottest parts of the engines upwards and, with the large flap, somewhat shields them from heat-seeking missiles.

As I pull the throttles back to idle, the noise reduces a

little, and, with the combined forces of the drag produced by the flap and gear, the aircraft pitches down. The sky disappears, and all I can see is ground. Disked propellers now mean we are stable and 'in the slot', descending quickly at a low ground speed. As the pilot flying, I am completely focused on the aircraft, while the co-pilot and navigator are calling out heights against distances to go, and where we are against the optimum profile. This will allow me to make micro adjustments to the path. The flight engineer is also making micro adjustments, in his case to the engines, to ensure we maintain idle until we need them. The air loadmaster, meanwhile, is in the cupola and, were this a real-world scenario and not just training over Wiltshire, would be constantly looking for threats.

A couple of racetracks, and we are turning towards the runway. Both my co-pilot and instructor, Merky, and I are looking out now and, through our goggles, we can see the dark image of a runway surrounded by different shades of green. With a timely reminder from the navigator, I duly push the power up from the six-degree path to the normal three degrees and the propellers bite the cold Wiltshire air, immediately reducing our rate of descent. The navigator, flight engineer and co-pilot all offer inputs, then the flight engineer alone counts down the feet to touchdown. Fifty, forty, thirty, twenty, ten . . .

And we certainly *are* down. With something of a clatter too. I pull the throttles back and up into reverse and there is a sudden burst of sound, throwing us forward in our straps as braking and reverse take effect. Then we stop, and the sound abates as I return the thrust to idle. I have done it. A new and important skill learned.

This was the first of many NVG landings I would go on to make, in both Iraq and Afghanistan. But this was in the mid-2000s; the technology had been proven and developed across many conflicts and operations since its introduction in the 1970s, and was now augmented by better definition and colour grading, giving a much more defined picture to aid situational awareness.

NVGs are essentially just electronic binoculars that take a small amount of light and enhance it. There is no magic beyond this, but they were a game-changer. Without them, it would be almost impossible to land an aircraft on a dark, hostile runway, as the plane would have to use landing lights, which would make it a target. (Many a drug cartel aircraft has tried to smuggle at night. To my knowledge, it's a skill the smugglers are still trying to master.)

The use of night vision goggles for approach and landing had become commonplace during my time on 47 Squadron, and continues to be today; rather than a niche capability confined mainly to specialist crews, by 2004 it had become standard, allowing all crews to approach unlit airfields in a covert fashion, and to offload and depart without giving the enemy too much of a chance to shoot at them.

This was far from the case decades earlier. Not only were night vision goggles still in their infancy, but just the business of landing a C-130 on an airfield to start an assault was something nobody had ever done, or even considered doing. Why would they?

That was until the summer of 1976, when an aircraft hijack, and the taking of many hostages, caused Israeli forces to consider exactly that. And in particular one man, a Hercules pilot in the Israeli Air Force: 31-year-old Lieutenant Colonel Joshua Shani.

On 27 June 1976, an Air France A300 jet carrying 190 passengers left Tel Aviv Airport. Bound ultimately for Paris, it first made a stopover in Athens where four hijackers were among the fifty-eight additional passengers who boarded; two from the Popular Front for the Liberation of Palestine, and two from extreme left-wing revolutionary cells.

The hijackers' demands were specific. Having now diverted Flight 139 to Entebbe Airport in Uganda, they stated that, in exchange for the lives of all Israeli and other Jewish passengers aboard the aircraft, plus the crew, they required the release of forty Palestinian militants currently imprisoned in Israel, as well as a further thirteen incarcerated in four other countries, by 1 July.

On arrival at Entebbe, they were met by three further accomplices, and offloaded everyone on board to a disused airport building. Supported as they were by the then Ugandan government, they were personally welcomed by the country's dictator, Idi Amin.

Though the hijacking was officially France's responsibility, with over ninety Israelis among the hostages, Israel was also paying very close attention. One of those following the unfolding of the drama was Lieutenant Colonel Shani. Indeed, he was doing rather more than following the action: as the commander of a Hercules squadron in the Israeli Air Force, he was already considering the available options – range, navigation, fuel requirements, payloads they could carry – should the IAF be asked to step in and effect a rescue.

Forty-eight hours later, they were. Shani was attending a family wedding when he received a phone call from the chief of the IAF, Major General Benny Peled. 'Tell me, is it possible – can you fly to Entebbe?' the chief asked him. 'How long will it take? What can you carry?' The very questions Shani and his crews had been asking themselves. For Shani, it was a slightly surreal situation. The C-130 was still fairly new in the IAF – it was very much a fighter jet air force. But with the answers to the major general's questions already at his fingertips, Shani left him with the impression that yes, they perhaps could mount a rescue mission. Operation Thunderbolt, as it was officially named, was go.

Joshua Shani already had good cause to trust his squadron's aircraft. Though there was much to consider – how they could fly beneath the radar between Saudi Arabia and Egypt, the weather patterns they would encounter – his faith in the Hercules was absolute. Having previously flown the notoriously difficult and unforgiving C-97 Stratocruiser, Shani had been responsible for bringing the first C-130 Hercules to the Israeli Air Force ten years earlier. Then a young IAF pilot, with only very basic schoolboy English, he'd spent three challenging months at Little Rock Air Force Base in Arkansas – the largest C-130 Hercules training base in the world – and Pope Air Force Base in North Carolina, where, after piloting the demanding C-97, the placid nature of the Herc was both a joy and a revelation. He'd then gone on to train every C-130 pilot in the Israeli Air Force. The C-130 was his baby; an aircraft he knew back to front. An aircraft he had developed such a close relationship with that he trusted it completely to deal with any problem that was thrown at it and carry on.

They had been through the Yom Kippur War together, had evaded SAMs and MiGs together, and he knew that if any aircraft could do the job, the Herc could.

The day after the wedding, and by now the third day into the crisis, Shani and his crews set to work. That the rescue attempt was happening was no longer in question; the question now was *how* could it be done? Locked away in an operations room, Shani and the squadron team began planning in earnest, their minds focused on the fact that by this time the hijackers had separated the hostages, dividing them up as if they were animals going to market. They had then released all those who were neither Israeli nor apparently Jewish, and repeated their intention that, were their demands not met, the remaining 106 hostages (ninety-four passengers and the twelve Air France crew) would be slaughtered.

An initial plan was tabled, to attempt the rescue over water. To drop naval commandos into Lake Victoria, who would then make their way by rubber boat to the airport (which bordered the lake), take the terminal, kill the hijackers and effect a swift release, and then call on Uganda to assist in flying them all home. In response to information from Mossad (Israel's institute for intelligence and special operations), however, this plan was swiftly vetoed. It seemed that Ugandan forces were now actively assisting the hijackers, and deploying their own soldiers to help guard the airport, so any assistance from President Amin would be far from assured. There was also the not insignificant complication that Lake Victoria was full of crocodiles, so the commandos' survival was far from assured either. They were not at all happy.

Plans for an airborne operation were therefore quickly escalated, and Shani and his crews worked round the clock to both formulate a plan that seemed feasible, and mitigate for every complication they might encounter.

Over the next forty-eight hours, every detail was scrutinized and tested, with Shani serving as lead pilot. The name *Operation Thunderbolt* had been chosen as a homage to the James Bond movie, *Thunderball*, and, as details were pored over, and challenges discussed, it seemed worthy of any plot devised for the fictional spy. They would have to fly just under 2,500 miles, at night, and in radio silence, to avoid being detected. They would then somehow have to covertly, on a possibly unlit runway, and at a highly hostile airport disembark some 200 soldiers of the Israel Defence Forces (IDF), all while still remaining undetected. In order to surprise the terrorists, they would also need to land close to Entebbe's old terminal building; and, having freed the hostages, immediately fly them back to Israel.

As Shani had predicted, the Hercules had quickly topped the list of contenders to perform this mammoth task. Though the IAF had both Boeing 377 Stratocruisers and Boeing 707s, it was only the Herc that could reasonably cope with the demands the audacious nature of the mission would place upon it. It could fly consistently low enough to evade any detection; it could carry far more than any other aircraft being considered; and, perhaps most importantly, given all the unknowns in the situation, it could land and take off on a short or non-existent runway.

Once the decision had been made to deploy four C-130s, Shani was faced with perhaps an even tougher quandary. As commander of the squadron, it would be his responsibility to select the crews. Everyone was a veteran of either trans-port or fighter aircraft, and all were highly proficient. And, naturally, every one of them wanted to be involved. Once again behind closed doors, he carefully made his choices, putting names on a blackboard. Some of the chosen had flown before to Entebbe or (in the days before Idi Amin expelled his Israeli helpers) been instructors to the Ugandan Air Force. Inevitably, however, some would not make the cut, which Shani knew would be a bitter blow.

That task complete, it was time to coordinate with Say-eret Matkal, the elite commando brigade whom they'd be carrying. Led by Lieutenant Colonel Yonatan Netanyahu, they would be responsible for storming the old terminal, killing the terrorists, and freeing the hostages held inside.

Time was critical. The terrorists had by now already extended their deadline to 4 July, at which point there was little doubt in anyone's minds that the mass slaughter they had threatened would be carried out. That left just forty hours to minutely plan every element. An operation such as this would normally be scrutinized and rehearsed for several months. There was no choice, however, and as the hours ticked by, Shani could only accept that they would have to leave 98 per cent of it to improvisation.

Still, they tried to cover as much as they could in the short time available. In case the runway at Entebbe was not illu-minated and they couldn't make out the runway on radar, one of the crew prepared a script: 'We are East African Air-ways flight number 414. We have wounded on board. Please illuminate runway lighting.' Shani felt certain that, under such circumstances, there wouldn't be a single air traffic controller who would not have turned on the runway lights.

Equally crucial was the matter of where they should land at the airport. Shani would have to get the commandos as close to the old terminal building as possible, yet taxiing too close to it would obviously alert the terrorists, who might take it as a cue to open fire on the hostages. Ironically, it was the Ugandan president himself, Idi Amin, who helped suggest one possible solution to this dilemma.

Along with many others, Shani and the IDF intelligence teams watched CBS news every evening, to pick up all they could about how the crisis was unfolding. Seeing the president visit the airport, and the mocking way he 'welcomed' the hostages, might have been chilling, but it also gave them an idea. Amin clearly enjoyed being the centre of world media attention, and he made a big show of his trips to the airport. He'd arrive at the old terminal building in a big black Mercedes, escorted by two Land Rovers. If, along with all the troops, they could bring with them three similar vehicles, then the sight of the 'presidential' cavalcade would give the Ugandan airport guards pause for thought, as opening fire on their commander-in-chief was obviously unthinkable. It might only work for a matter of seconds, but those seconds could mean the difference between life and death.

Finding two Land Rovers at short notice wasn't difficult, but procuring a black Mercedes proved impossible. So, instead, they managed to persuade someone to lend them a white one, and in a matter of hours a group of the commandos had given it a convincing black paint job. Convincing enough, at least, which was all they needed.

There were still many unknowns, so a senior officer would be required at the scene in case critical decisions had to be made on the spot. Operation Thunderbolt commander Brigadier General Dan Shomron would therefore fly with Shani in the lead aircraft. They also took two Boeing 707s, one with responsibility for command and control, and the other as a flying hospital, since many casualties were expected.

The military leaders were still concerned about the runway lights being cut. Could Shani *really* land his C-130 on a completely unlit runway? It was something none of his crew had ever been trained to do. Assurances were one thing, but to prove it would obviously be better, so they organized a practice landing without runway lights at Sharm el Sheik, to demonstrate – though Shani didn't attempt it unprepared. He took the Herc out a few hours earlier to be sure he could do it, and to familiarize himself with the topography of the area. No, he wouldn't have that same advantage when it came to Entebbe, but persuading the chiefs, and so not giving them cause to cancel the mission, was the thing that mattered most.

He also completed two night-time practice runs with the Chief of the General Staff, Lieutenant General Moredechai 'Motta' Gur, Major General Peled, and the head of air force operations, Avihu Bin-Nun, in the cockpit alongside him, all three of whom were breathing down his neck. These were also dark landings, on unlit airfields, carried out using only the primitive night vision goggles that had been developed by that time, along with the aircraft's radar. The practice runs didn't go particularly well, because the aircraft's radar picked up the base's metal fence, which looked much like a runway. But Shani pointed out that Entebbe was by a lake edge, which would be easy to identify, and that helped to calm his eminent passengers' nerves – along with the fact that Shani himself by this time felt unexpectedly calm, so focused was he on the aircraft's performance. This was vital; everyone involved was 100 per cent committed to the mission, and Shani saw his job as doing whatever needed to be done to help them make the decision to approve it.

The next evening, Shani had an unexpected visitor to his office: the Prime Minister of Israel, Yitzhak Rabin. There had been no warning, and he had no entourage with him – just his driver. It was almost as if he had turned up on impulse. He knocked and entered and immediately sat down opposite Shani.

'Look into my eyes,' he said. 'Can you do this? Can it be done?'

'Prime Minister,' Shani answered. 'Go home and get some sleep. We will bring you the hostages tomorrow.'

For years afterwards he would ponder what he said. Was he stupid? Was he crazy? In that moment, he believed every word.

The intention was to land at Entebbe at midnight (Israeli time) on 3 July, which meant a departure the following afternoon. That left enough time for the crews to conduct a final dress rehearsal at night, using a hastily erected mock-up of the old terminal building at Entebbe Airport, pulled together by the ground crew using whatever they could find around the base. With that having been completed successfully, it was time for everyone to try and get some rest. They had done all they could do.

The following day, the commandos and infantry having finalized their own preparations, and with everything loaded, the convoy flew to Ophir Air Force Base in the Sinai Desert, where they would depart for Entebbe at 1530.

The take-off was dicey, to say the least. They were flying with almost 30 per cent more weight than the maximum allowed by Lockheed for take-off, and Shani genuinely did not have a clue what would happen; all he did have was the promise he had made to the PM, and his dogged refusal to believe the mission would not be a success. It was a big ask for his Hercules as well. The temperature was hovering at around forty degrees Celsius, which, in terms of the extra stress put on the aircraft, was equivalent to losing an engine. Shani gave it maximum power, but by the time they had reached the end of the runway (beyond which was the sea) they were just two knots above stall speed and his professional instinct was screaming at him to abort. With the stakes so incredibly high, though, that wasn't an option. He had to lift off and use the ground effect – flying at just fifteen to twenty feet above the water – to gain a few more precious knots of airspeed and keep the struggling aircraft in the air. He then had to turn – they had taken off to the north, but their destination was south – and he struggled to keep control. He kept the faith, though. He knew his aircraft and, something more, that his aircraft knew *him*. It had feelings; it knew the mission could not be allowed to fail.

Incredibly, the operation was well under way before official approval was granted; they knew their strict radio silence would only be broken in the event of them being recalled. As it was, they had turned off the radios, so heard nothing, and the formation of four aircraft, flying in a loose diamond pattern with Shani's aircraft at the front, just 100 feet above water, continued on their seven and a half hour journey. At some points, where the risk of detection was very high, they were flying as low – scarily low – as thirty-five feet. It felt surreal to Shani to be flying in such close formation yet unaware (you cannot see behind you in a C-130) if the three other aircraft were even still there. But from time to time, as if sensing reassurance was needed, the other aircraft would briefly fly out and show themselves so he could see them, then return to their place in the formation. On reaching Ethiopia, however, where they knew there was no radar, they could at last climb up to 20,000 feet and speak freely on the radio for the remainder of the flight.

Shani and his crew left the rest of the formation at the Kenyan–Ugandan border, and while the other three aircraft remained in a holding pattern, his C-130 flew on, the plan being for him to land covertly at Entebbe before they joined him seven minutes later – the time they had calculated they would need to offload the vehicles and commandos, and storm the old terminal building. As they neared Uganda, however, the weather worsened, and storms began to rage over Lake Victoria. This made the flying even harder and, for those crammed in the back, very unpleasant – it was already hot and uncomfortable, and several of the soldiers threw up.

Shani was in no doubt about the challenge now before him. There was no Plan B; his job was to land quietly, and to do it in one shot – not go around and make more noise. And for this he used the Hercules' airborne radar. It's a weather-mapping radar, not designed for blind landings, but they had calculated that they would be able to identify the contrasting surfaces of the runway and its surroundings, and do an airborne-radar approach. They were assisted in this complicated procedure by Mossad, who had taken some photographs of the airport from a three-degree approach angle, so the navigator could compare the radar picture with something real.

Shani now felt under tremendous pressure. It was not fear of being killed or wounded, but fear of the mission failing, and the responsibility now sat heavily on his shoulders. Though he had an excellent crew, a commander providing remote support in one of the 707s, and now, at least, communications with the VHF radio, he was clear that, in the end, everything came down to him. Perhaps it had all along, ever since that phone call at the wedding, and the confident assurances he had given. One mistake and he knew the enormity of the disaster. All those lives – so many lives – now in his hands. He could hear it in his voice, in the constant chatter on the intercom and in the cockpit; his voice was fast and high-pitched. Yet, almost by instinct, he knew he must not let it show to certain people. When the chief of the air force was talking to him, asking him if he could see the runway, if he was okay, if everything was under control, he took several deep breaths, and answered him in a slow, soft, confident voice. Yes, he told him, everything was under control.

Though the storms had abated, a light rain was still falling as they made their approach to the airport. The runway *was* illuminated, which was a relief, but they continued as if it wasn't, and also refrained from illuminating the Hercules' landing lights till the very last moment, to give the least amount of warning of the aircraft's approach.

They touched down at 2300 Ugandan time, in the

77

middle of the runway, just thirty seconds behind schedule. The cargo ramp was then lowered, the Mercedes' and Land Rovers' engines started, and a group of paratroopers jumped out and marked the runway with electric lights – just in case they were recognized as hostile and someone in the control tower extinguished the airport lighting.

Leaving the paratroopers to take the tower, Shani turned the aircraft right and taxied towards the old terminal building, stopping far enough away from it that the hijackers wouldn't hear his engines, yet close enough that the Mercedes and Land Rovers would only have a short trip to reach it. The three vehicles drove out from the cargo door, and the commandos stormed the old terminal building.

When a pair of Ugandan sentries challenged the motorcade, the assault team opened fire. Fearing the terrorists might be alerted by the shooting, the commandos raced towards the terminal building. They exchanged gunfire with both terrorists and Ugandan troops. Coordinating the assault from outside, Sayeret Matkal's commander, Yonatan Netanyahu, was fatally struck by a shot from a Ugandan soldier in the control tower. Another soldier was badly wounded, and, in the crossfire, three hostages were killed.

By the time the other three C-130s began landing, seven minutes after Shani's aircraft had touched down, all seven terrorists had been killed and the hostages freed. Some forty-five Ugandan soldiers also lost their lives. While Hercules No. 3 was approaching, the Ugandans did cut the runway lights, but it still landed safely. The last C-130, whose job was to pick up the hostages, landed with the aid of the lighting laid out by the paratroopers, and taxied close to the old terminal building.

Armoured personnel carriers and infantrymen then offloaded and took up positions around the airport; the APCs secured the area near the old terminal building while the infantry sealed off access to the airport and took control of the new terminal and control tower. There was a problem, however, for the aircrews: they needed fuel to fly home. One option – still unconfirmed as being safe or viable – was to fly to a nearby destination to refuel, ideally Nairobi. But they had also brought a fuel pump, as their preferred option was to fill up at Entebbe from the underground fuel tanks found in all international airports. This they began, but not long into the refuelling, the Ugandan soldiers lost control of the airport and were shooting all over the place with tracers. So when a communication came from the command aircraft overhead telling the aircrews 'the Nairobi option is open', Shani ordered the refuelling to stop and the C-130s to depart – it would take only a few holes in the fuselage to ground them.

They were, however, still far from being out of danger. There were several MiG-17 fighters based at Entebbe Airport, and as the Hercules prepared for take-off the air force chief called over the radio network to remind them. The threat was only theoretical: the MiGs had no night capability. But Major Shaul Mofaz of the Sayeret Matkal was tasked with destroying them anyway – something Idi Amin's collusion deserved – and Mofaz's force took out between eight and twelve aircraft. It was a nerve-wracking few minutes for Shani and his crews as the explosions lit the sky, revealing their aircraft on the tarmac, but there was no further firing and, after almost an hour on the ground, he gave the order, 'Whoever is ready, take off.'

Shani watched the silhouette of Hercules No. 4 – the aircraft carrying the hostages – as it climbed into the night sky. He felt relief and satisfaction – that was it, they had done it. The mission he had had no choice but to believe would succeed had indeed been successfully completed.

The short stopover in Nairobi provided the first moments in the entire mission for everyone to relax, the hour or so they had to stretch their legs being much welcomed after all the tension and time spent aboard the aircraft.

Shani took it as an opportunity to go and see the hostages. It would prove to be a life-changing encounter. He walked the short distance from his own aircraft to the Hercules they'd been flown on. They were all still inside the plane; some were seated, but others were lying on the floor. And though he tried to talk to some, none were able to make even basic conversation. They were confused, in total shock, and what he saw he would remember for ever. Casting his eyes over the sea of faces he saw every emotion, all the way from hysteria, fear and exhaustion, to relief, happiness and exhilaration. All the expressions that seemed to exist in the world were contained in this group of just over a hundred people. It was a moment he would never forget.

The crews were now exhausted but still had an eight-hour flight ahead of them, though at least they could now use their radios. It was a shock to learn that the rescue was already being talked about by the French media and the British BBC. It was also being talked about in Israel. They were still only in Ethiopia when they heard the Minister of Defence, Shimon Peres, confirming that they were on their way back from Entebbe with the hostages.

After flying with an escort of four Phantom fighter jets to give them security over Egypt, three of the four Hercules eventually landed at Tel Nof Air Force Base. Hercules No. 4, with the freed hostages, would continue on to Ben Gurion Airport, where they would be reunited with jubilant family members.

Shani was to have a reunion of his own. He'd only just put his tired aching feet on the tarmac back in Israel when he saw someone familiar approaching. It was the Prime Minister, Yitzhak Rabin, walking up to him . . .

Shani frowned. He had been in his flying suit for twenty-four hours straight, in temperatures of around forty degrees Celsius, he was sweating, he was smelly, and here came the Prime Minister and – even worse – with his arms wide open. *Please don't hug me,* Shani thought. *You might die from this!*

The Prime Minister hugged him anyway, for what felt like a full minute, and said only, 'Thanks.'

A military man, Shani did not spend a lot of time thinking about Entebbe, and neither did he feel like a hero; he'd simply done what his job and his training had dictated he should do. But in the military what you mostly do, by definition almost, is involve yourself in the business of killing. You drop bombs, transport arms, fire missiles. So to conduct and carry out an operation to *save* lives did make him feel very proud.

Life moved on, however, as did Shani's career. And, to his delight, came new-found respect for both the Hercules and the IAF Transport Wing. Some ten years later, he was to get a powerful reminder of just how important that audacious mission had been. Shani and his wife were at a dinner, and he was chatting to a French doctor, a Dr George Teichner, who'd recently emigrated from France to Tel Aviv. And the doctor was complaining. About pretty much everything. How difficult everything was. How expensive it was. How hard it had been to get a job there.

'So why on earth did you come to live in Israel?' Shani asked him.

'Because ten years ago,' the doctor answered, 'I was on a plane from Tel Aviv, going back home to Paris, and we were hijacked and Israeli soldiers came to save me.'

Shani's wife interjected. 'Joshua was the pilot!'

The floor soon became wet from their tears.

They would also go on to become close and dear friends, till Dr Teichner's sad death from cancer in early 2022.

Operation Yonatan, as it was renamed in memory of Yonatan Netanyahu, greatly increased respect for the IAF Transport Wing. For Lieutenant Colonel Joshua Shani, whose hair had turned white shortly after the mission, it was a career highlight. In his thirty-plus years serving in the Israeli Air Force, Shani would accumulate 13,000 flight hours, among them 7,000 in C-130s. During that time, Shani commanded three squadrons and a mixed base of four squadrons and eight ground units. He retired as a brigadier general, after serving as the air force attaché at Israel's embassy in Washington DC.

While Joshua is humble about his role in this mission, he is rightly proud of the fact that, despite being a member of the armed forces, often perceived as merchants of death, he was able to save lives that otherwise would have likely been lost. His incredible vision, and his confidence in the Hercules as the platform to deliver it, were proven by the skill and bravery of the entire team. Although two hostages had already been shot, and one, Dora Bloch, would later be murdered on the orders of Idi Amin, none of the captives were lost as a result of Shani's raid.

The rescue at Entebbe was one of the first times airfield assault in a C-130 was used successfully. Now it had been proved that the C-130 could be deployed in such a way, it led the USA in April 1980 to try to emulate that success with Operation Eagle Claw, to rescue US hostages seized during the Iranian Revolution. That mission used a combination of C-130s and helicopters, but a tragic crash on the ground at a staging post, resulting in the loss of eight lives, meant it failed before it ever really started.

Not to be discouraged, the US planned a second operation, Credible Sport, that was to land a C-130 fitted with retrorockets on a sports field in Tehran. These rockets were part of a new system specifically designed for the mission; they would both slow down the aircraft from a landing speed to an almost vertical landing, with further rockets cushioning the touchdown, and then allow the C-130 to take off again. This concept led to one of the most modified C-130 aircraft ever built – one that could take off in 100 feet and land on a sixpence – but this too was a failure. The idea was scrubbed after a test flight in which the rockets fired in the wrong order, causing the aircraft to essentially stop in the air and fall. This fractured a wing between the engines, immediately engulfing the aircraft in flames. It was only the quick thinking of a helicopter pilot, who used the downwash from his rotors to blow the flames away from the fuselage, that saved the lives of the C-130's crew.

Despite these disasters, the reality was that conflicts, or other unexpected global events, often allowed innovation to flourish, as the normal constraints of defence procurement or design didn't apply. As a consequence, roles that were never envisaged for platforms would go on to become the mainstay of their capability. While the development of short take-off and landing C-130s using rockets may have been a step too far, it did show how the amazing flexibility of the aircraft could be technically adapted to many roles. Later in this book, we will hear of many such innovations, but also about a fatal flaw – an open secret for decades – that eventually led to the loss of an aircraft on operations.

The Entebbe raid itself remains a Hercules story of legend and has been celebrated by the motion picture industry in a series of films over the years, the latest as recently as 2018. But, as Joshua Shani pointed out above, the real star of the show was the aircraft itself. And for the RAF, which had never envisaged the C-130 having a role at the forefront of battle, the rule book was thrown out of the window. After all, the Hercules had just proven itself to be hugely capable in a tactical environment.

This shift in focus and understanding of just what a Hercules could do wasn't solely confined to the highest RAF powers. Hercules crews from right across the service could see it too: a sea change that was about to play an unexpected but vital part when UK forces were faced with an enemy halfway around the world, and with nothing but the Atlantic between them . . .

6. Long Way South: The Birth of the Flying Petrol Station

A colleague once fondly described air-to-air refuelling – or AAR, as it's commonly known – as 'the sport of kings; aerial ballet at its best'. I've since heard many others speak of it in similarly effusive terms – although other descriptions are, of course, available. For me, it was closer to standing on the edge of a cliff with no rope, then trying to thread a needle with your eyes shut.

Throughout my career, I have refuelled behind some of the RAF's best: the Handley Page Victor and Vickers VC-10. Both aircraft are now museum pieces but, at the time, and at least to me, they seemed cutting edge. As, in my ignorance, did the concept of this kind of refuelling in itself – a process I thought was still very much in development. Little did I know that the first successful air-to-air refuelling had taken place on 27 June 1923, a whopping forty-eight years before I was even born.

Early attempts were typical of the age of barnstormers and the pioneering aviation spirits of the 1920s, with one biplane dropping a hose to the pilot of another, who just opened the normal fuel cap on his engine and filled the tank. It was both straightforward and effective. So much so that, in October 1923, it was used to set a world record for a continuous flight of thirty-seven hours, when two DH-4s flew from the Canadian–US border in Washington

State to the US–Mexican border near Tijuana – a journey that in a modern airliner would now take about three.

It was an exciting time in aviation. Air-to-air refuelling was immediately seen to be the key to opening up trans-oceanic commercial flights, and Sir Alan Cobham, a veteran of the Royal Flying Corps, was keen to develop it even further. With his UK based company, Flight Refuelling Ltd, launching in 1934, he soon began making his mark.

Cobham had developed a design that used a grappled-line looped hose, which required the tanker to trail the refuelling hose, which was then grappled by the receiver and pulled into the aircraft to allow fuel to transfer. Once attached to the refuelling coupling, the tanker would climb above the receiver and, with a bit of help from good old gravity, the fuel would then flow.

This new system was equally simple, and trials in 1939 confirmed it; sixteen Empire flying boats crossed the Atlantic without needing to land for fuel. Just as commercial success beckoned, however, the outbreak of World War II suspended any further development. But Cobham was not to be deterred. He could see the advantages his system might give military aircraft, particularly if fitted to bombers, and he lobbied government and the Air Ministry relentlessly.

It wasn't until the closing months of the war, however, that the penny dropped and the RAF realized the value of AAR, finally agreeing to fit the system to some Lancaster and Lincoln bombers. The ones they chose, given the very late stage of the conflict, were those intended for the Tiger Force, the RAF's ultra-long-range bomber force intended to strike at the heart of the Japanese homeland.

Once again, however, progress was suspended. The use of the atomic bomb in August 1945 meant there was no need for the aircraft, so they were never deployed operationally. Cobham therefore still needed to prove his system added operational flexibility in a defence sphere.

In 1949, Cobham's looped-hose system was used to allow a USAF B-50 bomber to fly around the globe in ninety-four hours and one minute, starting and finishing in Fort Worth, Texas. Although this flight was publicly lauded as a success, in private, the technical challenges of the system left much to be desired, and Cobham directed work to be started on a new 'probe and drogue' system that would hopefully reduce complexity. There was also now a big shift in focus. With the improved range of aircraft in the fast-moving post-war aviation landscape, the focus would now be fully back on military applications.

While Cobham continued to develop his probe and drogue system, the USAF had instructed Boeing to develop a new system to replace the trailing hose, and so the 'flying boom' method was born. This led to a split in technologies that largely endures to this day: where the majority of US systems are now flying boom, all UK systems are probe and drogue.

The major difference is that, in the boom system, the receptacle is on the receiver and the tanker flies the controllable boom into its hole. On the probe and drogue, the receptacle is on the tanker, a basket that looks like a shuttlecock, and the receiver flies their probe into that. Both systems use a physical lock that secures and then allows fuel to flow from the tanker into the receiver. As with most things, though, there are always exceptions to the rule, and the US now has drogue systems for helicopter refuelling and adaptors to allow other NATO aircraft to use the boom with a basket fitted to the end.

While air-to-air refuelling systems had become commonplace on the fighters and bombers of the early 1980s, there were no plans at that time to extend the range of any transport aircraft, particularly for the RAF, which rightly argued that there was simply no need.

Until, that was, 2 April 1982, when Argentina invaded the Falklands.

The invasion of the Falkland Islands, a British Overseas Territory, by Argentine forces came as something of a surprise, not least to the then UK Prime Minister, Margaret Thatcher. While being aware of the tensions around whom the Falklands actually 'belonged to', she was as shocked as anyone, if not more so, by Argentina's audacity.

'I never, never expected the Argentines to invade the Falklands head on,' she told the subsequent Franks Committee. 'It was such a stupid thing to do, as events happened. Such a stupid thing to even *contemplate* doing.'

Still, they went ahead and did it, starting a seventy-four-day undeclared war between the UK and Argentina, one which would necessarily take place at the very limit of the geographical capabilities of the UK's forces. Even so, the response from the British government was decisive. The first assets to be deployed, one day after the invasion, were four Hercules, which quietly slipped away from RAF Lyneham to Gibraltar, with a secret plan to set up an air bridge between the UK and the pivotal strategic outpost of Ascension Island in the South Atlantic, through Dakar in Senegal. A day later, the submarine *Conqueror* set sail from its base in Faslane, followed the next day from Portsmouth by the two aircraft carriers, *Invincible* and *Hermes*, and their group of ships.

The big challenge for the UK waging war in the South Atlantic was one small detail that had up to now seemed largely an irrelevance: the RAF aircraft that could potentially be involved in the conflict did not have enough range, or 'legs'. Consequently, it was initially thought implausible for the RAF to support a naval mission of that magnitude that far south. Wideawake Airfield, on Ascension Island, was already 4,000 miles from the UK, and the Falklands were another 3,800 miles beyond that. Even flying empty, this was beyond the best range of the Hercules, so a solution was needed quickly. The finest engineering brains in the RAF were therefore set the task of finding the solution . . .

Like everyone on 47 Squadron, RAF Lyneham, Harry Burgoyne had been eagerly looking forward to the Easter weekend, and a well-earned break after a particularly busy period. His extensive experience flying missions on Op Agila meant the 30-year-old flight lieutenant knew the capabilities of the C-130 inside out. By now the longest-serving captain on the Flight, he had spent all of February on exercise with a squadron of elite troops in Africa conducting parachute training, including high altitude drops. He had then spent most of March working up the Hercules tactical demonstration for the summer air-display season, and planning and preparing for a 'coup de main' raid on RAF Laarbruch in Germany, for the station's tactical evaluation exercise. This had involved delivering a team of thirty hardened soldiers and two of their unique 'Pink Panther' Land Rovers onto Laarbruch's runway in a surprise night attack. Once on the ground, the troops had simulated blowing up the pilots' briefing room and 'exercise-killed' all the aircrew and support personnel within it. As a result, one of the RAF's main NATO fighter bases had been rendered completely inoperative.

Well, at least hypothetically. Though the exercise had been judged a success, Harry had his reservations. He knew his aircraft had been spotted by Laarbruch's radars, engaged by its Rapier air-defence missiles and, in effect, been shot down about two miles out from the runway. If this type of operation was ever going to be used for real, upgraded equipment and improved tactics would need to be evolved.

Busy with their training, the members of the Flight had not paid much attention to the news of the Falklands invasion. After all, it was already apparent that the UK forces would not be allowed access to any South American airfields, and the nearest usable one, Wideawake Airfield on Ascension Island, was well outside the operating range of the RAF's C-130 Hercules aircraft. Consequently, Harry, along with the rest of the C-130 aircrew, considered it extremely unlikely that the unfolding events would have any impact on their Cold War role of supporting covert activities.

However, others had different ideas.

On 3 April 1982, the morning after the invasion, the Flight's commanding officer, Squadron Leader Max Roberts (having survived that career-limiting moment with the monarch) was ferried by helicopter to Stirling Lines in Hereford, to discuss the situation in the Falklands with Lieutenant Colonel Mike Rose, the commanding officer there, and his staff. Many ideas were put forward, a few of them a little wild,[1] and Max was left with much to consider after the meeting.

A huge airlift of personnel and equipment to Gibraltar and Ascension Island was now under way and all the Hercules fleet were involved, including 47 Squadron aircrew. So it was not until the morning of 9 April that Max, having thought about the ideas promulgated at the Hereford meeting and formulated a plan for the required training, managed to get all his aircrew together for a briefing.

He explained that they would definitely be involved in covert ops, but that details of how and when were still sketchy. Max pointed out that the recent airfield assault at Laarbruch had been done using only one Hercules, and went on to lay out the bones of a proposed operation that would involve a two-aircraft airfield attack. Each C-130 would carry around thirty men, two Pink Panthers, and motorbikes, and both would be required to land simultaneously onto either Port Stanley Airfield on the Falkland Islands or an as yet unknown airbase. Once on the ground, they would unload the troops and vehicles ASAP and either depart immediately or wait on the runway for the troops to hit their targets and return. How they would get to either target was still to be decided.

Two Hercules-sized aircraft landing simultaneously at night, without landing lights, on a possibly unlit runway, and only 2,000 feet apart, had never been done before. An operation of this sort would require very careful planning and the evolution of completely new standard operating procedures (SOPs).

Max then announced that they would commence training for the approach and landing phase immediately. He also confirmed that it would most certainly not be a 'bring a bottle war' – as the Rhodesia op had been dismissively and unfairly nicknamed by those not in the know – and was likely to make huge demands on them.

As he came to the end of his brief, Max told them that one of the crews would be deploying that evening to Ascension to conduct resupply parachute drops to the ships of the British Task Force as they steamed steadily southwards.

That afternoon, the remaining four crews began an intensive programme of mission rehearsals, plus devising the new SOPs that would be required to meet these and other operational plans still being developed at the Northwood HQ of Operation Corporate, as the task to retake the Falkland Islands had now been named.

They flew to the nearby airfield of RAF Colerne, just outside Bath, and began to familiarize those who had not been involved in the assault on Laarbruch with the procedures and tactics involved. Unfortunately, it was a beautiful Good Friday bank holiday, and this unusual activity at the normally quiet airfield quickly drew a large crowd of civilian spectators to the perimeter fence, keen to watch these unexpected proceedings – not exactly ideal for crews trying to rehearse a top-secret mission.

It was also less than ideal that on this first day of training they narrowly avoided suffering their first casualty when a communications breakdown led to an early brake release as one of the aircraft powered up for take-off. This resulted in Air Loadmaster (ALM) Flight Sergeant Mick Sephton being toppled off the rear ramp of the Hercules and then blasted down the runway by the fierce propeller wash. As if this was not bad enough, Mick was quickly followed by one of the seventy-pound, five-foot-long, metal toe-ramps that were used for loading vehicles onto the rear ramp and into the freight bay. It had also been caught by the 80-mile-an-hour wind and similarly dislodged from the aircraft. As Mick tumbled down the runway, the toe-ramp hit the ground between him and the plane, bounced over him and missed him by inches. It was a very close call and could have caused him very serious injury or worse had it hit him. It could only be hoped that the huddle of perimeter-fence spectators assumed this was all part of the performance.

Thankfully, bar a few scratches and bruises, Mick was okay; but, as a result of this incident, procedures were altered and tightened up and the toe-ramps from then on were secured to the rear ramp so that they could not come loose.

Further training was carried out over Saturday and Easter Sunday, but relocated to the more remote RAF Marham in Norfolk to avoid unwelcome public attention. As SOPs and tactics continued to be refined and developed, it was announced that the target would not be the Port Stanley option, but a heavily defended Argentine airbase and its Super Étendard jets, their pilots and Exocet missiles.

On 12 April, Harry Burgoyne and his navigator, Flight Lieutenant Jim Cunningham, were summoned to the office of the Lyneham station commander, Group Captain Clive Evans, for a classified briefing. When they arrived, they were met by Evans and Squadron Leader Graeme Young, who had been Max Roberts's immediate predecessor and was now a staff officer at the transport fleet HQ at 38 Group.

'We need a reconnaissance team on the Falklands,' he told them without preamble, 'and you've been selected to insert it.'

A top-secret mission was to be mounted from Chilean-owned Easter Island in the Pacific Ocean. 'Ostensibly,' the squadron leader went on, ' it will look like you'll be delivering the Sea Skua missiles to the Chileans that were already ordered before the Argentinian invasion.'

A good cover, but there was a lot more to it than that. They would route from Easter Island to Punta Arenas in southern Chile to deliver the missiles and then return to Easter Island. However, at a suitable time, some hours after departure from Punta Arenas, the crew would 'discover' the fuses for the missiles had been inadvertently left on board and would then notify ATC that they would need to go back to Punta. This was where things would take a different turn.

The crew would actually descend to low level, route below radar cover round Cape Horn to East Falkland and parachute drop an eight-man recce patrol before returning to Punta Arenas. They would then unload the fuses and continue back to Easter Island. The whole mission would take around thirty hours.

Evans instructed Harry and Jim to prepare a detailed plan and start conducting any extra training that would be required. 'But do not tell anyone about this,' the squadron leader ordered them, 'not even the other members of your own crew.'

Once out of the briefing, Harry and Jim discussed this latest piece of news, and realized that they would not be able to conduct the planning and training required for this complex task without taking co-pilot Flight Lieutenant Bob 'Bumper' Rowley, air engineer Flight Sergeant Steve 'Sluggie' Sloan and ALM Mick Sephton into their confidence, so they did.

Concurrently with the work-up for this secret mission, Harry's crew also joined the other three crews in training for the other operation. Both were fraught with danger, but this one in particular was looking increasingly hazardous, as flying in formation at night and landing two large aircraft only 2,000 feet apart was, by its very nature, very dangerous indeed. Especially at the point where the two aircraft approached the runway, both completely blacked out bar the formation lights on top of the wings and with the second aircraft frequently losing sight of the leader in any ground lighting. And once on the runway, a collision was also a real possibility, as both aircraft braked heavily to a halt.

As the training progressed, various RAF airfields around the UK were 'attacked', but always with the same result: the aircraft could not fly low enough at night to avoid detection by the target airfield's radar. New techniques, plans and procedures were introduced as a consequence, but it often seemed that negating one problem only uncovered another, fresh one. And all the while, time was ticking away, and the grim reality began to sink in that, for the aircraft and the human guinea pigs aboard them, this mission could easily become a one-way trip.

It also became apparent that to undertake either of their missions the crews would need new equipment and/or upgrades of their existing kit. However, their many previous requests prior to Op Corporate had not been supported by the upper echelons of the RAF, a niggling annoyance whose roots were historic. The higher command of the RAF was selected from fast-jet pilots; transport pilots rarely made it to the highest ranks. As a result, the focus of the RAF's equipment-procurement budget tended to be concentrated on fighter aircraft, leaving little or nothing for the Hercules fleet. When (or if) these decisions were challenged, a common response would be that 'the Hercules will never be deployed to, or used within, a high-threat environment'.

This was, of course, nonsense. The Hercules was being used continuously in high-threat environments. In ferrying troops into and out of Northern Ireland, where the IRA were known to have man-portable, heat-seeking SAM-7 missiles, and lots of small arms, to boot. The RAF's C-130s had also been used in 1979 to evacuate UK and allied refugees from Iran following the fall of the Shah. And as recently as the following year, in Rhodesia, several crews had frequently spotted tracer close to them, and at least one Hercules aircraft had been hit by small arms fire.

Even within the Hercules fleet HQ at 38 Group, and despite frequent requests from the Flight, there was a reluctance to create a 'mini-fleet' of dedicated, better-equipped Hercs. It was argued that equipment such as an improved navigation suite, a radar warning receiver

(RWR), chaff and flare dispensers, cockpit armour or fire-suppressant-foam-filled fuel tanks could not be fitted, mainly on grounds of cost and maintainability. So there was no option but to go to war lamentably short of equipment.

The resourceful aircrew were not daunted, however, and ended up acquiring lots of equipment themselves. A hand-held RWR, designed for use in helicopters, was procured from the Fleet Air Arm at Yeovilton. Sea-survival suits, as worn by passengers on oil rig helicopter flights, were purchased, basic cockpit-seat armour was manufactured from steel sheets in the Lyneham workshops, parachutes were 'liberated' from the Parachute Training School at RAF Brize Norton, and old flak jackets were brought in from the army. Two extra flight-deck observation cupolas (known as 'bubbles' and fitted in the cockpit-roof escape hatch to spot enemy fighter aircraft) were eventually tracked down, one from the RAF stores at Carlisle and the other from Lyneham-based 30 Squadron's crew room, where it was being used as a punch bowl.

Thanks to the support of Group Captain Evans, and his station's unstinting engineers, everything was obtained and fitted in record time. And eventually, after much pleading, other key bits of equipment, such as an inertial navigation system (INS) and NVGs – things they could not procure themselves – *were* obtained through official sources.

As is so often the case, however, these necessary new fits came with their own complications. Good as it was to have an INS, it was subject to navigation drift error. A minimum of two was the usual fit – ideally three – to allow for comparison of their accuracy in order to identify if one was malfunctioning. So the aircrew had to conduct their own trials to establish the drift rate of their solitary unit and how accurate it would be during the very long flights they would be conducting.

Similarly, flying with NVG equipment (then known as ANVIS – Airman's Night Vision Imaging System) was still only in its infancy in 1982, and the only people doing it in the UK at that time were test pilots in specially adapted fighters. Because the normal cockpit white lighting was too bright for them to work, the Hercules lighting had to be specially adapted by fitting blue acetate filters to all the lights in the cockpit.

But there was no time – or enough acetate filter material – to modify over 150 dials and gauges (some 250-plus bulbs in total) to make them all compatible with NVG. So the aircrew and the Lyneham aircraft engineers compromised. Every instrument or gauge with internal lighting had its face covered with the acetate filter, which was taped in place, and the dozens of external 'p' bulbs located above individual gauges were removed. The 'p' bulbs that illuminated the pilots' essential instruments – such as airspeed indicators, altimeters and compass – were then carefully fitted with minute blue laminate filters and put back in place. Other high-priority lights, including the 'low' warning lights on the radar altimeter indicators, were also fitted with filters.

To help further, the engineers constructed a rudimentary lighting 'harness' using balsa wood and straps, which had filtered floodlights incorporated into it. This was suspended from the coaming above the pilots' instrument panels. This new, Heath-Robinsonesque lighting system was far from ideal, but at least it worked, which was as much as could be hoped for.

On the night of the first flights, a test pilot from Farnborough came down and briefed each crew in turn. They all then taxied to the blacked-out Lyneham runway and, while focusing on a star and/or the surrounding terrain, each adjusted their NVGs until they achieved the best picture they could. It was very scant training but time was very short. Once all the crews had had a go, the test pilot basically left them to it.

As the training progressed, they learned about flying with NVGS. The equipment needed a minimum of a quarter moon at thirty degrees elevation to work effectively: anything less and the picture deteriorated markedly. Plus the goggles were particularly prone to shutting down in rain, fog or cloud, which was exciting when flying close to the ground!

Undeterred, they pressed on, finding solutions to the problems NVGs kept creating. The navigator's station at the rear of the flight deck, which still had normal white lighting, for example, had to be screened off by a heavily lined curtain. The existing one, which had been too thin to block out sufficient light, was removed by the engineers, relined and replaced, then taped to the cockpit walls and floor. But despite their best efforts there were still occasionally leaks of white light from inside the cockpit itself. To cure this, two-inch strips of 'bodge' tape were prepared before flight, and stuck to the pilots' flying helmets. If a leak was detected, the flight engineer peeled a piece of the tape off the pilot's helmet, passed it forward and the pilot covered the offending leak point. Reflections of white light in the cockpit windows were more tricky, however, and it sometimes took considerable effort to locate the source and cover it. And all this was generally happening in the dark, while flying at 250 miles per hour only 250 feet above the English countryside.

This was the first time NVGs were ever used by regular aircrew on RAF fixed-wing aircraft. It was demanding and tiring flying and the Flight were basically making it up as they went along, all the time working at the very edge of safety. They had several close calls, but considered themselves fortunate not to have suffered an accident other than Mick Sephton's 'adventure' at Colerne on the first day of training.

By mid-April, the Task Force ships had sailed well south of Ascension and would soon be beyond the range of the Ascension-based Hercules that were still airdropping supplies to them. However, a potential solution to the problem of range had, at least in theory, been found.

The RAF's fleet of Andover twin-prop transport aircraft were, by 1982, approaching the end of their service life. They had used internal fuel tanks to extend their range during ferry flights, such as flying across the Atlantic, with each internal tank able to hold about 7,000 pounds of fuel. There were twenty-eight of these tanks, which had effectively been scrapped and put into storage, but someone realized they could still be useful.

To increase the range of the Hercules, the 'retired' fuel tanks were hastily retrieved, and four of them were mounted in the freight bay of Harry's aircraft, complete with rapidly designed and installed pipework. They now had to prove this rudimentary system actually worked, and over the next few days experimental trial flights of over ten hours became commonplace for Harry and his crew, alongside training for their top-secret mission from Easter Island.

The trial flights could be hair-raising. On one of Harry's, the auxiliary fuel system piping burst and flooded the inside of the freight bay with gallons of fuel. As there were no procedures in place for such an emergency, the problem was solved by simply opening the rear door of the Hercules and then climbing, so that the fuel poured out of the back. But in just over a week, remarkably, the internal-tank fit was cleared for service – something that, in peacetime, would have been done by highly trained test pilots and would probably have taken more than a year. Yet it still wasn't enough.

Towards the end of April, it became apparent that the plan to use the internal tanks to resupply the Task Force would be short-lived. The ships were now at the extreme range of the Ascension-based Hercules – even those fitted with the repurposed Andover fuel tanks. A means of further extending the range of the aircraft had to be found, and the answer was air-to-air refuelling.

Although some USAF special operations Hercules were capable of being refuelled in the air using the American boom system, AAR using the British probe and drogue system had never been envisaged for the RAF's Hercules. Now it was – and it was needed quickly.

The decision to proceed with modifying the Hercules to become AAR-capable was made in late April, and

Marshall of Cambridge, the designated Lockheed UK engineering authority, set to with a will.

Plans and system blueprints were quickly drawn up and XV200, a C Mk1 Hercules undergoing scheduled maintenance in the Marshall's hangar was chosen to be the guinea pig. On 29 April, it emerged, now with an air-to-air refuelling probe fitted directly above the co-pilot's position, connected to a hastily faired-in fuel pipe running along the top of the fuselage and into the ground refuelling manifold located just aft of the starboard wing. After a test flight by Marshall, the aircraft was flown to the Aeroplane and Armament Experimental Establishment (A&AEE) at Boscombe Down, for RAF acceptance trials.

On the morning of 6 May, Max and Harry, plus a composite crew, assembled in a briefing room at A&AEE, both to prove the system, and to learn how to conduct AAR operations under the tutelage of test pilot Squadron Leader John Brown.

Once they were airborne, they quickly met up with the Victor tanker aircraft and established that the Hercules AAR system worked. But, as they proceeded with further trial flights, they encountered a very large problem – one that nobody had anticipated.

The Victor's refuelling hose was held out in the airstream against spring pressure by the shuttlecock-shaped basket at its end, and required a minimum speed of 230 knots to keep it in position. As the fuel increased the weight of the Hercules, however, it became obvious that the turboprop C-130 could not maintain this speed. A solution was required and it was Co-Pilot Bob Rowley who came up with the answer – refuel while descending, giving the Hercules the extra energy to keep up with the sleek, jet-propelled Victor. They tried it, it worked and, as it involved 'sliding down hill at speed', the technique was known thereafter as 'tobogganing'.

A trial such as this would normally have taken years but, only five days later, the Hercules was cleared to refuel by day or night from a Victor tanker aircraft at weights up to 175,000 pounds (in peacetime, the normal maximum oper- ating weight of the C-130 was 155,000 pounds), on four and three engines, and Max and Harry became the first two Hercules pilots cleared to conduct AAR operations.

Already an experienced RAF qualified flying instructor, Max Roberts was appointed as the first Hercules AAR instructor and began teaching AAR to other Hercules pilots, and forming what would become Lyneham's Tanker Training Flight.

On the afternoon of 12 May, Harry and his crew were ordered to RAF Brize Norton to board a VC-10 aircraft bound for Ascension Island, from where they would start resupplying the Task Force using their newly acquired, and definitely unrefined, AAR skills.

When they arrived at Ascension mid-morning on the 13th, Wideawake Airfield appeared initially to be a scene of total chaos. It was hot, dusty, and the noise was ear-shattering. Apron space was at a premium, with Victors, Nimrods, VC-10s, Hercules, Belfasts and even a visiting USAF C-141 apparently shoehorned into their parking slots, while overhead a never-ending stream of buzzing heli- copters went about their business ferrying equipment out to Task Force ships moored just offshore.

The predatory shapes of two Vulcan bombers parked to the south of the apron seemed to preside over this hive of activity. And the Shrike anti-radar missiles, slung men-acingly under their wings, only added to the sinister image.

After extracting all their bags from the pile at the side of the VC-10, and an interminable wait for transport, the crew were driven four miles over the stark volcanic plain and up a winding hill road, bound for the bungalow that would become their home for the next few months, in the relative calm and marginally cooler surrounds of Two Boats village. Here they would meet up with the two other crews that had already been detached to Ascension to con-duct the increasingly long-range resupply parachuting task as more and more Task Force ships sailed south.

Since long flights of over twenty-four hours were now being contemplated, the captain and navigator from one of those crews had been selected to augment Harry's crew and share the workload. The pilot, Flight Lieutenant Jim Norfolk, and navigator, Flight Lieutenant Tom Rounds, had already flown several long-distance sorties to the Task Force. During a very detailed briefing, the two stalwarts passed on a wealth of knowledge and experience regarding naval procedures, weather and, especially, the techniques of operating the Hercules well in excess of the manufac-turer's absolute maximum guaranteed safe weight of 175,000 pounds.

Jim Norfolk, the Flight's training captain, also explained that aircrew fatigue had already become a major consider-ation and was causing some concern. Normal peacetime rules stated that 120 flying hours per month should be the absolute maximum, but Jim's crew had already exceeded that by a considerable margin, having flown almost 190 hours in the previous thirty days. In addition, most of the other crews, including Harry's, were hovering around the 130–140-hour mark, and these were just the airborne times. They took no account of the pre- and post-flight duties that each crew carried out.

Consequently, rules of engagement for the use of the bungalow's two available bedrooms, and their four single beds, had been devised to ensure that everyone got the best rest possible. As there would now be over twenty personnel sharing the limited facilities, the ROE were simple – outbound crews heading south had priority; crews in post-flight rest were next; and if neither of these were factors, the rule of 'first come, first served' applied. In fact, most people just elected to sleep in the crowded living room or found a quiet area in the garden, where, given the personnel and vehicles active around the bungalow during the day, 'quiet' was a relative term.

To help the crews sleep, the RAF's Institute of Aviation Medicine had hurriedly cleared temazepam sleeping pills for aircrew use, and the 'yellow perils', as they were affectionately known, became a vital aid to sleep in the crowded, noisy, non-air-conditioned environment of the Flight's accommodation, their efficacy speeded up by being washed down with a can of beer, or 'Dr McEwan's exported amber sleeping draught', as it generally became known.

The moment of truth for Harry and his crew had arrived, as the Task Force had now entered the Total Exclusion Zone (TEZ) – an area of 200 nautical miles radius centred on the Falkland Islands, which had been declared by the United Kingdom on 30 April. Within this area, any sea vessel or aircraft, from *any* country, could be fired upon without further warning.

The morning of 15 May started in the same way the previous one had, with a long queue outside the bungalow's one bathroom, following which the crews cooked themselves breakfast, then crowded round the radio for the daily eleven o'clock 'intelligence update', which came courtesy of the BBC World Service. They then, in anticipation of the challenge ahead, retired to the garden to read, sunbathe or write a bluey home.

By now, despite the brief nature of the training he'd received, Harry felt confident in both his and his crew's ability to conduct any AAR long-range drops to the Task Force. He felt similarly confident about doing the parachute insertion. After all, it was what he had been trained to do over many years. However, he was fairly convinced that they would not survive their other mission – the airfield attack – and that they would either be shot down approaching the target, as had happened at Laarbruch and during their UK-based rehearsals, or shot to pieces on the runway if they managed to get that far. There were just too many obstacles and unknowns on such a long-distance raid, and the likely winter weather in Tierra del Fuego and lack of a moon during the proposed period of the operation, nullifying the use of NVGs, were just some of them. It was a very tense and stressful time for all the aircrew.

At 1300 hours, after getting what scant rest he could, Harry was ordered to report with his crew to Air Transport Ops. Following a lengthy transport delay, they finally reached the airfield, where the detachment commander, Squadron Leader Nick Hudson, briefed them for their first AAR mission. Hudson was concise and to the point.

'You are tasked to conduct an airdrop of eight para-chutists and 1,000-pounds of stores to the Royal Fleet Auxiliary ship *Fort Austin*, some sixty miles north of Port Stanley Airfield. Drop time is 1500 Zulu tomorrow after-noon. My staff will offer you any assistance we can, but my resources are tight. Commence your planning and let me know your take-off time as soon as you have it. Good luck!'

Only the crew knew that the eight elite troops were the recce team for a covert operation and that, after being dropped to the Task Force, they would later be helicop-tered into Argentina to gather intelligence and report back to headquarters.

Harry, Bob and Jim set to work immediately and quickly had the sketchy outline of a plan they could work with. As the drop was scheduled for mid-afternoon the following day and transit time to the drop zone would be almost thirteen hours, this meant take-off at 0245, just over twelve hours away. Time had suddenly become of the essence. Because the detached Lyneham ground crew were fully committed to unloading and refuelling the constant stream of transport aircraft bringing supplies from the UK, it was left to the aircrew to prepare their own plane. They needed to move parachutes and survival equipment into the air-craft, order and collect rations, prepare and load the drop stores, liaise with the Victor AAR planners to devise the AAR plot, and then plan the actual flight, ensuring that they complied with the Task Force security procedures as they approached. And, of course, after that, try to get some sleep before the wake-up time of 2330.

Harry's air loadmaster, Mick Sephton, and flight engineer, Steve Sloan, aided by two other ALMs, Pete Scott and Roy

Lewis, began the lengthy process. While the pilots and navigators started their initial flight planning, fuel tanks were filled, aircraft equipment checked, and the crew's survival suits, life jackets and parachutes were stowed and secured. Though the likelihood of ditching in the waters around the Falklands was small, with Argentine fighters scouring the area they couldn't discount the possibility. If their aircraft was hit, Harry hoped to get his crew out by parachute close to a Task Force ship, to minimize the time in the water. The survival suits were probably good for sixty to ninety minutes in the freezing ocean, but the aircrew life jackets contained a radio, flares and a light to aid being located quickly, so if they were lucky they'd be picked up much sooner.

The 1,000 pounds of specialist equipment was finally loaded into two waterproof containers, carefully rigged for parachuting, and then positioned on the aircraft ramp by the two 47 Air Despatch Squadron army soldiers who would be flying with them.

Three hours later, and with the sun sinking towards the ocean, all the preparations were complete. Well, with the exception of the all-important fuel and AAR plan. As nearly all the Victor tanker aircraft were currently airborne, refuelling a long-range Nimrod sortie, there was no way of knowing how many of them would be available for the Hercules task until they returned some hours later. Without hesitation, Jim Cunningham came forward.

'Harry,' he said, 'I'll stay here at the airhead in the AAR cell and complete the planning when I can. The rest of you can get back to Two Boats and catch some sleep. I'm more than happy to kip down here when and if I can.'

Harry was not surprised by Jim Cunningham's selfless

gesture. It was absolutely typical of him. Very grateful, Harry readily accepted, and hastily arranged transport for the others back to their accommodation so they could hopefully get some rest before their pick-up time of midnight.

Harry found it difficult to sleep that evening. It was noisy, it was hot, and he was extremely nervous; he knew the success of the forthcoming mission depended entirely on his ability to complete a successful AAR. However, at the appointed time, all the crew, minus Jim, assembled outside their accommodation to await the transport – which duly arrived forty minutes late . . .

Despite this inauspicious start, and having forgone breakfast to make up the lost time, they rushed through an intelligence brief and eventually arrived at the flight-planning tent at the side of the aircraft parking apron. Here they rejoined Jim, who had worked tirelessly throughout the evening and had only completed his fuel planning some forty minutes earlier. The number of Victor tankers available was limited, and the only plan that worked meant they would have to uplift all their fuel in one go, some six hours after take-off. Not ideal, but there seemed little choice.

Harry managed to work through the aircraft's performance manual and to calculate all the required speeds for their expected take-off weight of 181,000 pounds. Unfortunately, the graphs only went up to Lockheed's maximum safe operating weight of 175,000 pounds, so Harry had to extrapolate and the resultant speeds were nothing more than educated guesses. Again, not ideal.

What Harry, somewhat unsettlingly, *did* know for certain, was that if they lost an engine immediately after take-off, the remaining three engines would be unable to produce enough power to keep them flying – taking them directly to the scene of a very nasty crash landing, either on any remaining runway or, if they couldn't make it to the ocean, on the mile of very rough and unforgiving volcanic rock that lay between the two. Under normal, peacetime regulations, this 'overload situation' would not have been allowed and the weight of the aircraft would have been reduced so that flight on three engines would enable the aircraft to keep flying and safely climb away.

Harry was also concerned about the structural integrity of the aircraft wings as they were required to support such heavy weights. Jim Norfolk, however, offered some welcome reassurance, saying he had already made several take-offs at similar weights on his previous long-range drops using the internal tanks. Plus, Harry knew that several of the USAF Hercules aircraft that had participated in the abortive Iranian hostage rescue attempt in April 1980 had taken off at close to 190,000 pounds. There was also Harry's confidence in his aircraft. Over the nine years and 3,000-plus hours he had flown it, he had come to trust the Herc, and was sure Fat Albert wouldn't let them down.

Still, the atmosphere was strangely quiet as the crew walked out to the waiting aircraft and each man set about his individual pre-flight tasks. Survival suits were unpacked, parachutes checked, flak jackets issued, and everything positioned ready for immediate use. Harry then went into the freight bay to check on progress and was immediately struck by the lack of space.

The four Andover fuel tanks obviously filled the main cargo area, and the ramp area was now stacked with the boxes containing the parachutists' equipment. So tight was space, that the chemical toilet that normally sat there was now in the middle of the freight bay, offering no privacy to anyone who might have cause to use it – as, given the twenty-three hours plus that they would be airborne, they surely would.

The eight troops, meanwhile, had spread out along the red webbing seats adjacent to the fuel tanks and were trying to create an area that might offer some comfort during the thirteen hours they were going to be on board. Having got to know a couple of them during training, Harry said a quick 'hello' and then formally briefed the whole crew, including the two army air despatchers and the two parachute jump instructors who would supervise the troops during the drop. He then took the opportunity to enjoy a swift smoke outside before finally returning to the flight deck. As far as they could be, Harry felt, everyone was good to go.

As the last few minutes before departure ticked away, there was little of the normal friendly banter. Everyone was engrossed in their own world, preoccupied with their individual thoughts. However, at the appointed time, the familiar ritual of the start checks concentrated minds and the sleeping Hercules was slowly nursed into life. Bob Rowley contacted ATC.

'Wideawake Tower, Ascot 4622 request taxi.' Significantly, he used the standard air transport 'Ascot' callsign so as to blend in with all the normal resupply flights; they would revert to their tactical trigraph callsign of 'DFR 68' once south of Ascension.

The American Wideawake controller responded

immediately. 'Ascot 4622, cleared to taxi to Runway 14, and enter and take off when ready. Altimeter two niner eight eight. Have a good flight.'

Harry pushed the throttles forward and the Hercules slowly taxied out and into position on the threshold of Ascension's 10,000-foot runway. Then, as he applied full power and released the brakes, he noted the time as 0240 and idly wondered when – or if – they were going to get back to Ascension.

Such thoughts quickly vanished as the aircraft gathered speed, however. As Harry had anticipated, the take-off roll had been much longer than normal, but in answer to his tentative pull on the control column, XV200 rose slowly into the warm night air. Once away from the island, the sky was pitch black with no discernible horizon, so Harry concentrated hard on his flight instruments. He had never flown the Hercules that heavy before but, reassuringly, it seemed to behave as normal; the only really noticeable difference was that everything seemed to be happening a little slower than usual.

Wanting to have plenty of speed in hand before attempting any manoeuvres at such a heavy weight, Harry levelled at 2,000 feet and allowed the aircraft to slowly accelerate before easing into a gentle turn and, as they rolled out on course, engaged the autopilot and started the climb. Now able to look outside, he noted that the Southern Cross was slightly off the nose, clearly visible among the multitude of stars twinkling in the deep purple-black of the night sky.

With the aircraft stabilized in a cruise climb, the next few hours passed fairly routinely as the crew kept busy carrying out hourly fuel calculations and checks. Mick

Sephton had by now opened the aircraft's small galley and, amazingly, produced freshly made egg and bacon sandwiches, which were swiftly despatched.

At just after 0600, the sun finally rose under the left wing, bathing the cockpit in the subdued, warm pink hue of the dawn – a privileged view only granted to aviators in flight. The increased light, combined with copious amounts of hot, sweet coffee, restored energy levels as they continued southwards in preparation for the airborne refuel. The atmosphere, however, was growing tense. Harry, in particular, was very conscious that the success of the mission was totally dependent on him being able to hook up to the Victor and get the required fuel on board.

By 0800, they had burned off about 32,000 pounds of fuel, had climbed to just over 22,000 feet, and were approaching the refuelling rendezvous point. Harry noted that the area was clear apart from some cumulonimbus clouds far below. They wouldn't be a factor, he thought, with some relief.

As he pondered the job ahead of him, Harry was roused from his reverie by the harsh intrusion of the radio call from the approaching Victor.

'Delta Foxtrot Romeo 68, Alpha Lima Mike 23 is with you approaching the RV.'

Having taken off from Ascension sometime after the C-130, the much faster tanker had gradually closed the gap and was now only five miles behind. Co-Pilot Bob Rowley responded immediately.

'Alpha 23, this is Delta 68. Flight level 222 on one zero one three, ready for RV.'

And so the ballet of air-to-air refuelling began. As Harry

adjusted his seat and restraining harness, he mentally ran through the procedure he was about to undertake for only the sixth time in his life. His palms were glistening with moisture as he slipped on his flying gloves; in contrast, his mouth felt distinctly dry.

But there was no time to mull over the enormity of the task, as the slim, elegant shape of the Victor, captained by Squadron Leader Martin Todd, swiftly overtook the slower Hercules and stabilized 1,000 feet above, just forward of the Hercules' right wing. They were now maintaining formation, and Bob Rowley transmitted again.

'Alpha 23, Delta 68 visual.'

'Roger, Delta 68,' came the reply from the Victor. 'I have the lead. Commence toboggan, ready, ready, go! Delta 68, you're clear astern.'

'Delta 68. Roger, clear astern.'

Simultaneously, both aircraft began a gradual toboggan at about 500 feet per minute. Trying to keep his control inputs to a minimum, Harry carefully manoeuvred into a line-astern position and began moving forward on his hook-up run towards the Victor's trailing refuelling hose. Under Bob's calm directions, and with Steve Sloan, the flight engineer, monitoring the engines, the two giants slowly closed until the refuelling probe on top of the Hercules and the Victor's basket were only ten feet apart.

'Delta 68, Alpha 23. You're clear contact.'

As well as aerial ballet, AAR has also been described rather more pithily as 'trying to take a flying fuck at a rolling doughnut'. This was no exception. Twice Harry edged his aircraft forward, but each time the basket, dancing around in the turbulent airflow between the two aircraft,

23 August 1954. The prototype Hercules takes to the air for the first time.

In 1963, a Hercules landed and took off from the USS *Forrestal* to become the largest aircraft ever to fly from a carrier.

C-130s flew on operations throughout the Vietnam War.

The first Hercules for the RAF was delivered in a bare metal finish and painted at Marshall of Cambridge.

The Hercules entered service with the RAF in 1967 and was soon in action supporting Britain's withdrawal from Aden.

In 1973, RAF C-130s flew famine relief missions in Nepal as part of Operation Khana Cascade.

The RAF deployed the Hercules to Antarctica in support of US bases.

Dropping supplies in Rhodesia in 1979/80 as part of the Commonwealth monitoring force.

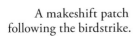

Birdstrike! Hercules crews in Africa faced unexpected hazards from local wildlife.

A makeshift patch following the birdstrike.

The author with Brigadier General Joshua Shani, lead pilot for the
Israel Defence Force mission to rescue hostages from Entebbe in Uganda.

IDF commandos hoped to buy valuable
extra seconds by arriving
in a Mercedes similar to the one
used by Ugandan VIPs.

The wreckage of a C-130 at
the Desert One base during the
disastrous attempt to rescue US
hostages from Tehran in 1980.

A Hercules takes fuel from a Victor tanker. The capability was rushed into service during the Falklands War in 1982.

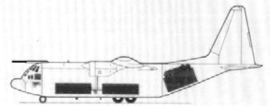

Long-range tanks were also fitted inside the Hercules cargo bay.

Too close for comfort! The view refuelling behind a Victor.

After the war. A Hercules flies low over the
South Atlantic, escorted by two RAF Phantoms.

All that remains of the harness that nearly
dragged Loadmaster Roy Lewis out of the
back of a C-130 into the South Atlantic.

The low-flying regulations in the Falklands were open to interpretation!

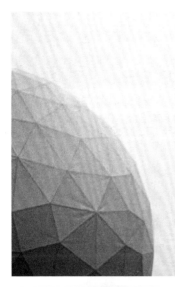

Showing off next to the radar site at Mount Kent in the Falklands.

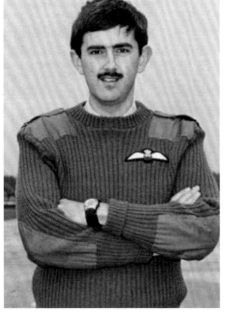

'The name of the Nile will be an omen of your strength'. Crest for 47 Squadron.

Simon Footer was at RAF Akrotiri with 47 Squadron when he helped evacuate personnel injured in the 1983 bombing of the US Marine Corps barracks in Beirut.

Chasing shadows during the first Gulf War in 1991.

Yours truly standing guard as a 47 Squadron loadmaster, Mogadishu, 1992.

With my wife, Sharon.

Somalia, 1992. Renegade by name …

I completed my basic flying training in a Slingsby Firefly T67 M260.

Alongside the red, yellow and blue 47 Squadron patch, I was rare in also earning both a Loadmaster brevet and pilot's wings.

moved away and he failed to get his probe into it. Although his frustration was building, he had to keep on trying, always conscious that valuable fuel was being used up and the formation was getting lower and lower. Finally, as they passed through 18,000 feet, it was a case of third time lucky – a successful contact was made, and the precious fuel began to flow.

To transfer the 37,000 pounds of fuel took over thirty minutes and, towards the end, it was touch and go. By that time, both aircraft had descended through 1,500 feet and were having to dodge around the dark cumulonimbus clouds that Harry had assessed earlier as not being a problem. Furthermore, the weight of the Hercules was back up to around 178,000 pounds. Just maintaining contact in the turbulent, low-level air was extremely difficult, and Harry was aware that if he accidentally disconnected before the requisite fuel had been transferred, he would not have sufficient power or altitude to reconnect and the mission would be lost.

Thankfully, Martin Todd in the Victor was on top of his game and skilfully led the airborne duo around the worst of the big clouds and showers until, after what seemed like an eternity, Steve Sloan announced that the refuel was complete. With an enormous feeling of relief, Harry could at last ease back on the power and, with a soft clunk and a slight spray of fuel from the basket, a clean disconnect was achieved.

As they started their climb back up to cruising altitude, Harry passed control to Co-Pilot Bob Rowley, wiped the sweat from his face and eyes and, while the Victor completed an elegant sweeping turn away northwards to

Ascension, gulped down three large cups of water. Having established that Bob had steadied their aircraft and that the compass needle had settled once more on south, towards the Falklands Total Exclusion Zone, he then extricated himself from his perspiration-sodden seat and retreated to the crew rest bunk, feeling absolutely drained but also conscious that an air of euphoria now pervaded the flight deck, and spirits were high.

It was over three hours before Harry returned to his seat, having spent two of those in the crew bunk in a futile attempt to sleep. Meanwhile, the rest of the crew had swapped roles in order to gain what rest they could. Just about one hour before the descent to the *Fort Austin*, each man resumed his normal station having donned his survival suit, life jacket and parachute.

To avoid detection by the Argentinian radar on the hill overlooking Port Stanley, the descent had been initiated about 250 miles north of the Falkland Islands. The Flight's specially devised 'combat entry checklist' had been completed to set the aircraft up in its best fighting configuration and, as Harry levelled the Hercules at 2,000 feet – just below the cloud base – the two army air despatchers checked in on the intercom from their observation positions in the open parachute doors, ready to alert the crew if they spotted enemy fighters. Bob Rowley now established radio contact with the Task Force.

'Zulu Whisky Romeo Tango, this is Delta Foxtrot Romeo 68.'

'Delta 68, this is Zulu Whisky Romeo Tango, go ahead.'

'Delta 68, approaching the gate, squawking as instructed. Request clearance to continue.'

Silence.

Bob, however, was calm. He had done an exchange tour with the Royal Navy, flying F-4 Phantoms off the *Ark Royal*, and was thus well acquainted with naval procedures. He explained to the rest of the Hercules crew that their message would probably have to be relayed to the bridge and the Task Force marshaller before a reply would be forthcoming. And a few moments later the reply duly came.

'Delta 68, this is Zulu Whisky Romeo Tango. We have you on our gadget. All ships have you identified as friendly. You are clear to proceed. Contact Golf Sierra Echo Victor on 322.4.'

'GSEV' was the callsign of the *Fort Austin*, but it would be a few minutes before the aircraft would be in range to make contact. As the aircraft entered the TEZ, the tension had become palpable; conversation had diminished, and all eyes scoured the horizon for enemy fighters.

Conditions were not ideal. It was a bitterly cold, grey day, with a cloud base of about 2,500 feet and visibility of about four miles, which decreased markedly in the widespread, squally showers, as Bob Rowley established contact with the *Fort Austin*.

'Golf Sierra Echo Victor, this is Delta Foxtrot Romeo 68. Seven miles, running in.'

'Delta 68, this is Golf Sierra Echo Victor. Identified, surface wind fourteen – one four – knots, sea temperature plus two, call running in for live drop.'

Fortunately, the wind speed was just within limits for the drop and, since the parachutists were wearing wetsuits, it all looked reasonable. As the aircraft homed towards the ship, the hastily installed, primitive hand-held radar-warning receiver chirped and squeaked, indicating that several radars were illuminating the Hercules; but, thankfully, no fire-control radars, either friendly or hostile, had 'lock-on'.

Harry then spotted the *Austin* about three miles ahead, riding on a grey sea and with its recovery boat already in the water. They descended to the drop height of 1,200 feet, opened the rear ramp and door and completed the final dropping checks.

Bob called again. 'Golf Sierra Echo Victor, this is Delta 68, running in, live drop.'

After a few moments came the reply. 'Delta 68, this is Golf Sierra Echo Victor. Cleared live drop.'

They were good to go.

All the parachutists were despatched on the first run, but the process of plucking them from the icy ocean into the recovery boat immediately ran into problems. A thousand feet above them, the Hercules circled overhead, the crew confused as to why the recovery of the men was taking so much longer than expected from training drops.

Forty-five minutes later, the last man was finally dragged aboard the recovery boat; three quarters of an hour during which the Herc had been burning precious fuel. By the time they had been cleared to drop the two stores containers, they were close to the minimum fuel required to return to Ascension; as soon as a faint voice on the radio confirmed that all the men were safe and that the stores were being hoisted on board, the Hercules immediately set off north into the gathering dusk. Shortly afterwards, that same faint voice came back again.

'Delta 68, this is Golf Sierra Echo Victor. Thank you

for the mail, it means a lot. Godspeed. Golf Sierra Echo Victor out.'

The modest amount of personal mail that the ALMs had managed to squeeze into the stores containers had been a small thing for the aircrew to do, but it obviously meant a great deal to those so far away from their homes and loved ones. It was a good note to leave on.

By the top of the climb, darkness had descended, and a new problem had arisen. Very strong northwesterly head-winds had developed and seemed likely to continue for some time. As they had very little fuel to spare after the delayed stores drop, a solution was required ASAP. It was Jim Cunningham who offered a possible way out, by using a technique borrowed from sailing ships – tacking. Instead of applying drift to their heading, and thus lowering their ground speed as they turned into the wind, they should maintain their track heading for thirty minutes, allow the aircraft to be blown east, then turn towards Ascension or directly into the wind to regain track.

It sounded a bit strange, but Harry could understand Jim's thinking. They were in uncontrolled airspace and thus free to proceed as they pleased. Plus the alternative options of asking for a precious Victor to be scrambled from Ascension and attempting an emergency night AAR some eighteen hours into the flight, or diverting to the South American mainland, were not inviting. Harry agreed to try Jim's idea and, amazingly, it worked. And continued to do so until the wind finally abated about two hours later.

As they continued the eleven-hour night flight back to Ascension, seats were once again swapped, and further meals eaten, but that was more to combat the ever-encroaching fatigue than from hunger. Games were devised, but they soon discovered that there was a limit to the number of times you can play 'I Spy' in a Hercules. Meanwhile, the BBC World Service News continued to provide hourly updates on the overall progress of the British forces' operation to restore the Falkland Islands to their rightful owner – Her Majesty the Queen – and to their inhabitants.

About an hour out from Ascension, it seemed that the most demanding and potentially hazardous portions of the flight had now passed, and they allowed themselves to relax a bit. However, the calm was soon shattered.

'Radar contact,' Jim suddenly announced. 'Ten o'clock, five miles. Potential threat.'

Intelligence briefs had mentioned the remote possibility of an Argentine Air Force Boeing 707 being equipped with air-to-air missiles and sent out on reconnaissance patrols, and although Harry and his crew had heard a rumour that it had already been intercepted by one of the UK's Sea Harriers, this had not been confirmed by intelligence.

Harry looked to their ten o'clock, and acquired a visual sighting almost immediately. 'Tally,' he confirmed. 'It's an aircraft turning towards.' This could be a game-changer, Harry thought. This could be that very 707 turning to get a bead on them.

Crews of the embedded unit were the only Hercules aircrew trained in fighter evasion. They practised it regularly, were good at it, and had shown that they could outwit enemy fighters on many exercises. That was, as long as the Hercules crew saw the fighters first. Having done so, Harry immediately took action. He disengaged the autopilot, reduced the power and started a high-bank-angle, high-G turn towards this apparent threat, to shield the hot engine exhausts from any heat-seeking missiles.

Jim Norfolk shot forward to Harry's side. 'Harry, it's friendlies!' he said, pointing at the lights. 'It's a string of Victors, departing Ascension!'

It was a fortunate intervention. What had appeared to Harry's very tired eyes as an aircraft in a turn was, in fact, a mass formation of tankers setting out on another mission – one which had not been known about when the Hercules aircrew had been briefed some twenty-seven hours earlier.

Following these hair-raising few minutes, the approach and landing were, in comparison, relatively straightforward. However, fatigue ensured that everyone monitored everyone else very closely as, some twenty-four hours and five minutes after take-off, XV200 finally touched down on Wideawake's runway.

Mission accomplished, the Hercules slowly taxied past two quick reaction alert Harrier fighters that were parked just off the edge of the taxiway to Runway 14. Steve Sloan wiped the grit from his eyes and passed his last fuel reading to Jim Cunningham, who duly completed his navigator's log and placed it in his bag. Harry continued taxiing into their parking slot on the crowded airfield apron and, as the aircraft came to a halt, Mick Sephton opened the crew door, stepped down onto the tarmac and filled his lungs gratefully with the fresh, salt-laden island air.

Harry called for the shut-down checks and, as the propellers of the Hercules slowly wound to a halt and the all-pervading noise of the engines faded, extracted his aching body from his seat. Stretching stiffly, he reflected inwardly on everything that his crew had been through in the lead up to their record-breaking flight. No RAF Hercules had ever been airborne for longer, and this was the first time AAR had been used operationally by one.

Bob Rowley, the co-pilot, had other things on his mind.

'Oh, wouldn't it be great,' he said, nodding towards the Harriers they'd just passed, 'to have a nice, safe job – like being on a front-line fighter squadron.'

7. Friend or Foe

As the Falklands War went on, the business of dropping troops and supplies to the Task Force – always a hazardous operation – became ever more complex and dangerous. This wasn't just about the obvious threats, either. The incredible innovations that would go on to become standard practice were accompanied by an often ad hoc decision-making process that was part and parcel of trying to militarily, and unexpectedly, take back this faraway place. There was also the multi-force, multi-agency nature of the whole business, with many top-secret missions executed alongside the war being documented for and seen by the general public.

War is terrible, and brutal, and necessarily fought on many fronts; but the added complication of the Falklands invasion having taken place so far from home brought an extra layer of jeopardy to all those fighting to defeat it. And, for the C-130 crews, this made the statement that 'the Hercules will never be deployed to, or used within, a high-threat environment' feel more than a little ironic.

By mid-May 1982, the Task Force had reached the Falkland Islands and battles were being fought on land, sea and in the air. Ships were being sunk, aircraft on both sides were being shot down, and the British Army had landed in San Carlos Bay.

With so many different forces and operations involved –

some highly secret – the Hercules crews were all too aware that they had to keep their wits about them, conscious that armed Argentinian aircraft were possibly roaming the South Atlantic, and that as they approached the TEZ to carry out their drops to the fleet, they came within range of Argentinian fighters.

When the Americans decided to use C-130s aggressively in Vietnam, they installed specialist defensive equipment, and even armed some of them. By contrast, when the RAF took delivery of its sixty-six Hercules in 1967, they were 'bog-standard' off-the-shelf models for strategic and tactical roles only, which were intended to be used mostly post-war, in 'friendly' environments away from any threats. Despite this, some crews had close shaves on operations, such as the evacuation of civilians from Dhaka in 1971 during the Pakistan Civil War, or, as Harry Burgoyne had discovered, positioning soldiers and personnel in Rhodesia following the unilateral declaration of independence by Prime Minister Ian Smith, to name but two. As a small flight within 47 Squadron evolved, prior to 1982, it was clear that, in order to get the customers to where they wanted to go, and to do what they had to do, it was necessary to fly lower, faster, almost exclusively at night and possibly behind enemy lines. Requests were therefore made, and papers were submitted, for better navigation and defensive equipment, just for a few aircraft – but, as previously noted, they were robustly turned down.

However, in what would arguably become one of the defining features of prosecuting the Falklands War, it wasn't just enemy threats the Herc crews had to worry about.

*

On 25 May, the same day that the *Atlantic Conveyor* was struck by two Exocet missiles, Max and his crew – Co-Pilots Nigel Watson and Dan Macintosh, Navigator Dave Musgrave, Augmentee (extra) Navigator Ken Bull, Flight Engineer Dick Ludford and Air Loadmaster Roy Lewis, were tasked with their second air bridge, 'Drop Mary', to the Bristol group of ships joining the Task Force, headed by HMS *Cardiff*. Because of the C-130's basic nav fit, the navigator had to be working *all* the time, so on these 24-hour-plus flights, they needed the extra manpower so crew could rest in rotation while others covered.

Also on board the aircraft would be four elite troops – replacements for some of those tragically killed in a Sea King helicopter crash near HMS *Hermes* on 19 May – plus containers of vital supplies, including some of the first mail the Task Force would have had for many weeks.

Married, with three sons, 35-year-old Max had by this time been a Hercules captain, training captain and instructor since 1971, and had been involved in most things the Hercs had been up to – wherever there was famine, drought, floods, earthquakes or unrest, he'd been there. However, he'd only taken over command of the small unit within 47 Squadron on 15 March 1982 – just two weeks before the invasion of the Falklands – so this undeclared war had already been a baptism by fire for him.

Max, Nigel and Dave briefed at around 1 a.m. at Operations HQ while Dick and Roy went to prepare the aircraft. During this briefing, the Victor AAR planners mentioned that one of their crews had reported the day before that they had had to take avoiding action from a surface-to-air missile, most probably a Sea Wolf fired from one of

Cardiff's picket ships, HMS *Penelope*. The navy maintained it had fired at the Argentinian 707 aircraft that was flying missions in the South Atlantic, but whatever had *actually* happened, this 'friendly fire' was worrying news.

But it was not insurmountable. Among the mass of planning paperwork were things called 'authentication tables', which provided one-time codes, related to time and date, which were used for replying when verbally challenged by Royal Navy ships. But because the crew knew that Task Force ships were really trigger-happy, and that, as transport crew, they knew nothing of the fine art of fleet penetration procedures – including broaching their missile engagement zone (MEZ) – Max also asked HQ for the Nimrod detachment on Ascension to supply the crew with an air electronics officer, or AEO, to be on board the flight, to guide them through this more than tricky part of the airdrops to the fleet.

With full wing and pylon tanks, plus the internal tanks and the cargo, they were nearly 10 per cent over peacetime maximum weight by the time they lined up on the runway for take-off. Still, the pre-dawn departure was uneventful, as was the first outbound AAR. However, in what would be the first of several potential disasters to dog the mission, the second refuelling, some eight hours south of Ascension, was slightly less so, there being significant weather, with a lot of cloud around their height of 23,000 feet. So finding the Victor in the first place wasn't easy. Once hooked up, and refuelling while descending in the toboggan, the Victor captain began weaving them around the cloud formations, in order to keep visual all the way down.

The refuelling required intense and sustained concentration as, after some twenty-five minutes 'in contact', they would likely be down 1,000 feet above the raging Atlantic, but could not afford to break contact till they had completely refuelled their wing tanks. Whatever the conditions, the margins were so tight that, if they did break contact early, they wouldn't have sufficient fuel to fly a further three to four hours, descend to low level for some 100 miles (where fuel consumption was very high), remain 'on task' for the drop for thirty minutes, then finally climb back out to maximum height for the twelve- to thirteen-hour long-range flight back to Ascension. Even with full tanks, they would still have to take care to conserve fuel, to ensure at least thirty minutes' flying in the event of bad weather back at base.

Ten minutes into the AAR, however, it became clear that they were dicing with disaster. The weather was so bad that it was becoming impossible to avoid; suddenly plunged into a bank of thick cloud at one point, Max completely lost sight of the Victor. All he could see was the end of the hose, some ten feet ahead. He knew he should break contact – safety protocols demanded it. But since that would have meant the failure of the mission, he decided to hold both his nerve and his position until the Victor reappeared ahead, thankfully only a few seconds later.

That potential disaster averted, they carried on, feeling greatly relieved. Some eleven hours after take-off it was time to descend, post the lookouts throughout the aircraft to watch for unfriendly 'bandits', and initiate pre-drop procedures. So far, so good. They now had the fleet on their radar, and as they approached at low level in the mist and rain, above a very rough and cold-looking South

Atlantic, it was the now infamous *Penelope* who interrogated them first.

Once again, despite their careful planning, they were potentially in great danger, because their reply codes, inexplicably, did not match the ones they had been given. The Nimrod AEO suggested that *Penelope*'s signaller was probably using the previous day's codes, which presented a problem. So high were the tensions, and so real the risk of enemy attack, that Max knew that if they continued to try, there was a real possibility they would receive their own 'mail', in the form of a decidedly unfriendly motorized explosive tree trunk, aimed right through their flight-deck window.

But, having flown for so many hours, and with such vital cargo, was the next step to simply give up? They had to get through with their men and supplies somehow, so Max turned round in his seat to the Nimrod AEO on the bottom bunk. Already out of his comfort zone (given that he was aboard a tactical flight on which all were carrying personal weapons and flak jackets, and currently taking measures to avoid being shot at or downed), he was now looking rather green as well.

'What do you suggest we do now?' Max asked him. 'We really need to come up with a solution – and ideally before we get shot down.'

The AEO spent a few moments apparently deep in thought. 'Just tell them we've got all their mail,' he suggested. 'And that we're happy to take it straight back to Ascension.'

It was a novel approach. And given everyone's high state of alert, it was potentially extremely risky. But it was the only idea anyone had.

'Do it,' said Max to his co-pilot. And Max's co-pilot

transmitted in no uncertain terms: '*Penelope*, do you want your fucking mail or not?'

Thankfully, not least for the AEO, it worked, because *Cardiff* then transmitted – rather wearily, Max thought – '*Penelope*, let them through.'

But the problems didn't end there. Normal safe procedure was always to drop containers before troops, but because of the cramped conditions down the back due to the internal fuel tanks for the twenty-four-hour mission, it wasn't logistically possible; they had to drop the troopers before the containers. And given that they only had thirty minutes on station, or face running out of fuel and having to ditch short of Ascension, it all required a lot of improvisation.

So, with time and fuel running out, they dropped the four men (who, being communications experts with only basic parachute training, had little para experience to draw on) on *Cardiff*'s starboard side, and set to run in on her port side to drop the supply containers. And their unlucky streak followed them. Max was busy turning the aircraft onto its run-in to the drop zone, while Roy the loadmaster was working feverishly down the back positioning the large container for the stores drop. Once the Herc was running in, and the nav called, 'Red on,' Roy duly acknowledged it; but when the nav, at the critical moment, then called, 'Green on,' the reply wasn't as expected. '*Fuck!*'

This was followed by a string of muffled and worrying-sounding noises from down the back, none of which sounded remotely like 'Green on'. What the hell was happening?

'Roy!' Max shouted. 'Roy! What the fuck's going on down the back, Roy?'

Three agonizing seconds passed. Then came the answer.

'Load gone.' He seemed to be breathing very heavily. 'And,' he continued, 'I very nearly went with it!'

'Oh my god,' Max said. *'What?'*

But there was no time to find out what had happened. He was too busy trying to fly accurately (and manually) at 115 knots, straight and level, at 800 feet exactly, in appalling weather. By then, it was also becoming clear that *Cardiff*'s helicopter still hadn't found the troopers, and maybe thought they had to pick up the container first. This apparent miscommunication was further compounded by the fact that *Cardiff*'s phonetic callsign was something like 'HZSA' and the helicopter's 'HZ1' – not the easiest to differentiate between, anyway.

With the Herc by now having reached its fuel limit, they could only circle once before having to depart. And do so while listening to what was an almost comedic radio conversation between ship and helicopter, with 'HZSA to HZ1, leave the load and pick up the troops!' being misheard, and 'HZ1 to HZSA, say again pick up the parachute??? . . .'

The situation was potentially too grave for levity, however. It took twenty-two minutes before the men were eventually picked up, and, given that the sea temperature was no more than about five degrees Celsius, they nearly didn't make it.

Having said goodbye to *Cardiff*, Max and the crew climbed out northwards and on into the darkening dusk. It was only now that Roy could come up to the flight deck – and with what remained of the safety harness that it seemed had nearly taken him to a watery grave. Because, in the confusion between dropping the troops and the stores, he had forgotten to click on forward of the static line for the stores load. At green on, when the load started to move towards the exit, Roy was towed along with it, and it was only his quick thinking and swift deployment of his dinghy knife that had saved his life.

With so little fuel, they were now having to fly the aircraft for maximum range, a delicate technique in engine handling, in order to milk absolutely everything out of the little they had left in the tanks. It was a task made even more difficult when they encountered a completely unforecast 150-mile-an-hour westerly jet stream, which threw their Doppler navigation equipment offline. Was their luck ever going to change?

Apparently yes, because, against all the odds, no further dramas unfolded, and they landed safely back on Ascension twelve hours later. Though after more than twenty-four hours of flying in total, it was with little more than vapour in the tanks.

It is impossible to overestimate the role the Hercules fleet played in Operation Corporate or just how much had been achieved in such a short time, particularly given that it was the Air Transport Force's biggest operation since Khana Cascade. In the first three months of Op Corporate (April–June 1982), the Lyneham Wing flew 214 per cent of its normal, peacetime authorized flying task and carried 7,000 tons (15 million pounds) of freight, including 114 vehicles and 22 helicopters, and nearly 6,000 troops plus support personnel.

The introduction of AAR was also done in ridiculously

short order, and would go on to become an enduring capability throughout the rest of the Hercules' time in RAF service. Likewise, the introduction of a Hercules tanker in a matter of weeks was an astonishing achievement. And one that would consign the tricky business of tobogganing to history.

There is no doubt that the Falklands conflict was one of the pivotal moments in the development of the Hercules and its tactical capability. While other aircraft, like the Harrier and Vulcan, were much lauded during and after the fighting, the Falklands War could not have been won without the bravery, innovation and sheer bloody-mindedness of the C-130 crews, and both Harry Burgoyne and Max Roberts were rightly awarded Air Force Crosses. Training Captain Jim Norfolk would also go on to receive the AFC in December 1984 for his work integrating the use of NVGs into Hercules operations.

There was, however, still one elephant in the room: the continuing lack of defensive equipment fitted to C-130s, despite the mantra that 'Hercs would never be used in threat situations' sounding increasingly hollow. The world, and the political order of world powers, was changing. Preparedness for a Cold War, important as that had been in recent decades, was not only proving to be far from the whole story; it was, arguably, no longer the story at all.

So being prepared was key, because there was no knowing where the next threat to peace was going to come from.

And perhaps because no one was looking at the lessons of history, neither could anyone predict what form it might take.

8. Beirut: Suicide Bomber

On 23 October 1983, at a little after six in the morning, a big yellow Mercedes lorry drove into the public parking lot at Beirut International Airport. The lot was adjacent to the four-storey barracks where some 350 marines lay asleep. From the US Navy's Battalion Landing Team, they were part of the 1,800-strong peacekeeping force that had been established there the previous year, as part of a multi-national effort to try and restore the sovereignty of the government of Lebanon.

The truck entered the compound largely unremarked. Heavy trucks and lorries were a common sight at the airport, and as the truck circled the lot, the sentries on duty, their weapons unloaded, as per normal peacetime rules of engagement, initially gave it little attention. By the time the hostile intentions of the driver became clear, it was too late; before they had time to slam rounds into their guns, the truck had veered off and was now headed straight for the BLT building, where it smashed through the entrance.

The truck came to a halt in the middle of the lobby, and, after a second or two of silence, it exploded. The blast was so massive that the whole building lifted into the air, before completely collapsing, like a house of concrete cards.

The destruction didn't stop there. Even as people rushed to the scene, ash and debris raining down on them from the enormous mushroom cloud above, a second bomb was detonated at the nearby French barracks. Many of the occupants, paratroopers from 1 Parachute Chasseur Regiment, were out on their balconies, having heard the first explosion. They too did not stand a chance.

The new era of suicide bombers had begun.

For Flying Officer Simon Footer, a young co-pilot who had been selected to join an elite unit within the fabled 47 Squadron, 23 October had begun with a slight hangover. It was a Sunday morning, after all, the second day of a weekend that, following an intense period of flying since his arrival in Cyprus a week earlier, had already seen its share of fun and games.

Si had come to RAF Akrotiri after many months of training, which had represented a significant career change. Following a short spell flying Jaguar fast jets, a minor health issue had meant a medical downgrade from fast jets for the young officer, and a role change to Hercules. Having joined the Hercules fleet at RAF Lyneham in December 1982, he was now delighted to be posted to 47 Squadron, as it was widely recognized as the best of the four C-130 squadrons at Lyneham. He had spent most of that summer being trained on a wide range of niche skills, some resulting from the Falklands War of the previous year, which had proven essential for the deployment, resupply and extraction of specialist troops in that kind of operational theatre: night low-level flying, using NVGs, air-to-air refuelling, parachute dropping, airdropping, and tactical landing techniques, all in minimum light levels, to simulate the conditions that might be encountered in a hostile environment.

Si's first 'proper' detachment had started on 17 October, and had been challenging and intense. So, as a first-timer at Akrotiri he was particularly pleased to find that they weren't required to operate during the weekend; it would tie up too many people on the station who, understandably, would rather be at home or on the beach. The weekend had therefore started on the Friday evening, with a few brandy sours, and, this being Cyprus, had finished off with late-night kebabs washed down with the local tipple, Kokineli. This had been followed, on the Saturday, with a day on the station beach.

Even though there had been a few sore heads, the day had gone well. Footie and beach volleyball, pre-lunch beers, more beers after, then riding bikes as fast as possible along and off the rickety jetty into the sea, with marks awarded for the most spectacular launch, war cry and splash.

Despite the embarrassment of having to bare their pink aircrew bodies alongside the honed, suntanned physiques of the marines, it had turned out to be great fun. And after a quick kip, they were all back in the mess for further jollity, including more beer, more brandy sours and, once again, kebabs down in the village. Si knew, having signed up to fly with the Flight, that there would be challenges ahead, but for now life for the young aviator felt good.

After the 'socializing' of the previous day, to wake up and not feel completely shite was, Si reflected, something of a bonus. Yes, he was feeling a bit ropey, but the prospect of another beach day was enough to lift his headache, and, with the weather again glorious, he and the rest of the crew were soon on their way down to the beach and looking forward to finishing the weekend with another relaxing day off.

By 10 a.m., the crew were all nicely settled into beach mode, towels laid out on the warm sand and the day getting going with the football they'd brought down with them being kicked around. They were just thinking about sun cream to cover already stinging shoulders when they spotted a Land Rover careering down the beach road, a cloud of dust swirling in its wake. It screeched to a halt just short of the sand, and out climbed the Station Ops corporal. With his long socks and empire-builder shorts he attracted a couple of covert sniggers, but the smiles soon faded as he made a beeline straight for them. Something serious was clearly going on.

'Are you the Herc crew?' he asked them.

'Why?' Tony Evans, the skipper, wanted to know. At twenty-nine, he was already a veteran of the conflict in Rhodesia, and knew that no one in their right minds would volunteer that kind of information without understanding what the consequences might be.

'We have a situation,' he told them. 'We need you back at work. Grab your stuff, sirs, and jump in the Land Rover.'

He ushered them into the back of the vehicle to go to Station Operations for a briefing. But, during the drive, clearly agitated, he began to fill them in. 'A massive bomb's just gone off in Beirut,' he explained; 'apparently there are many dead and wounded American marines. The RAF has been asked to help evacuate the worst of them.'

It took a moment for the five men to take in the enormity of the situation, but they quickly rallied, keen to get on with it, and to know more. And there was more. As they arrived at Station Ops, they were met by OC Ops with the news that a second bomb had also been detonated, at the French paratroopers' HQ. 'Which is only five kilometres from the airport,' he added. 'So there's concern that our own guys with the peacekeeping force might be targeted too.'

Their focus now, though, must be on the wounded US Marines. Their Herc, they were told, was already in the process of being turned into full stretcher fit for about seventy potential casualties, and speed of deployment was, of course, critical.

Station Ops was a windowless concrete building; though only a couple of miles from the sunny beach they'd just been relaxing on, it felt like a world away. The five men could immediately feel the chill from the air-con as well, which only added to the contrast between the day they'd envisaged and the grim task that now lay ahead. Within ten minutes, and feeling decidedly underdressed for such an important briefing in their shorts and T-shirts, they were updated on the situation by the station intelligence and ops officers, along with the station commander.

The briefing itself was fairly sketchy. The bomb, which was apparently huge, had been detonated by a suicide bomber at 0622 in the HQ and accommodation of the US Marine Corps element of the peacekeeping force. The worst injured were being flown out to the USS *Iwo Jima* and USS *Eisenhower* of the US Navy's Task Force, which were both sitting offshore. Once aboard, they were being triaged, and the most desperately wounded would then be flown back to Beirut Airport in big Sikorsky CH-53 'jolly green giant' helicopters, for immediate emergency air evacuation to a US military hospital in Germany. The only problem was that the American Nightingale DC-9 medivac jet that had flown into Beirut earlier to make the transfers had subsequently become unserviceable. They were now asking that the RAF Herc crew take over, flying the worst injured back to Akrotiri to be transferred to waiting aircraft which would take them on to Germany instead.

The crew's orders from the US military were also made clear. Once en route, they were to talk only to the *Iwo Jima* for control into Beirut. As the airport was now effectively closed to non-military aircraft, they were told to ignore Beirut International Airport controllers; they were going into a war zone, with a definite threat, and though nothing was said, the crew knew they were going in not only without equipment on the aircraft to defend it and them, but in only light summer flying gear, without personal protection kit or weapons.

The briefing over, they then hurried to get changed into that kit; the Hercules was by now ready to go, and there was no time to reflect on what they might be faced with.

At 1120, the crew climbed onto the waiting Herc. By this time, a number of nurses had been grabbed from the nearby British military hospital, and though none of them were aeromed qualified, let alone had any experience of dealing with casualties of war, they were in the same frame of mind as the crew, the sense of urgency uppermost among them all. There was also an experienced army doctor on board, plus the Herc crew's own two ground engineers, as to break down in Beirut would be hazardous. The two parachute jump instructors had been called in to help too, as they were au fait with fitting the stretchers.

Driving to the aircraft in the crew bus, Si could see that the back end of the Herc was a hive of activity, everyone chipping in to prepare the freight bay for emergency medical evacuation as best they could. Large boxes of medical stores were being loaded, and rows of stretchers were still being fitted – four across and two high, along the entire length of the bay. Incredibly, despite the unexpected nature of the coming mission, there was even a packed lunch in a brown paper bag provided for each of the crew. Every army marches on its stomach, after all.

Being a Sunday, the airfield's ramp was almost empty, apart from a parked-up Nimrod and a couple of Chinooks. However, there was no intention of launching any other aircraft in support, as this was an ostensibly straightforward medical evacuation mission.

With everyone still a bit dazed but now totally focused, they took off for the thirty-minute flight to Beirut. It had only been around ninety minutes since they'd been relaxing on a sunny beach, and in another thirty they would be landing amid a very different scene. Si had been into Beirut on routine trips a couple of times over the summer, to resupply the small British peacekeeping contingent there, but this was to be a different matter altogether.

There was no time to reflect on the kind of horrors they would surely witness, however. They were busy doing the job they'd been trained for and their principal emotion was adrenaline-fuelled excitement. This was the first time Si, just twenty-six, would find himself heading into this kind of environment, and he said so.

'Me too,' said Tony.

'Me three,' said Dave Wood, their flight engineer, which

surprised Si, as they were both such experienced operators. But with everything having happened so quickly,
there was no time to think about anything other than the
job that lay ahead. As soon as he could after take-off, Si
spoke with the control room on the *Iwo Jima*.

'*Iwo Jima*, this is Ascot 456, RAF C-130 inbound to
Beirut. Request picture.'

'Welcome cousins,' came the response. 'Picture is clear, but
busy with friendlies. Proceed as requested. Squawk 5431.'

He wasn't wrong. It all sounded pretty chaotic on the
radios, with lots of US helicopter activity and generally a
hubbub on the airways, and from about ten miles off the
Lebanese coast they could finally see why. Though it was a
hazy day, the size of the bomb quickly became obvious; a
veil of smoke was still drifting across the sky over Beirut,
and, below it, sitting offshore, was the *Iwo Jima* itself, the
same US aircraft carrier that, back in 1970, had picked up
the crew of the Apollo 13 mission. They had been lucky.
Many, many more today had not.

Si had already been told it was best to dial up the instrument landing systems and fly an instrument approach into
the airport from the north, so Tony duly set himself up for
this, and down the glide slope they went. As the coast came
in sight, they were pumped up but focused, both on getting onto the ground safely and on keeping a lookout for
anything threatening; they had been briefed to potentially
expect a threat, in the form of anti-aircraft or small arms
fire. They were also very aware that the US Nightingale
had red crosses all over it, whereas their Herc was the usual
plain khaki, and so looked like exactly what it was – a military aircraft. Potentially hostile. A target.

Having had so little time to think about the situation they were going into, the crew remained calm, making the flight deck feel almost routine as they thrashed out a plan en route. Tony and Dave would stay in their seats, to monitor the engines. This was a hostile environment, so all four would be left running; if they were fired upon, they would need to make a quick getaway.

The Herc was ten miles away when the crew could make out the individual plumes of dust and smoke close to the airport, still coiling up from the devastated US Marines HQ. The building itself must have been blasted out of existence with scores of personnel inside, most of whom had almost certainly still been in bed asleep, or just in the process of getting up, ready to start their day. As they made their final approach, the dust cloud was now hanging in the air around them, incongruous against the deep blue of the surrounding sky. The crew in the cockpit looked around them for threats, eyes on metaphorical stalks; they could see debris still burning and lots of people with guns – and no idea who might or might not be friendly. It was one thing to worry about the threat of being shot down – there was an equally serious threat of being shot once on the ground.

On landing, Tony rapidly threw the engines into reverse thrust and they turned off the runway onto one of the high-speed angled taxiways, where lines of sandbagged trenches formed makeshift observation posts that were manned by US Marines. They were lucky to have been elsewhere when the bomb had been detonated earlier, but looked as miserable and wretched as anyone Si had ever seen; their faces pale and clammy, their expressions shocked, and their youth painfully obvious. Many of the men would not have yet even been twenty and would have seen some pretty horrible sights for the first time in their lives.

On the large international ramp where they came to a stop and parked, there were a couple of 'jolly green giant' helos, engines turning and burning, and the broken Nightingale aeromed aircraft whose job they had been called in to do. The noise was incredible, even with the engines idle; once the doors were opened, it was immediately bone-shakingly loud.

When Si had been to the airport before, they had been met by a couple of vehicles containing British soldiers – Union Jacks fluttering gaily, reassuringly friendly faces – but on this day there was nothing, which felt very eerie. Everyone they could see was too busy desperately trying to save lives.

Bob Mahoney, the loadmaster, opened the crew door and went out, using a long communication lead to talk to the crew while they waited for someone to come and tell them what to do. The destroyed barracks were now about 250 yards to their front. Against the backdrop of the collapsed building, exposed wires, shattered glass and jagged masonry, people were still swarming around, picking their way over the rubble, following cries and screams for help, in search of trapped marines. Closer at hand, trucks and flatbeds were making their way down to the taxiways and ramp, loading up with those who were to be taken to the *Iwo Jima* via helicopter for triage and initial trauma treatment.

On the ground the atmosphere was oppressive; dusty,

hot and smoky, and laced with the acrid smell of fuel. And something else, something Si had not experienced before. The sweet, sickening stench that came from burning human flesh. There was so much noise too, from the still running C-130 engines, that it was almost impossible to hear or be heard. A small price to pay, though, for the reassuring knowledge that, should things turn uglier, they could swiftly take off again.

From up on the cockpit, they could see two marines run across and speak to Bob.

'Okay,' he relayed back. 'They're going to send us some badly injured troops. We need to open the ramp and get ready.'

They duly did so, and as Si unstrapped and made his way down to the freight bay to help load the stretchers, a fresh blast of heat travelled through the aeroplane.

'What do you want us to do?' Si asked. He had to yell to be heard.

'Help get the stretchers on board,' one of the marines shouted back. 'They're backed up. Been waiting on your fellas to get here.'

It wasn't just stretchers that caught Si's attention as they entered the fray. Further up the taxiway, he could see long rows of bodies, some in body bags but others just in zipped-up sleeping bags.

Everyone began doing what they could, and despite the chaos, a sort of order was soon wrestled from the confusion. The most critically wounded were being identified and tagged by on-site medics, then carried on stretchers, or placed onto the back of the nearest vehicle, bound for the airport ramp, where the waiting CH-53s had now

143

disembarked the casualties bound for Akrotiri and were being loaded up again to ferry more of the injured out to the *Iwo Jima*.

Bar Tony and Dave, who had stayed on the flight deck, the RAF crew soon got into a rhythm, assisting in the business of getting those casualties returning from the ship and bound for Cyprus and then Germany safely onto the stretchers on the Herc. Si and the rest of the crew, new to this kind of emergency operation, basically did whatever they could do to assist the nurses. Doled out water, lit cigarettes, offered moral support by simply talking to the injured men, many of whom, their faces chalky-white from the clouds of dust and debris, were in a state of shock as well as in pain. Their melted uniforms, and the blood on them, now coagulating and crusted, lent a metallic tang to the dust-filled air.

Some were very talkative, others less so, the most seriously injured semi-conscious, oblivious to the hubbub of activity all around them. And as dressings were replaced, wounds tended and precious painkillers (mainly morphine) administered, a stream of new casualties, fresh off the jolly green giants, were one by one settled and strapped into place.

That Si was now in a war zone could not feel more obvious. Huey Cobra gunship helicopters were whizzing up and down above the airport, a powerful show of force intended to keep enemy heads down, along with intermittent high-decibel booms. No one was sure where the latter were coming from, but they were thought to be shells fired by US forces into the surrounding hills, presumably to deter any thought of adding to the miseries already inflicted. The crack of small arms fire could also be heard above the cacophony of other noises, though whether in celebration or with intent to harm was anyone's guess. The most insistent, chilling sound, though, which would cut through all the others, was the sound of shouting and screaming from in and around what remained of the marines' barracks. In contrast, the sound of the Herc's engines, still dutifully humming away, provided at least a measure of reassurance.

Just as Si was returning to the flight deck to prepare for departure, he felt a touch on his arm. He turned to see a marine who'd been stretchered up front, a big black guy, almost right up against the cockpit. 'Hey buddy, can I get some help here?' he said.

While Si gave him water, lit his cigarette and issued him with autoinject morphine, they talked. His name was Joe and, having been on gate duty, he had been near enough to actually see the lorry drive towards the building. 'Even saw his hand go up' – he tried to illustrate, with a grunt of pain as he did so – 'like this, so he could pull the handle that would detonate the bomb. *Man*, did I run,' he went on. 'Did I *run*. But,' he shook his head slightly, his expression suggesting he still couldn't quite believe what had happened, 'I was too late.'

The explosion had hit Joe with sufficient force to break both his femurs. He had looked down when he'd come to from the effects of the blast. 'And my legs, man,' he said, 'sticking out at right angles. At *right angles*.' He'd been bandaged up, but his thighs were swollen to a massive degree now. They had a girth almost as wide as they were long. 'And look,' he said, raising his filthy, bloodstained arm to show Si his shattered watch. 'Stopped dead on the dot of 0622.'

The desperate work continued. The crew had been on the ground for over two hours when they were asked to depart with the thirty or so seriously injured they already had on board, who were by now in critical need of transfer to hospital. With the flow of casualties now reducing, it was agreed that once those on board had been delivered to Akrotiri, they would turn around and come back for more.

Minutes later, the crew having taken up their positions, the Herc taxied past the same very forlorn looking marines in the trenches, one of whom had even fashioned a make-shift sign, which seemed to speak for them all. It simply said: 'Take Me Home!'

The aircraft was promptly positioned onto the runway and took off without hesitation (or any clearance) before turning out to sea initially at very low altitude. Si got back in contact with the *Iwo Jima* and they set heading direct for Akrotiri. When he asked to change frequency to Cyprus, the controller on the *Iwo Jima*, in a southern US accent, said, 'Thank you to you Brits –'preciate it!'

By the time the Herc landed back in Cyprus it was late afternoon. A fleet of ambulances had been sent to meet them, and once again it was all hands on deck. While the crew completed their shut-down checks in the cockpit, everyone else set to work, offloading the casualties to take them to the nearby military hospital – all except one marine, who had died of his injuries while in the air. The crew were then told that they would not be going back to Beirut. Despite the measures taken by US forces, it was considered too 'hot'; the airport was now being fired upon.

The crew slowly got themselves off the aircraft with their kit and were immediately bundled onto the crew coach to go to Station Operations, so they could debrief the intelligence officer with anything they could remember about what they'd seen that could potentially be of use to the intel community.

They trooped once again into the windowless concrete room.

'Are you guys okay?' the station commander asked them. Then, satisfied that they were, he asked them to give him some more detail; though, despite copious questions being asked and copious notes being made, there was little to tell of any practical use.

By then, the crew to a man could really only think about one thing: their first beer. They eventually got back about 5 p.m., and beers were duly cracked open, but there wasn't the usual post-exercise euphoria. Instead, everyone was quiet as they processed what they'd seen and done.

What Si needed more than anything was to get his head straight. A good strenuous bike ride, he knew, would probably help, but his bike, brought out to Akrotiri only a week previously, had already become another casualty of war, after the high jinks of the previous day. It seemed a very long time ago now.

Keo beer, then – the famed Akrotiri elixir – it would have to be. Slowly but surely the crew began to feel more normal; and with that, finally, also came a sense of achievement. They had pitched in when called upon and had done what they could. And though all agreed they'd never seen that kind of destruction close up – and that included those crew members who'd seen action in Rhodesia and the

Falklands – they felt they'd handled it well and were proud of their efforts.

It was the first time Si had seen the horrible reality of war. How could any human being possibly and willingly want to inflict such devastation, damage, death, pain, suffering and misery on any other human? But it had also been satisfying to be able to help, and there was a sense of fulfilment in having been able to put his extensive training into practice. And pride – that being Si's principal emotion by the time he got through on the phone to tell his wife and his mum about his day, even if the former was shocked, and the latter upset, to find out he'd spent his Sunday afternoon in a dangerous war zone.

Once Si had finished his calls to his family, it was time to meet in the bar for a sharpening brandy sour. Later, they agreed, they'd see if they could drum up one of the base Land Rovers so they could go to the hospital and visit the marines they had been unable to say goodbye to. First, though, it was dinner, where they were seated with a couple of the military nurses who had been with them. They too were sombre and reflective. It was hard not to contrast having dinner with friends and colleagues with the carnage they'd witnessed just hours ago, which was beginning to feel slightly unreal. After all, only a scant eight hours had passed since they'd been on the beach that morning, about to crack open a beer.

Just as Si was remembering he didn't have a tie on, one of the mess committee came over – a crusty squadron leader, wearing a cravat and a disapproving expression.

'Can I just say,' he said sternly, 'that you are improperly

dressed for dinner, young man, and I'm going to have to ask you to leave the dining room.'

Though going by the mess rules, he was strictly correct, it was the closest Si had come to physically picking up a medium-sized guy by the scrotum and throwing him through a plate-glass window.

Luckily, Tony Evans, seated next to him, could see how seething he was. 'Si,' he said, touching him lightly on the forearm. 'Let it go. It's not worth it. Don't bite.'

Si knew he was right and duly did as instructed. But not wanting to share a dining room with such an insensitive knob, he got up and marched out nevertheless.

He stood for a while on the patio at the back of the building, watching a goat trying to eat the mess garden furniture. His anger having dissipated now, he began to feel calmer, and with that came a growing sense of gratitude. For his job, which he loved, for his Hercules mates, who were second to none, and, perhaps for the first time in his life, just for *being* alive. Those six intense hours had been extraordinary.

That day would also turn out to be an era-defining moment. Laden with an estimated ten tons of TNT, the bomb which had destroyed the barracks at Beirut Airport would turn out to be the biggest conventional bomb detonated anywhere on earth since World War ll.

The combined death toll of both bombs was chilling: 241 US Marines, 58 French paratroopers, 6 civilians and, of course, the 2 terrorists. In all, 307 people dead. Many more with life-changing injuries. By February 1984, the whole multinational peacekeeping force had been with-drawn from Lebanon. Many say the 'War on Terror' started not on 11 September 2001 in the USA, but on 23 October 1983 in Beirut.

Though the crews of 47 Squadron didn't know it at the time, this was the first operation in what would turn out to be a four-decades-long involvement in the Middle East, as terrorism became a weapon of war the like of which the world had never seen before.

More immediately, however, another equally destructive force was gaining traction some 2,000 miles to the south – one which would again see the C-130 need to evolve. And though the agents of death this time included participants in a bloody civil war, at the heart of this new menace was a very different enemy. Mother Nature.

9. Ethiopia: Feeding the World

The famine in Ethiopia was one of the biggest global news stories of 1984. It was brought to a shocked world's attention in late October through a now iconic BBC News report by Michael Buerk, with footage by cameraman Mohamed Amin. It galvanized the pop musician Bob Geldof into masterminding one of the most famous fundraising events in history, the December 1984 Band Aid single 'Do They Know It's Christmas?' Together with the follow-up Live Aid concert in the summer of 1985, it would go on to raise many millions of pounds for famine relief.

For the Hercules crews of 47 Squadron, 'feeding the world' would also represent a new challenge, one that would lead to innovations in how they provided humanitarian aid. The abundance of goodwill, and also guilt, that had resulted from that BBC News broadcast needed translating into food in tens of thousands of actual mouths, and few doubted that this would be a massive task. With so many displaced and living in terrible conditions due to Ethiopia's ongoing civil war, there was also a desperate need for blankets, tents and sanitation and medical supplies. All of this had to be delivered somehow to a far-flung and dangerous country, and into areas that were remote, at high altitude and not conducive to safe landings.

When it became apparent the RAF was going to assist in the famine relief mission in Ethiopia, it was initially envisaged that this would be an operation where the crews would be landing on remote, unprepared strips, and off-loading the aid on the ground.

Tony Evans, just turned thirty-one, and still a captain with 47 Squadron, was as aware as anyone else of the scale of the problem, having watched Michael Buerk's report on the BBC only the previous week. However, with his experience in Rhodesia as part of Op Agila, he was already aware of the problems inherent in such a large-scale and urgent operation. There was no issue with getting aid to hubs of Asmara and Assab, but getting it to where it was needed was more tricky. The road network was patchy, and the roads themselves dire, plus having to transit through a country that was in the middle of a civil war meant the risk of violence and potential hijack was very high. As an interim measure, therefore, it was decided that food and supplies would be transported by air.

Tony was assigned to the task and he immediately set up a detachment in Addis Ababa – under Wing Commander Barry Nunn – of two aircraft and three tactical crews, from both 47 Squadron and LXX Squadron (as 70 Squadron, the sister tactical Hercules squadron, is always styled). Though there would be no direct threat from ground-to-air missiles, they would not be allowed to stay overnight at any of the airstrips as, with the ongoing war, the risk of attack was considered too great.

On 3 November 1984, Tony and his crew, along with another 47 Squadron Hercules, arrived from RAF Akrotiri to Addis Ababa. Though first billeted in a hotel in Addis, they were soon moved to the more salubrious environs of the International Livestock Research Institute, not out of concern about the standard of accommodation, but because of the risk of gastrointestinal illness, which was substantial, and would severely compromise the operation.

Tony loved Africa. He loved the scenery, the history and the people. And though it felt strange to find himself part of an International humanitarian response to a disaster he had been watching unfold on TV at home in the UK only a few days before, as soon as he flew into Ethiopia he felt that familiar sense that he was back in a very special place, and honoured to be able to step up and do his bit.

On first arriving in Addis, two of the four crews did an afternoon recce of some of the strips, to see if there were any obvious problems. Like half the developed world, they had seen the many images on TV but, in reality, most of the camps that had sprung up as starving people tried to flee the civil war were away from the airstrips, and as the relief crews could only operate in daytime, taking time to travel to a camp and back (as well as being exposed to more potential risks) would have compromised their ability to get three trips in during the day – their proposed day being likely to consist of flying from Addis to a coastal port, loading up, and then flying three shuttles between the coast and an airstrip such as Mekele, Gondar, Axum or Alamata, before returning to Addis. In this way, it was envisaged that they could deliver some 85,000 tons of desperately needed grain, as well as tents and blankets, and vital medical supplies.

Addis itself is an elevated city. At nearly 8,000 feet above sea level, it's one of the highest capitals in the world, and that altitude was going to put an added strain on the missions, since the thinner air would reduce the performance of the C-130s' engines, which would make both take-off and landing a riskier operation. Though, as a veteran of Rhodesia, Tony was already familiar with this problem, and had total trust in the Herc's ability to deliver.

That evening, they had their first detachment briefing, using the maps of the area they had been supplied with, and discussing weather, fuel and potential routings to the various airstrips that had already been identified. And with the world's eyes watching, eager to see the aid being delivered, they were also joined by Michael Buerk himself and a BBC camera crew.

The next morning, they began operations. Tony and his crew flew the first trip to the coast, with Michael and the filming team on board with them. They first picked up supplies from Assab, where they'd been delivered, and then flew them to the camps that had been established at Akele and Axum. Even for an experienced Hercules pilot who'd seen service in some pretty grim situations, Tony found it a lot to take in. The reality was shocking; the sheer expanse of the barren and almost lunar landscape, the sense of hopelessness and desperation in the hordes of starving people, the pitiful crying of listless and emaciated children. And along with all his crew, rather than just hearing about the threat of danger, Tony was now feeling and experiencing it. An atmosphere of incipient violence seemed to permeate everything.

Flying at altitude with a fully laden aircraft, however, was challenging enough to help keep the crew focused.

And the 'airstrips' themselves were even more so. They were very basic, with no lighting, and little or no air traffic control either: at Makele, it was literally a man sitting in a hut with a microphone.

From their first two aid drops that morning, they could immediately tell that operating from these unprepared airstrips was always going to be risky. They were usually short, or very short, and, with safety parameters much reduced, there would be little margin for error, even in a Herc, which could land on the proverbial sixpence. Unlike Tony's experiences in Rhodesia, where remote strips could be deeply rutted or slicks of mud, the strips in Ethiopia were dry, hard and rough, and mostly covered in loose stones and gravel. This meant there was a substantial risk of damage, both to the underside of the aircraft and to the tyres, so after each landing one of the ground engineers, who would be carried on every flight, would have to get out and crawl under the aircraft to inspect everything.

Still, with a couple of runs under their belts by the middle of that first day, they felt reasonably confident that they could do what was required of them to help with the immediate crisis, while a more sustainable method of delivering aid could be found. They could see how vital the work was. They also felt well supported by the ground personnel, who made short work of unloading the pallets from the Herc and organized those locals who were keen to help and get involved, many of whom had rarely seen, much less been up close to, an aircraft.

The first two drops completed, the crew set off for their final run of the day, to deliver their last lot of aid to the airstrip at Axum. They had just landed, and Michael Buerk was interviewing Tony for a BBC News report, when a second Herc arrived, crewed by LXX Squadron. On touching down on the rocky strip, it immediately burst a tyre and now lumbered along forlornly, listing slightly to the left, while the crowd of starving locals looked on, mostly incuriously; they were beyond any spark of interest beyond getting food in their bellies.

Fortunately, Tony's ground engineer had additional training, so was well placed to advise how they might get the Herc airborne again. But there was no time before it grew dark to get back to Addis and fetch any equipment that might help, and the crew of the stricken Herc obviously couldn't stay overnight. Neither was it an option to take the crew and leave the aircraft; the villagers might not be interested, but there were others who most definitely would be, so if they wanted to see it intact again they had to get it back to base. Though they were able to contact Addis via HF radio and fill them in on the situation, there was little that anyone could do. There was also nothing at Axum itself they could make use of, bar the stirrings of interest that were now beginning to become evident.

Dusk would soon be encroaching, and though it all made good content for the television news back in the UK, a solution urgently needed to be found. In these equatorial regions, the transition from day to night was very swift, and with news travelling fast about the stricken aircraft too, including to the wrong sort of people, it wouldn't be long before they would be facing real jeopardy. Eventually the flight engineer came up with a germ of an idea. Highly risky, and certainly not officially sanctioned, but couldn't they perhaps wind the wheel with the blown tyre up into its bay?

'I've got some "get you out of trouble" notes,' he explained, 'from Vietnam. I pinched them from when I was training with the US Air Force in Texas.'

He duly climbed back aboard the aircraft and retrieved them from where they were stashed. Based, as they were, on notes made by US airmen as a result of their experiences flying C-130s during the war in Vietnam, these were in fact very far from official indeed (and recognized by neither the USAF nor the RAF), but everyone seemed happy to turn a blind eye to that tiny detail, as they had been proven to get aircrew out of some pretty tight predicaments.

Once the two ground engineers were satisfied the strategy might work, every bit of remaining freight was then unloaded, to make the aircraft as light as possible. The late afternoon heat was now intense. It was a hot day to do even the simplest of tasks, and this was definitely not the simplest of tasks, despite the cheery optimism of the notes. Eventually, however, the damaged wheel was wound up, and Tony and his crew, together with Michael Buerk and his crew – who were pleased to have obtained another tranche of useful footage – felt able to leave the other Herc crew to finish the job, so that at least one aircraft could return to Addis before nightfall.

There was still the business of the damaged aircraft taking off and landing safely, however, so once back in Addis, Tony stayed in the control tower till it appeared. This was long after dark, because the unfortunate Herc had sustained some electrical damage too, and had to make the entire hour's flight with the remaining wheels down.

Thankfully, they landed without incident. But they were only a single day into the stopgap operation, and it was obvious to everyone that a less fraught and dangerous solution was going to be needed as soon as possible for a problem that could well happen again and again. Although using parachutes to drop the aid in might have seemed the obvious answer, parachutes were expensive and they would need more than they had, because they almost certainly wouldn't be able to recover any of them.

A new plan was needed. They needed to drop aid *without* parachutes. Which meant they'd need to go lower. A *lot* lower.

Like the 747 Jumbo jet, the C-130 has one of those iconic, immediately recognizable shapes. People tend to know it when they see it. Ditto that distinctive, one-of-a-kind noise. For such a colossal transport aircraft, it also has amazing speed and manoeuvrability, and I guarantee that anyone who sees one flying at low level, weaving its majestic way across the landscape, will feel compelled to stop and watch. As a pilot, you never forget what it's like to fly one at low level either. There is simply no sensation quite like it.

Flying at 250 feet is the normal height for UK low flying and the minimum drop height for small stores. Most stores, however, require you to 'pop up' to a much higher altitude to drop them (most go at 400–800 feet), in order for the parachute to open and slow the descent. Like everything in the military, however, there are always exceptions to the norms and in the case of airdrop, there are two. Ultra-low-level airdrop (ULLA) is a very specialist drop used for extremely robust loads (like ammunition in steel boxes) which are essentially dragged out of the aircraft at fifteen feet above the ground, and at a minimum speed of 140 miles per hour – an extremely dangerous undertaking. There is also 'free-dropping' of similarly robust stores, which uses the very low-tech method of throwing them out from fifty feet and hoping for the best.

When I was an air loadmaster, the latter method was something that we practised regularly and was often a challenging but fun airdrop.

Flying a training airdrop sortie with a number of loads on board was commonplace, because the air despatch crews and loadmasters had to maintain currency in each drop discipline, as, of course, did the entire crew. The last drop during these sorties was often the free-drop, and, as we flew downwind on one of the many Salisbury Plain drop zones, we'd configure the aircraft with 50 per cent flaps to allow low-speed flying with the cargo door and ramp open at the rear.

We'd line up on the drop zone from about three miles away, at about 900 feet, and, by reducing the power, start a shallow descent. At about a mile away, the aircraft passing through 200 feet and still descending, the flight engineer would then call out the radio altitude (100, 80, 60, 50 . . .) until a small application of power arrested the rate of descent and we'd be flying across the field at just fifty feet.

Game on. The navigator would call 'Fifteen secs', which I'd follow with 'Action stations!' which would be acknowledged from the loadie on the edge of the ramp. At the rear, they'd be watching the world fly past at about 140 miles per hour, and as they perched on the very lip of the ramp, would look and feel as if they were floating on air. Then it would be 'Red on', then 'Green on', and then a shout from the back, 'Load gone!' was my cue to apply the power and start a climb away from the Wiltshire countryside as the doors closed. The last words in the sequence would come from the drop zone controller. On a good day, our load – normally a sack filled with twenty-five kilograms of pebbles – would be dropped so expertly that it would obliterate the drop marker completely.

Although this drop was always fun to practice, in reality dropping stores in a bag had no practical use – not unless what you wanted was twenty-five kilograms of pebbles – because the bags often split on impact, throwing the precious cargo everywhere. There was also the issue that we only ever dropped one of these twenty-five-kilogram bags on each pass, that being the maximum load the two-person crew could literally throw out the back – not, at any rate, without following it themselves.

The crews and the army teams involved in the Ethiopia operation looked to the stable of current techniques to see if there were any solutions for the landing-strip problem. The use of the RAF's standard one-ton containers was an obvious solution, but they would take a long time to rig at the ports, they would need parachutes and netting to make them safe to drop and, as already mentioned, it would be unlikely that these would ever be seen again.

Free-drop was the obvious next solution, but dropping single bags from 50 feet would probably see the bags burst, and only delivering one or two bags per pass would require more than twenty-four hours each day to get any meaning-ful amount to the drop zones. Something completely new was clearly needed.

The first solution came from the army teams who were on the ground in Ethiopia itself. They would take a ply-wood base board like that used for one-ton containers, stack double-bagged flour or grain on it, and wrap it all up with cling film. This was simple, easy to rig, and all the materials required were in plentiful supply locally. It was then over to the driver's airframe to find a dropping solution.

Some of the crews in Ethiopia, trained to airdrop the ULLA loads, wondered if a hybrid solution of normal free-drop and ULLA techniques would work. Dropping much lower would result in less of an impact, and the board and cling film would help during the deceleration of the load. Why couldn't they drop at perhaps 30 feet or less with the gear down? Previously, due to the risks involved, only a few crews had been trained to drop at these extremely low altitudes. By now, the Lyneham Wing had six aircraft in Ethiopia, with many crews, and they would all be doing this numerous times a day in the challenging and dangerous terrain of the highlands. Was the solution simply to train them on the job?

It seemed worth a try. So, once it was approved, the tech-nique of 'heavy free-drop' was born, and, over the next few weeks, the switch from landings to airdrops was complete. Not that it didn't have its complications. Though there was no doubt that dropping aid in this way was a far safer option than the one they'd been using previously, the ultra-low dropping technique required both skill and experience.

By the time navigator and instructor Doug Marsh was deployed to Ethiopia, he had already gained experience in Rhodesia and Kenya, and was a veteran of the more recent Falklands War, so there was little he didn't know about the business of dropping things out of Hercs. But dropping grain at low level was unlike anything that had been done before, and one unintended consequence of this new method of delivering aid was that it didn't take much for it to inadvertently become a daily bird buffet as well.

Birdstrike was a risk at any time, particularly when conducting missions over areas with large wildlife populations, and Ethiopia, a country of densely wooded mountains, deep verdant valleys and wide plains, was more wildlife-rich than many. As well as large flocks of geese, ducks and other waterfowl, and the iconic – at least to 47 Squadron – demoiselle crane, there were also several species of vulture and eagle, whose defining feature seemed to be that, unused to humans and their airborne machinery, they were not at all afraid when face to face with a low-flying aircraft. In fact, so unafraid were they that, instead of flying away, they would keep going and bring up their feet, talons raised, as if about to strike prey.

This was quite a sight, obviously, but also dangerous. Only a few days into his first deployment, Doug witnessed one such bird actually punch a hole through the fuselage with its claws. The bird died on impact, and the crew were all stunned to see two sets of talons poking into the wall of the flight deck. Given that the Herc's speed at impact would have been some 125 knots, however, the fact that the bird's claws went straight through the metal was perhaps to be expected.

Fortunately, they were able to patch up the aircraft on the job, the engineer simply putting a plate over the hole till it could be properly dealt with back at Addis. But it soon became obvious that it was the flocks of smaller, less aggressive birds that posed the most risk.

The crews generally tried to fit in four sorties a day, and during each one, the system being good but not perfect, a small number of the double-bagged sacks of grain would burst open. This presented no problem on the first run, but was a major hazard subsequently, as so many birds by that time would have come to feast on their unexpected RAF-provided breakfast, and would take to the air in dangerous numbers when the aircraft returned and disturbed them.

The villagers soon learned that it was sensible to try and scare the birds away, but it wasn't just the birds causing problems. Corruption was rife, and it very quickly became common knowledge that sacks of grain dropped in remote areas to feed the starving people were ending up for sale back in the market at Addis two weeks later, as 'commissaires', armed with guns and kitted out with trucks, would wait for the sound of the C-130 approaching and simply help themselves to as much as they could carry. And, naturally, no one dared to take them on.

As the days passed, the crews began to see the pattern evolving: the pallets of aid would drop, the armed men would help themselves to what they wanted, and the villagers would only come out when it was safe, bringing bowls and buckets to gather up what was left, mostly the grain from any sacks that had split. Doug and the crew could only look down on all this shameless crime and profiteering in frustration. This was a war zone they were working in, after all, and the term 'trigger-happy' was never far from their minds. The only consolation was that, all too often, several sacks did, *very* unfortunately, split open on impact, despite the double-bagging and cling film system being so good. Curious. But this at least meant they were only of value to the people for whom they were intended . . .

The RAF left Ethiopia in December 1985, having carried out 2,152 sorties, a mixture of air-land and latterly airdrop operations. Each airdrop sortie would deliver about sixteen tons of cargo; for those receiving it, it really did represent the difference between life and death. While the crews may not have realized it at the time, they saved the lives of many thousands of people.

Innovation from the army, combined with the bloody-mindedness of the crews, meant the mission continued to save lives for many months too, and in far from ideal conditions, demonstrating again why Team Lyneham was, at that time, the go-to one-stop shop for government when any global disaster emerged. Indeed, though the famine relief effort in Ethiopia was an international operation, with aircraft from many different nations regularly dropping aid, the RAF, and specifically the Hercules crews of 47 Squadron, hold the distinction of having carried the most.

There are sometimes world events which turn out to be so significant that everyone can recall where they were when they happened. The 1985 Live Aid concert was one such. I was just thirteen, still in Scotland, and remember watching it with my parents at home, as I do the news images that distressed everyone so much – in my case, those of emaciated infants covered in flies, which I can remember in precise detail to this day. I also remember seeing footage of the C-130 which, adorned with its white cross, was dropping the vital stores that were supposedly going to help stem the appalling death rate. The sound of that aircraft, something that still gives me goosebumps, had once again been linked with the business of saving lives, through the delivery of humanitarian aid.

The C-130, though, had other roles to fulfil. All too soon it would be tested again. The lessons of Agila, Ethiopia and other operations apparently forgotten, Albert would soon find itself behind enemy lines, exposed to hostile fire, in a very different theatre of war: the Persian Gulf.

10. Gulf War 1: In at the Deep End

By May 1991, I had finished my training as an air loadmaster at RAF Finningley and had been given my first posting to an operational station, RAF Lyneham. There, in a week's time, I was to start the Hercules Operational Conversion Unit. I was a little sad to be leaving Finningley behind as I had made some amazing friends there, the bonds forged through the tough times that we found ourselves on during the courses. It felt a little like graduating from secondary school; we'd been together for a while, but were now going our separate ways as we moved on to the next challenges in our various careers. Well, not all going our separate ways – I was off to RAF Lyneham with my great friend Bob Mason, and we were both looking forward to a little time with our families before the OCU started.

Having decided to drive from Scotland to my new home in Wiltshire, I set off early in my banana-yellow Astra estate – my pride and joy – as I had agreed to pick Bob up from his home in Warrington on the way. Bob was a little older than me – he was married with a young son – but despite the difference in our age and life situations, today, and for the next few weeks, we would both be the 'fucking new guys', or FNGs. Which was not a compliment. The military is a very good leveller.

We loaded the items that every young sergeant needs to

make an impression at their first posting: highly bulled shoes, an ironing board, and – non-negotiable – a good steam iron, as standards were extremely high. So not for me the scruffy band T-shirts and torn jeans of my contemporaries who were at university – I was already, at the tender age of twenty, a well-oiled ironing machine. With everything loaded, we set off for RAF Lyneham.

The journey took a little over three hours, and as we were driving along the M4, towards the end of our travels, we saw a Hercules in the distance flying in the circuit above our new home. I felt all at once excited and not a little terrified. This was our last hurdle to overcome in order to get to the front line and, potentially, a lifelong career in the forces.

Lyneham had a very different feel to the training stations that we'd been at before. It had a real buzz to it and people seemed far more welcoming. Much as I suppose any trainee would anywhere, I always felt while at a training station like a second-class part of the RAF team. Even as a sergeant training at Finningley we had a separate sergeants' mess from the 'training staff' sergeants and warrant officers. But at Lyneham, we immediately felt a part of that big RAF family; and although I was as nervous as I had been on my first day at 'big school', everyone we met could not have been friendlier.

Having found our allocated rooms, Bob and I headed to the crew room for a coffee, where the talk was all of the ongoing war in the Gulf.

Iraq and Iran had been fighting each other for most of the 1980s, but once that war ended in a stalemate of sorts, Iraq's relationship with Kuwait became hostile. Saddam

Hussain, the Iraqi leader, had borrowed $14 billion from the Kuwaitis to fund his war with Iran, and they wanted it back.

To further fuel the fires of discontent, and distract from his internal political and social issues, Saddam accused Kuwait of stealing Iraqi oil and resources. Eventually, with nobody else left to pick a fight with in the region, Saddam invaded Kuwait on 2 August 1990 and, with an army of over 600,000 troops, quickly overwhelmed the country's defences. The seeds of the Gulf War had been sown.

Entirely by chance, the start of the Gulf War found one young Hercules captain, Flight Lieutenant Dave Fry, very conveniently placed. Having previously been with LXX Squadron, he was now a little over a year into his first tour with 47 Squadron and coming to the end of a month-long exercise with a large team of specialist ground troops in Kuala Lumpur. The day had been clear and, relaxed after a successful tour, Dave and the crew had decided to get some sightseeing in before catching some shut eye in Kuala Lumpur ahead of the final leg home to Lyneham via Dubai and Akrotiri.

The sightseeing done, Dave was now cruising at 25,000 feet over Oman, looking out of the cockpit windows. With almost no light pollution, the sky was particularly dark, making the stars feel even brighter; in the distance, the lights of Dubai were only visible as a soft, orange glow.

It was just passing 0200 locally and Dave was dreaming of his bed, unaware that at the other end of the Gulf, just a few hours before, tens of thousands of the Iraqi Republican Guard had poured across the border into Kuwait.

The landing in Dubai was uneventful, and as they turned off the runway they were given the instructions to 'taxi to cargo', followed by 'good luck'. Even for an expat Scottish controller, this seemed an odd turn of phrase. After all, once they had shut down, and the crew and the passengers they were carrying were on the ground, the plan was only for a swift beer and then bed.

'Dave, can I have a word?' asked one of the troop commanders, who'd been travelling in the back of the aircraft. 'The shit's hit the fan,' he explained, having obviously turned on his satphone. 'Saddam has invaded Kuwait. And there's a hint that he might have taken some hostages from a British airline, so we might need to stay put for a while.'

Dave was completely taken aback. Saddam had been throwing around some rhetoric recently, yes, but it hadn't seriously been entertained that he would actually invade Kuwait. Yet it seemed he had. And, soon after, more intelligence came through: the attack had begun with a bombing raid on Kuwait Airport.

Dave and his crew had stumbled into a pivotal moment in history. Not only that, they had done so while carrying some of the most capable fighting forces on the planet. A classic case of right time, right aircraft, right place. It was incredibly fortuitous.

The 'hint' of potential airline hostages was also confirmed to be true. And, it turned out, there were quite a number of them. In a case of wrong time, wrong aircraft, wrong place, a Boeing 747 airliner had landed, due to stop only briefly before flying to its final destination in India. When the airfield was unexpectedly attacked by Iraqi bombers, the airliner's captain, Richard Brunyate, had just started putting the aircraft 'to bed', ready for the handover to Captain Peter Clark for the next leg of the journey. With the Iraqi bombs rendering the runway unusable, at least for a Jumbo, both the crew and the passengers were now trapped on the ground, in what had, in little more than the blink of an eye, become an active war zone.

Unsure what was happening, and obviously scared for his crew and passengers, the captain of the Jumbo had immediately commanded the evacuation of his aircraft into the relative safety of the airport terminal, resigning himself to the fact that they would be going nowhere any time soon.

He was right. The 747, all eighteen crew, and all 367 passengers of Flight 149 were now the prisoners of Saddam Hussain.

Over in Dubai, the picture was becoming clearer for Dave and the soldiers he'd been transporting. Completely coincidentally, they were right where they needed to be. Perfectly placed to effect a speedy rescue. But the devil, of course, was in the detail. The 747 crew and passengers stuck in Kuwait were to be their immediate focus, and plans for deploying the Herc were discussed with military commanders back in the UK.

'What are the aircraft hours?' they wanted to know. 'What weapons do you have on board?'

'Not many', and 'Not many', were, in effect, the answers. Then it was just a case of waiting for orders. After two days of discussions, however, they were ordered to return to the UK. 'There's nothing you can do,' they were told. There were simply too many unknowns to make an intervention viable.

Within hours, Dave, his crew and an entire squadron of the world's most elite troops climbed aboard the C-130 to return home. By sheer accident, they had been right where they needed to be to be deployed, but now it was almost as if they had never been there. And as he piloted the Hercules away from the sandscape of Dubai, Dave thought about all those hostages and what would now become of them. There was little doubt in his mind, though, that it *had* been the right decision. The only ammunition they had on board were the smoke flares they used for parachuting, and he wasn't sure that would be much use against the Republican Guard, no matter how strong the commitment of the Hereford Gun Club.

Back in the UK, British forces were already moving to a war footing. The international community condemned the invasion and set about finding a diplomatic solution to the conflict which would get Saddam to withdraw. When it was evident after a few months that Saddam wasn't going to back down, stronger action was needed, and the US started to garner support for a coalition that would, once it had obtained the backing of the United Nations, move to forcibly evict Saddam's troops from Kuwait. On 29 November 1990, the UN signified its approval with the passing of Resolution 678, which demanded Iraqi troops leave Kuwait peacefully, and authorized the coalition 'to use all necessary means' to force Iraq to comply if they did not.

For the RAF C-130 fleet, the first Gulf War started long before that resolution was passed. Only a matter of days after Dave Fry's mission that never was, crews from four RAF C-130 squadrons, together with their support personnel and equipment, were scrambled to pre-position to RAF Akrotiri, in Cyprus. From there, they were spread across the allied countries in the Gulf, with a permanent central base and headquarters in Riyadh, Saudi Arabia, in preparation for the largest air bridge of UK forces' people and equipment since the Falklands. During these first few days, success was far from assured, as the gravity and scale of the airlift task was now becoming apparent. It would be more than a test of the coalition's ability to fight the Iraqi troops; the success of the entire campaign largely hinged on the ability of commanders to get equipment and soldiers into the correct places to fight, and to be able to support them for what could be many months. Like all wars before this, logistics were going to be key to winning against a well-equipped and highly motivated enemy. This is where air mobility comes to the fore – and, with that, the role of the C-130 as a tactical transporter, back on the front lines once again.

The entire theatre was soon riddled with C-130s, from the United States Air Force, Marines and Navy, as well those from the air forces of Australia, New Zealand, Saudi Arabia, South Korea and, of course, the UK. By 9 September 1990, just a few weeks after the Iraqi invasion of Kuwait, the US alone had ninety-six C-130s in the region, providing intra-theatre tactical delivery, or 'tactical air-land operations'. This number was to double as the coming weeks saw an enormous multinational airlift effort.

This logistical challenge was met by the USA using the well-rehearsed 'spoke and hub' model that had been used in Vietnam – the same method, incidentally, that the retail giant Amazon employs now for home deliveries, to some success. The US would use its larger cargo jets, such as the C-141 and C-5, to do the long-haul journey into the Gulf at major air hubs, and then use the smaller C-130 to deliver intra-theatre, i.e. the spokes. This methodology was employed at the peak of the build-up of coalition forces, and saw a C-130 depart a hub airfield every three minutes with a load for the front line of ammunition, food, spares or even fuel.

While the USAF focused on the hub and spoke method, the RAF lacked the strategic airlift capacity in its VC-10 and Tristar fleets to make any real impact using it, so instead started what is called a 'slip pattern' from the UK to the Gulf region, through RAF Akrotiri in Cyprus, using its C-130s. The crews would change (slip), but the aircraft would shuttle back and forth endlessly with their loads from the UK. This 'point-to-point' delivery of logistics without having to go through a hub, while asset-intensive, can often be a faster way of getting equipment to the front line. The C-130 was always designed as a tactical airlifter, optimized for the short flights intra-theatre, but it was also finding its feet in a new role as a strategic airlifter. Within a few weeks, the tempo of these operations was taking a toll on the crews and teams that supported them, and small errors were beginning to happen.

One such error involved a C-130 that was due to depart Akrotiri for the Gulf with a load of live 1,000 lb bombs on board. This load, like many others, was carefully planned in advance: they had received detailed instructions about stowing the bomb-laden trailers, and the quantity they could carry had been carefully calculated to ensure they didn't exceed the maximum wartime take-off weight of 175,000 pounds. This sortie, they knew, would be getting airborne at the heaviest weight for a C-130, but little did they know that they were about to set a record. With full power set, the aircraft started its take-off run, and straight away the crew's concern began to build. With the end of the runway fast approaching, they had not yet got anywhere near the take-off speed. By the time the captain was able to rotate the aircraft they were almost entirely out of tarmac, and it felt like an age before they finally lifted off.

The captain's reaction was understandably pithy. 'Something is fucked up,' was his first observation, and his subsequent command of 'Gear up', so familiar as to be automatic, didn't help the situation one bit. The nose gear door on the Hercules opens forward, which means it acts like a brake – not normally a problem in a fast-accelerating aircraft, as it only slows the speed by something like two knots, but in an aircraft that is already struggling to get airborne, those two knots can make all the difference. The Herc immediately began sinking back towards the brush on the periphery of the airfield and crossed the road beyond it at barely 100 feet above the ground. They were out over the Mediterranean before it started climbing sufficiently for the crew to feel able to breathe normally again. That was enough excitement, and the captain elected to dump much of his fuel over the sea before returning to Akrotiri for a review and a beer!

As ever, there was a reason for the aircraft's sluggish take-off. It emerged that the planned weights didn't include the tail-fin section of the bomb, so the actual load on the aircraft was over 200,000 pounds. No wonder Albert didn't want to get airborne. Yet, astonishingly, it had managed to, once again proving that the trusty C-130 could exceed its design limits to keep its crews safe. And a valuable lesson had been learned in the process. That planned weights perhaps needed to be double-checked.

While the logistics were a major challenge, the management of the airspace was also going to need some innovative thought. The airspace over Saudi was an aerial ballet of fighters, transport aircraft and tankers, as well as a modicum of civilian airliners still flying up and down the Gulf region. Every single sortie was timed and coordinated to the minute, ensuring that the airfields and airspace were used to capacity without being unsafe. This is colloquially called a 'frag' (or fragment) of the air tasking order, which is produced for every mission that is to fly on a given day. This is a hugely complex and secret document that includes thousands of sorties planned for the theatre, from air transport to strike missions. One such mission, on 31 January 1991, was callsign 'Spirit 03': an AC-130H Spectre gunship of the USAF, tasked to provide air support for US Marines in the battle of Khafji.

While many will only remember the invasion of Kuwait, Iraqi troops and armour did advance into Saudi Arabia, and entered the border town of Khafji on 29 January 1991. Coalition commanders saw this as a key strategic move by the Iraqis and part of a wider plan to push south into Saudi and capture their oilfields, hence it was imperative to repel it.

On the night of 30/31 January, a counteroffensive was mounted by British, American and Saudi ground forces, and this was supported from the air by the crew of Spirit 03. As dawn loomed, Spirit 03 was supporting US Marines in contact with the enemy, and decided to stay overhead, engaging them, despite the loss of the protection of

darkness. In the growing light, the aircraft became silhouetted against the blue sky, and the Iraqis fired an SAM-7
surface-to-air missile. It struck and fatally damaged the aircraft, resulting in a crash and the loss of all fourteen crew
members. During all of Desert Storm, the USAF lost only
twenty personnel; the crew of this aircraft, from the 16th
Special Operations Squadron at Hurlburt Field, Florida,
constituted the bulk of those losses.

The offensive actions of the USAF gunships were not
the only ones carried out by Hercules during the conflict,
as eleven BLU-82 bombs were dropped by C-130s during
five missions in 1991. This weapon, known colloquially as
the MOAB – the Mother of All Bombs – is one of the
largest conventional weapons in the world. The bomb is
dropped on a pallet from the rear of a C-130 at about
7,000 feet and drifts down on a parachute before detonating. It was primarily used in the first Gulf War to clear
minefields in southern Kuwait ahead of advancing troops,
though the effectiveness of this was never proven. But it is
also thought they were dropped for their psychological
effect on Iraqi troops prior to the ground offensive. Indeed,
a unit of elite UK troops that witnessed one of the blasts
assumed the US had just dropped a nuclear weapon and
radioed back to their HQ exclaiming, 'Sir, the blokes have
just nuked Kuwait.'

Meanwhile, the rest of the British forces had also been
busy. And just as 47 Squadron had been the first of the
Hercules Wing to forward deploy to a friendly Gulf nation
in preparation for the war, it was also the first RAF unit to
enter the conflict zone. A small group, which included

Dave and his crew, had already flown into a remote air-strip, a desert hideaway codenamed Victor, from where, it was planned, they would launch deep-penetrating missions to place British forces behind enemy lines.

This secret base was originally destined to be a brand-new training facility for the United Arab Emirates; when Dave arrived and was allocated his accommodation, it contained furniture so new it was still wrapped up in plastic. Though it was definitely a plus to turn up for war in an austere environment and enjoy such upmarket facilities, it also felt a little like a prison. Due to the nature of the work, which was to directly support covert operations, the crew were forbidden from even travelling to the nearby 'oasis', for a few pints of Mr Heineken's elixir of life. They did, however, manage to catch lots of news on CNN, and were able to watch the ongoing hostage situation play out, with both the passengers and crew of the 747 now being used as human shields, to help Saddam try and win the propaganda war. It made for frustrating and unedifying viewing. They'd been so near, and with the calibre of elite troops they'd been carrying, had been a whisker away from being able to save them.

Over the next few weeks, the crews flew constant training missions from Victor, flying ever lower, and at night, in the hope that they could evade what they believed would be the inevitable threat of ground-to-air munitions once they were operationally deployed. The remainder of the Hercules fleet, meanwhile, was accelerating rapidly to lift an army into the western desert in preparation for a ground war. The next few months proved that the entire military effort was, and would continue to be, reliant on the airlift capability of the Hercules and the flexibility of the crews. No operation had ever put this kind of strain on the entire fleet, and they needed to raise their game to get the job done.

Op Desert Storm started with an air war on 17 January 1991, when allied forces began bombing targets within Iraq and Kuwait. The ground war started just over a month later, with elite troops the first to see action, having been placed behind enemy lines by a combination of methods, including covert insertion by C-130s.

The Herc crews on the ground in Kuwait during the first Gulf War were experiencing conditions and threats the like of which they hadn't seen before. This was almost certainly the first time in British forces history since World War I that troops and crew faced the real threat of chemical warfare; Saddam Hussein had already used the Sarin and Tabun nerve agents in the Iran War and against his own people, after all. For many of the younger aircrew (some little older than I was), it was also the first time they could anticipate being bombarded – in this case, by Saddam's Scud missiles.

In true pragmatic Hercules style, however, they soon acclimatized to the level of threat. Martin, a C-130 flight sergeant loadmaster, and one of the aircrew who was there for the duration, speaks for many in his assertion that, after a while, it didn't even seem real; more like just another aspect of their training. Though people would tend to panic the first few times alerts sounded, familiarity soon bred, if not contempt, a certain *c'est la vie* attitude. If alarms went off when they were loading and unloading, they'd simply ignore them; and if they were billeted in their accommodation, they could often be found watching from hotel and hostel roofs, wearing nothing more than shorts and respirators, their G&Ts still firmly in hand as they cheered each incoming missile shot down by the US's Patriot defensive system. (A gin and tonic can be drunk through the straw on a respirator faceplate just as easily as water – Adapt and Overcome.)

As in any high-stress, high-jeopardy, high-risk profession, high jinks and childish humour helped keep people sane. But perhaps the pinnacle of adolescent behaviour – to put it mildly – was what happened after the swift ground war had ended. Facing defeat within just four days of the allies' ground troops going into Kuwait, Saddam ordered his retreating forces to set fire to hundreds of oil wells, creating infernos the like of which had never been seen before. With so many wells alight, they were burning through around 4–6 million barrels of crude oil every single day. The deserts turned black, the sky turned black, and what wasn't burning rained down from the sky, coating everything and everyone in its toxic pollution.

Saddam's thinking, of course, was that if he could no longer profit from the oil he had accused Kuwait of stealing from him then no one else should either, and with the hope that the fires would be impossible to put out.

It was something Dave Fry was to experience first hand. After a lot of 'on the bus off the bus' stuff during the previous months, on 24 February 1991, he and his crew were finally told, 'It's on.' As part of a historic, two-ship mission (Monty 66 and Monty 67), they were to prepare to be only the second allied aircraft on the ground at Kuwait Airport.

Their mission was to resupply coalition forces, which

by this time had already liberated the airport, with fresh troops, ammunition, fuel and guns. They would land on the battle-damaged runway in Kuwait and, essentially, see how things played out. The only thing they knew for sure was that they would fly at low level for the first portion of the route then climb above the smoke from the burning oil wells to transit to the airport. They knew it would be bad, but Dave had no conception of what the next few hours would see them do.

'Gear up,' he called as they climbed to a few hundred feet and departed their new home for the unknown. It was a bumpy ride in the heat of the afternoon, but not disturbingly so; they were galvanized by the thought of finally going into theatre, and the thermals actually made it feel pleasingly like being on a funfair rollercoaster. Well, at least for those on the flight deck, because they could see out. For the troops in the back, who were being pitched violently around with no visuals to warn them, it might not have been quite as pleasant.

As soon as they crossed the border into Kuwait, the smoke from the oil fires came into view. At first like low thundery clouds hanging over the distant horizon, it soon resolved itself into the hellscape it had become. They had all heard about Saddam setting fire to the Kuwaiti oil fields, but, as night fell, no one was prepared for the picture of Hades that was now presented to them through the Herc windscreen. By the time they were visual with the city of Kuwait, it had become increasingly apocalyptic – as if the product of some overenthusiastic disaster-movie director's sick imagination. The normally ochre desert was now black from all the oil that had rained down on it, and the smoke, blacker still, billowed up into the night sky like a living, breathing thing. A writhing, malevolent entity, fuelled by the fierce oil fires that were raging below. It was sickening to smell and to witness, but even more sickening was that the actions of a cornered, vengeful man were now destroying the planet's precious natural resources.

To reach Kuwait Airport, they now had to fly right through the middle of this toxic maelstrom. Having seen exactly what Dave had, Tony the navigator began to work feverishly at his nav station to come up with a plan to get them safely down on the ground at their destination. He was using a new, GPS-based navigation system called 'Skins' (SCNS: Self-Contained Navigation System), which had only recently been fitted to some of the C-130s, and the technology was pretty unfamiliar.

Dave glanced across and behind. 'Do you think you can come up with a way of getting us down safely?' he asked.

Tony nodded. 'I'm happy with the accuracy of the system,' he confirmed. 'If I set the threshold of the runway as a waypoint, I can build back an approach from that to descend us on a three-degree slope through the smoke.'

They had a brief crew discussion; they were going off-piste now. This was brand-new technology, and using this methodology was both unpractised and unproven. Could they trust it to get them down safely? It was going to be a very dangerous business, much more so than anyone had envisaged, so everyone needed to fully commit to it. If anyone said no, they would have to find another way.

Everyone agreed, however, so it was time to put both Tony and Skins to the test.

'500 feet is the limit,' Dave said. 'Nothing seen, and we

go around.' With everyone now ready, Dave followed Tony's direction to the start point for the descent.

At about seven miles from the runway and about 2,000 feet above the ground, they entered the wall of smoke. The immediate stench in the aircraft was nauseating, as if they were inhaling crude oil straight into their lungs. Dave looked over his left shoulder to where the wing was and couldn't even see their props, it was that dense.

'Five miles,' Tony said, '1,500 feet.' Dave looked down at his altimeter. Noticing that he was passing 1,600, he made the necessary adjustment. It was now not so much 'out of the frying pan and into the fire' as 'out of the frying pan and into the abyss', because the smoke still roiled around them, seemingly without end.

'Everybody okay?' Dave asked. The affirmatives were reassuring. The radar altimeter started beeping to signify that they were now down to 1,000 feet. 'Resetting 450 feet,' Dave said, twisting the bug around to their agreed minimums.

'700,' the eng called, reading from the radalt, '600.'

Dave still could not see the runway. He could see absolutely nothing, in fact, outside the window.

'500.' Still nothing. He pushed the throttles forward. 'Flaps 50,' he called, and the eng shouted out, 'Torques . . . 15 . . . 16 . . . 17 . . . 18,000,' as Dave initiated the go-around.

'Gear up,' he commanded, accelerating to 170 knots and climbing. Shortly afterwards, they broke out above the oily smoke that had engulfed them for so long.

'I'm still happy with the accuracy of the Skins,' Tony said as they assessed their options. 'I think we can go lower.'

It was not without risk. There was no ground-based instrument approach available to them here. They were relying on an unproven system to take them down through the smoke, to an imaginary point in space, less than a mile from the runway, at 200 feet. They were literally making it up as they were going along.

Dave twisted in his seat, and turned to the crew. 'You all happy for 200 feet?' Everyone nodded, and Tony gave them a steer towards the runway and their virtual glide path.

Dave configured the aircraft for landing, and they entered the smoke this time at 7.5 miles, and just a little under 2,500 feet. Almost instantaneously, the smell and the smoke engulfed the aircraft once more.

'*Beep beep beep!*' The shirl of the radalt hurt everyone's ears as they passed through 1,000 feet.

'I'm setting 180,' Dave called, as he twisted the bug again. Were it not for the droning of the four turboprop engines, you could have heard a pin drop on the flight deck.

'600 . . . 500 . . .' came the height calls from the flight eng. Dave still couldn't see anything out of the windows. '400 . . .' Still nothing. Except . . . was that something? In his periphery, he saw a pylon pass the aircraft, close enough for him to pucker his arse.

'300 . . .' said the flight engineer.

'I can see it!' Dave said, with perhaps a little more enthusiasm than he had intended.

So at least they had sight of the runway; but another problem was now horribly apparent. Every piece of glass on the aircraft was covered in a thick layer of oil, distorting the view as their forward speed pushed the slick up the windows. It was like trying to land while peering through a kaleidoscope. Dave pulled back when it felt right, chopped the power and, seconds later, Albert sat down on the Kuwait tarmac, the tension of the approach immediately forgotten as the job of delivering their precious cargo began.

As Dave taxied towards the ramp, the scene was reminiscent of something out of *Mad Max* the movie, and dominated by the burnt-out hulk of the 747 whose captive crew and passengers he had come so close to helping all those months earlier. As it was, they had all long since returned home; all bar one, a Kuwaiti national who had already disembarked before the plane was captured and was subsequently killed by Iraqi troops.

Two other RAF C-130s were already there. While they'd been airborne the plan had clearly changed. Dave shut the aircraft down and wandered across to speak with Al, the captain of Monty 66, who'd landed safely a few minutes earlier.

'Fuck me,' Dave said. 'I wouldn't be wanting to do that every day!'

After comparing notes with his buddy, Dave then went to speak with some of the UK specialist troops who had liberated the airfield.

'Don't go in the terminal,' they told him. 'We think it's booby-trapped.'

Dave looked through the terminal windows and saw the carnage inside. Everything smashed. Everything broken. Everything that could be destroyed had been destroyed. It looked as if a bomb had been detonated in the building, even though he knew it hadn't. It was not unlike the business of setting all those oil wells on fire. Such a needless act of vandalism.

He walked over to the shell of the burnt-out 747, ostensibly to get himself some pictures, but also because he felt pulled there, as if by a tractor beam. It was such an iconic aircraft and so heartbreaking to see it had come to such a sad end. Saddam Hussein, in his rage, had blown it up just a few days before. The fire had gutted it, immobilized it. Killed it. Yet the tail, as if defiantly refusing to accept its fate, still stood upright, reaching to the heavens. It was an eerie, disturbing, but strangely compelling sight. This was a passenger aircraft. A thing of business, of pleasure. It was never designed to be embroiled in the ravages of war.

As Dave returned to his own aircraft, he reflected that the broader mission, to liberate Kuwait, was now coming to an end, which was something to be thankful for. But, gazing into that terminal building and knowing what had happened, he couldn't help but think about the mission that never was, and the innocent passengers and crew who had suffered there.

With freedom restored to Kuwait, the then Prime Minister, John Major, was very keen to visit, and had come up with a singular plan. In order to show Kuwait that the United Kingdom was a friend – and, by extension, could be pivotal in helping the oil-rich state to rebuild after the war – his idea was to drive around the region in his pristine British racing green Jaguar saloon. He hadn't, however, figured on the mischievous antics of Flight Sergeant Loadmaster Martin, together with Flight Sergeant Stu, the crew's flight engineer.

Stu and Martin's little Hercules gang was on standby in Akrotiri at the time, and had turned up at the aircraft with their 'big green bags'. These contained essential equipment they might need, such as their nuclear, biological and chemical (NBC) protection suits, gas masks, 'whistling handbags' (aircrew respirators) and autoinjectors (like an EpiPen, but containing atropine, in case of a chemical attack involving a nerve agent). As the crew arrived, they loaded their personal bags down the back as usual. Martin let them know that they had a British racing green Jaguar loaded in the freight bay.

'Which belongs to the PM,' he clarified. 'He's coming to visit in the next couple of days.'

Everyone, of course, had to take a look. The loadmaster out of the UK would have made sure that the car had been prepared for the trip with little to no fuel, and disconnected the battery to reduce the fire risk on board, so it wasn't currently driveable, but it was definitely stunning. The whole crew wasted no time in inspecting the interior, making comments about the swish leather seats, the thickness of the doors, the stylish dash, and all the bulletproof glass. Who knew the PM would possess such a thing?

Departing out of Akrotiri, they headed south over Egypt and then the Red Sea, after which they would then be allowed to enter Saudi airspace to head towards Kuwait. Being over friendly territory, and at a low ebb, Martin and Stu decided they would take a little rest in the back seat of the car; just stretch out for a while and have a cup of tea, not just to escape the constant, teeth-grinding noise, but also just so they could say that they'd done it.

While in the car, and obviously not pretending to be the Prime Minister (that would, of course, be too juvenile), they noticed a small red button in the centre console. Being inquisitive, they pressed it to see what it did. A small red light illuminated, indicating there was still some kind of power source that should have been disconnected. *Bugger.* Thankfully, nothing terrible happened. Though they'd convinced themselves that the car would be fully tooled-up, James Bond-style, no seats were ejected, no missiles were launched and no clouds of smoke came billowing from the exhaust.

Thinking nothing of it (except for a little mild disappointment), they continued to sit in the back and finish their tea. About twenty minutes later, a face loomed. It was Captain Chris knocking on the rear car door. Since the glass was too thick, and neither man could read lips, they opened the door to find out what he wanted. The serenity inside the Jaguar was immediately vaporized, and not just by the racket from the freight bay rushing in.

'You two,' Chris barked, 'messing about in this car! Have you touched anything?'

'NO!' they said in unison.

The captain scowled. 'Are you *sure*? Because the security services in the UK are trying to figure out how the Prime Minister's car is doing 250 miles an hour at 25,000 feet over the RED SEA!'

It appeared that they had inadvertently activated the emergency alert and tracking system used if the car were ever under attack. Which it wasn't. They quietly closed the door and finished their tea.

But that wasn't the end of it.

The flight continued, and Martin and Stu got back to their respective flying duties. As part of those, on arrival in Kuwait they unloaded the Jag onto the apron. As it turned out, the battery hadn't been disconnected, just encased in a battery-safe bag, plus the car did have a small amount of fuel in it still, presumably to allow them to do a post-flight test drive, to ensure it was still in good working condition.

It seemed it was. Before bottling it, and parking it beside the other freight they had offloaded, they managed to get the very heavily armoured, and so extremely weighty, Jag up to a decent seventy miles per hour on the taxiway.

Thinking of it as nothing more than a fun story for the grandkids, Stu and Martin had an uneventful trip back to Akrotiri. The following morning, however, one of the jobs on that day's Kuwait flight was to pick up a racing green Jaguar.

Not a little anxious – would they soon be clapped in irons? – they arrived to find out what had happened. Fortunately, they were off the hook. Apparently, one of the locals had taken it to a local gas station and accidentally filled it with the wrong fuel.

Now comprehensively broken, at least until the fuel tank could be flushed out, the Prime Minister's Jag was duly reloaded. It had travelled about 4,000 miles from the UK to Kuwait, been driven for less than a mile *in* Kuwait, and was now travelling another 4,000 miles back again.

It is traditional and, I think, psychologically healthy, for veterans of conflicts – however traumatizing and stressful – to recall the high jinks that helped get them through. But it probably bears repeating that the Gulf War saw not just the loss of millions of barrels of oil; it also saw a lot of needless death. The allies suffered 290 deaths during the fighting, with forty-one of these being British. It is also estimated that 10,000 Iraqi troops died in the four days of the ground offensive alone. The fighting came to an end on 28 February 1991, with Kuwait liberated, and a formal ceasefire agreed; but, as we know now, this was not to be the end of conflict with Iraq and Saddam Hussain.

When the last Hercules crews left the permanent C-130 detachment in Riyadh, in March 1991, the seven in-theatre RAF Hercules, together with two from New Zealand, had carried out 2,365 sorties, moving 20,340,000 pounds of freight and 23,270 passengers.

The allies did, eventually, manage to cap all the oil wells. Over the following months, a coalition of US companies found a way to use the wells' own pipeline to the Gulf to pump in the vast amounts of salt water needed to extinguish the fires. Initially, they were capping the burning wells at a rate of only one every seven to ten days, hampered by unmapped minefields placed to protect them. Once these were cleared, however, the rate increased to two or more a day. The last well was capped on 6 November 1991. An impressive feat of engineering, coupled with human fortitude, in the face of what had initially appeared to be an impossible task.

The war proved to be another point of pivotal change in the utilization of the C-130 as a tactical tool, with the aircraft now a proven platform for operating deep within enemy territory, as well as for delivering masses of logistics to our own front lines. So central to the war effort was the Hercules that General Hansford T. Johnson, military airlift commander of the USAF, was moved to note: 'Without the C-130 there would have been no 100-hour victory.'

The versatile Herc even turned its hand to becoming a giant airborne environmental monitoring station, when the Met Office's C-130W Mk 2 – a highly modified aircraft known as 'Snoopy', normally used for meteorological research – was commissioned in its classified secondary role to 'sniff out' nefarious pollutants thrown up into the atmosphere as a result of the war, which could have a negative impact on human health.

Saudi Arabia, an alcohol-free country, had also, it was rumoured, become the world's fifth-largest importer of Scotch whisky in 1990. The Herc crews had not contributed to that feat in any way, of course, and had never landed with any contraband on board. They had, however, become big fans of fresh oranges, for some reason, and always needed resupplies of syringes for their first-aid kits. Weird. (Actually, a weird new take on the vodka and orange; but the less said about that the better.) Many have since wondered what the Bedouin wandering in the western desert would think should they ever happen across all the empty glass bottles strewn across the landscape from low-flying aircraft . . .

Back at RAF Lyneham, among the newly minted Gulf War veterans, my first day of the eight-week ground school started with a meet-and-greet over coffee in the 242 Operational Conversion Unit buildings – old Nissen huts that used to serve as airmen's accommodation. The single-storey buildings had now been converted to classrooms and offices, but, because of their original use, felt more like a labyrinth of dead ends than the centre of excellence for C-130 training in the RAF.

I met my crew for the course and sat for the obligatory military photos to mark the occasion. My crew was to be captained by the new Officer Commanding LXX Squadron, Chris Le Bas, and the co-pilot, pleasingly, was a fellow Scot, Dave Tully. The navigator was the incoming station commander, David Adams, a giant of a man. The flight engineer, who would normally be the other non-officer on the crew, was actually one of the few officer flight engineers, a guy called Martin Heal; so, all things considered, I felt slightly overwhelmed. Just eight months earlier, I had joined the RAF as an airman, and here I was training alongside a crew of heavyweights.

Our first day closed with an aircraft visit – my first time on the aircraft that I was about to fall in love with. This one was a little special: during the war in the Gulf, the C-130 engineers had adorned a number of the aircraft with nose art, and this was one of them.

Back before World War I, nose art had been used to identify aircraft from different units. In World War II, however, it evolved somewhat, to express the individuality not only of the aircraft itself, but also of the crews, who often felt constrained by the uniformity of the military. These paintings were frequently risqué in nature, and would evoke memories of home. But their appeal was further enhanced by the fact that, although they were officially unapproved, they were tolerated as a morale-booster. The most famous example from World War II is the Memphis Belle: a curvy female wearing only a swimsuit and high heels, who adorned the side of a US B-17 Flying Fortress.

In the era of *Loaded* magazine and *FHM*, the Brits were

now doing things a little differently. The C-130 that I was about to board was decorated with 'Sandra and Tracey', the 'Fat Slags' of *Viz* comic fame, both dressed in similar swimsuits.

Today, this nose art would probably result in a court martial – and a conviction in the court of public opinion (and quite rightly too). But at the time, as I boarded the aircraft, such things were far from my mind. For me, it summed up the humour of the gang I was joining. No, not the best-looking kids on the block, not the mighty USAF, but fun, full of humour and dependable.

I was going to fit right in.

11. Unexpected Item in the Loading Area

The movie *Black Hawk Down*, released in 2001, is one of those visceral 'once seen, never forgotten' war films. Focusing on the Battle of Mogadishu, after the US dropped 100 elite troops onto the main marketplace of Somalia's capital, it's rightly been lauded as a faithful representation of the events that happened there in 1993.

Back at the tail end of 1992, however, battles in African countries couldn't have been further from my thoughts. I was completely focused on a battle of my own: to come to terms with the gulf between my childhood ambitions and the reality now staring me in the face.

It's no exaggeration to admit that, by this stage in my young life, I was feeling pretty bruised. My confidence had been bumped so comprehensively during my time in the RAF already that, at just twenty-one, I had fully accepted the truth: that I did not have what it took to become a Hercules pilot. Or, indeed, any kind of pilot. It had taken a long time and a lot of soul-searching to accept this.

But I still loved being in the RAF. I loved my new squadron. And, by now, I was definitely in a long-term relationship – with a very large lump of khaki-coloured aircraft. So, since arriving at Lyneham in the spring of 1991, a change in career goals had taken place. If I wasn't going to be allowed to drive the machine I'd so comprehensively fallen in love with, I was determined to become the best air loadmaster the RAF, indeed the world, had ever seen.

By mid-December 1992, I was very much on track with that ambition. I had reached the final hurdle, and was about to finish the last test of my tactical training course, where my skills as an ALM had already been taken to the next level. I had just the double medium stressed platform (MSP) drop left to do.

It had been a tough course, particularly the discipline of airdropping loads under canopy, something I hadn't done up to that point. We were fortunate to have some legendary air loadmasters as the instructor cadre, but they had a fearsome reputation for being scrupulous, and for giving absolutely no quarter in their role as the gatekeepers to these new skills. And rightly. If you're going to drop anything very heavy from a very great height, it's obvious you need to know what you're doing.

As anyone who knows me will testify, I have never been a details guy. I'm much more about ideas and the bigger picture. Sadly, this course was entirely about details. About procedures and checking the minutiae of stuff – stuff that could mean the difference between success and failure, life or death.

So I found the course very hard, but it had at least been incremental in nature. To my relief, you always started with the smallest loads – a few jerry cans strapped together with a harness and a small parachute, launched from the side door – before progressing up to the largest: a brace of MSPs, weighing several tons each. The latter was spectacular to watch leaving the aircraft, but the hard bit was the loading and rigging, i.e. all those little details.

But here I was, finally. About to jump that last hurdle. After which I was done till the New Year.

With just four hours to departure, I arrived at the aircraft accompanied by Henry – one of the legends – who would be coaching me on my first ever double MSP drop. It was the qualifying drop too. Get this wrong and I wouldn't be, so I was already extremely nervous, not just about the drop, but about being watched doing the drop – which, as I had never done one before, I was literally doing from a book.

My checklist in hand, I started to pre-flight the aircraft for this unusual load and inspected everything, from the width of the roller conveyor in the freight bay to the position of two anchor points that would be crucial to the load sequence. The MSP, essentially a large metal skidboard and frame which only just fitted inside the freight bay, had flattened airbags fitted to the bottom. These would inflate as the load descended, then cushion the majority of the impact on landing, with a honeycombed cardboard called Dufaylite taking up what was left, allowing the vehicle and stores to survive this epic plummet to earth. Atop the frame were up to three enormous parachutes, which supported the load as it swung towards terra firma. To give a sense of scale, for it was vast, a single MSP could hold a Land Rover, a trailer, ammunition and a gun, and we could drop two of these behemoths simultaneously. (Normally, the load would be around the three- to four-ton mark for each platform, but they could actually carry up to eight tons.)

Once I'd prepared the rest of the aircraft, I set the ramp at the horizontal position, so that the load would have a continuous line from the lip of the ramp onto the main cabin floor. I made sure that the ramp was supported by a hugely over-engineered piece of steel, colloquially known as the 'elephant's foot', which prevented the entire aircraft from tipping on its arse when you put a huge amount of weight at the back. The MSPs were ready and waiting behind the aircraft, on something called a 'condec', a specialist vehicle used for loading cargo onto planes. I checked the security of the load in the frame of each MSP and then took time to align the condec perfectly with the end of the ramp. The platforms were slowly pushed onto the aircraft by an army loading team, by hand; then, to avoid damage to either the condec or the aircraft as the MSPs made the final transition on board, the loader was pre-emptively lowered. Once we had put our collective backs into shoving both loads into their predetermined positions in the freight bay, the aircraft was full – much like your fridge when you've bought your Christmas turkey.

The task so far had involved dealing with a host of details, but there were still plenty more to pore over. While half a dozen soldiers clambered all over the loads, rigging them ready for airdrop, I was back into my checklist and following the army lead around as we made sure that all was correct. The sequence of this airdrop had been explained to me many times in the classroom. As I had been told repeatedly, 'If you get this one wrong, the tail will be pulled off the aircraft,' I had both it and the contingencies memorized. The checks complete, we had a briefing with the rest of the crew, then it was a case of shut up, start up, and take off on our low-level trip to the drop zone on Salisbury Plain.

In what seemed no time at all, we were approaching the drop zone. By now, I was about as nervous as I would be if I were I dropping myself. The flight engineer had started running the pre-dropping checks, and Henry and I were at the front of the freight bay, both attached by an umbilical safety line to a cable running the length of the aircraft. The rear then opened and, increasingly silhouetted against the incoming light, the monolithic loads looked even more impossibly huge. It felt like a miracle that science and technology could combine with something seemingly designed by Heath Robinson to produce a system that would ensure that both would almost certainly hit the ground intact. (And, by extension, that it would be my fault if they didn't.)

It was time, then. Stationed at my post by a manual release arm (backup if the electronic launch from the flight deck didn't work), I was about to launch two Land Rovers on the trip of a lifetime.

In my head, the carefully memorized sequence of events was quite sedate. *Press the button, the drogue chute swings from a bomb rack in the top of the gap between the ramp and door, then it opens in the air and pulls the three larger chutes off the ramp* (these are deployed in what's called a 'reefed' condition, which is about a third of their normal size), *and when enough drag is generated, the small cable holding the platform in the aircraft breaks, and this drag pulls the first platform out of the aircraft.*

The reality, of course, was very different. The flight engineer pressed the button, then it was *clunk!* then *whoosh!* and the first platform was gone, followed almost instantaneously by the second. I could only stand in awe; it was stunning to think that both platforms were accelerating to 150 miles per hour from a standing start in no more than about a foot. Needless to say, it was all over before I could even let out the breath I'd been holding, and, after a walk to the end of the ramp, safely tethered, I watched the loads that were already so far below us. After their first seconds of plummeting, they were now under canopy, but still descending at about a pretty hefty thirty miles per hour.

'Load gone,' I said. It was all I *could* say in that moment. I knew I'd passed. But I was also transfixed by the physics. Essentially, we'd deployed a chute or three, the massive load had seemed to stop in space, and the Herc – well, it had basically just flown away from it.

It was the most spectacular thing I had ever seen go out of an aircraft.

Meanwhile, my other love life was going well too.

Sharon and I had met in a pub in Chippenham, near to the airbase, and following two blissful years in which it became apparent that, remarkably, she felt the same about me as I did her, I had activated my pre-Christmas plan and plucked up the courage to ask her to marry me. To my great relief, she had immediately accepted.

On the squadron front, other pre-Christmas plans were in full swing: the Guinness and Mince Pies party, which was always pretty raucous, and the altogether quieter and more 'family friendly' option that was the Squadron Review. This was a sketch show put on by the 'Squadron Players' – essentially the show-offs who liked taking the mick out of the bosses.

Fresh from my tactical training and with my brand-new fiancée on my arm, I couldn't have been happier. With Christmas now imminent, Sharon and I were dying to spend a few days at home together, sharing the joy of our engagement with our families.

The Review was not long over, however, when I was namechecked by the boss. So was Sharon – and then the penny dropped; word was now out. As was tradition, we were both duly ushered onto the stage: my fiancée, to accept a glass of bubbly to toast our engagement; and me – because this is what 47 Squadron's like – to accept a yard of it. Yes, a whole *yard* of champagne.

I managed to drink it – my male pride saw me through – but it wasn't very long till it made a reappearance, along with most of the beige buffet I'd eaten earlier. Still, undaunted, I returned to the dance floor. And was right in the middle of throwing some rather uncoordinated shapes when I heard my name for a second time. What fresh hell was *this* likely to be? I only needed to see the boss's expression, though, to realize it must be a little more serious, and it was. A group of five crews were to be deployed to support operations in Somalia, where the UN were providing famine relief.

'As in when?' I asked hopefully.

As in tomorrow.

It seemed Christmas, for me at least, was cancelled.

Being in the forces involves the tacit understanding that you can be called upon to do anything, at any time. So all of us accepted this development with grace and got back to enjoying the party. As did Sharon, who, instead of having her new fiancé home for Christmas, would now have to wave me off for six long weeks. Welcome to the RAF family!

Up to now, I had only heard snippets of something

happening in Somalia on the evening news – I had yet to learn that breaking stories in the media of an overseas disaster, famine or conflict are often an early indication of where the fleet will likely find itself going next. I also, in my relative innocence, had no clear idea where Somalia even was, other than 'somewhere in Africa', and I certainly had no conception at this point of the problems that had precipitated the need for our mission.

There were to be two aircraft deploying, with two crews apiece, and I was to be deploying as part of a fifth crew, for operations support – a ground-based role, working for the detachment commander, where I'd help coordinate the movement of all the aid, and be mostly based in neighbouring Kenya.

It was a first for me in a couple of ways. Other than supporting the efforts in the Gulf, which were still ongoing, this would be my first operational deployment. Was I ready? I wasn't sure. I was pretty naive still, pretty wet behind the ears. But, after the bashing my confidence had taken since joining the RAF, I was also *very* keen to impress.

It would also be the first time I had ever travelled to Africa, as so much of the focus of the RAF had been in the Gulf for the first part of my career. So, despite the downer of leaving Sharon, I felt excited.

Though this was probably a good time to find out what the hell I was going into.

Unlike Ethiopia, Somalia under the dictator Mohamed Siad Barre had been relatively stable as a state (at least in African terms). Having come to power in 1969 through a bloodless coup, he had imposed autocratic rule based on what was essentially a personality cult of sorts combined with a form of 'scientific socialism'. By 1990, however, human rights abuses had hurt Barre's internal and national standing, forcing him to promise free elections and reforms. When, inevitably, these never came, his own two most trusted generals turned against him and ousted him from office.

This plunged the country into civil war, as the two generals each sought to establish himself as the leader of Somalia. This incessant conflict led to the destruction of the country's agriculture, and, by the autumn of 1991, the UN had declared that 4.5 million Somalis were on the brink of starvation, and appealed for international help. A UN effort called Operation Provide Relief was launched, and the delivery of aid by road started almost immediately.

The task wasn't straightforward. It was, sadly, being hampered by various rival militias, who were hijacking the aid convoys and preventing their supplies from getting through to those in desperate need. Enter President George H. W. Bush, who, during his last weeks in office, in December 1992, proposed to send the US military into Somalia to stabilize the area and deliver aid by air. They would be assisted by troops from a coalition of the willing, including UK forces.

And now including me. So, before dawn the following morning, I said fond farewells to my new fiancée and headed over to the squadron building for our intelligence, security and medical briefings.

The intelligence brief is formal, and uses professionally formal language. But it is – and was – easy enough to translate. 'There will be fighting. There will be shooting. There will be people shooting *at* you. It will be lawless. It will be just like the Wild West. Everyone has guns, both the "good guys" and the "bad guys". You won't, by the way, know which is which. There aren't even "good guys" or "bad guys", in fact. Not in any meaningful sense. And though the villagers *are* "good guys", you won't know who they are, since everyone wears the same clothes. Oh, and did we say? You will be shot at.'

This was a lot to take in, but one thing was crystal clear. For the first time in my life, someone might try to shoot me.

If I survived Africa itself, that is. The doctor who briefed us, and who was going along himself, wasted no time in making us aware of the many natural dangers that also awaited. Chief among these was malaria, for which he was already providing pills, but he was also keen to emphasize that nasty bugs lurked everywhere. 'So do not,' he ordered grimly, '*ever* drink the local water. And that includes ice in your drinks. And *on no account* ever go near the local seafood.'

Duly warned, we headed off that afternoon for our overnight stop at RAF Akrotiri.

Akrotiri has figured heavily in every RAF C-130 crew member's life at some point. From the early days of the Suez Crisis, through the evacuation of Beirut, to oper-ations over three decades in the Gulf, Syria and Afghanistan, Cyprus has been the key point from which to launch oper-ational sorties and logistic support. It's also been a high-profile base for the CIA's 'Detachment G' and its U-2 since the early 1970s, and is the site of a huge, almost science-fiction 'over the horizon' radar. This array, which comprises a collection of large masts and reflectors, uses shortwave radio transmissions to refract the signal off the ionosphere in order to track targets at exceptionally long ranges. Where ground-based conventional radar can see surface targets at about fifty kilometres, this system can accurately track them at many, many hundreds of kilometres beyond the visible horizon.

Not that any of this was on our minds during our layover en route to what we stoically accepted would probably be a very un-Christmassy and apparently very bug-ridden Kenya. No, while we still could, we were looking to eat, drink and be merry.

We landed in Cyprus that evening to find it was still a pleasant seventeen degrees Celsius. It was then time to enjoy the Ascot Shuffle. Named after the callsign prefix used by all RAF transport aircraft, this involves a period of 'hurry up and wait' milling about; a theme of military life familiar to many. Eventually, however, after a long wait on a bus, we were off across the apron towards the small, one-storey building that housed the engineers of the visiting aircraft section. Not to discuss engineering matters, but rather to visit the small back-room off-licence the engineers ran, which sold crates of cold beers to the visiting transport crews. The small premium charged for this excellent service then went back into their tea fund.

With beer duly purchased, it was off to the officers' mess to be allocated our accommodation. Normally, at bases, the officers would stay in their mess and the sergeants in theirs. However, Akrotiri has so many transient crews that only the permanent staff stay in the mess buildings. Everyone else stays in one- or two-storey communal blocks with shared toilets, rather like the university halls of residence of yesteryear. And the high jinks, it must be admitted, tend to be similar too.

Tonight would turn out to be no different. Perhaps even more determined than usual to make the most of our last night of freedom, we returned to our accommodation some hours later that evening extremely well-oiled.

Some, at this point, very sensibly went to bed. We would be flying to Africa early tomorrow, after all. Others, however, myself included, headed straight for the sergeants' mess before it closed. Since it was nearly Christmas, and we were already far from home, they were happy to oblige us with a final jug of beer, which we shared while morosely pondering the fact that no one had thought about Christmas decorations. It would be sad enough spending the festive period under the hot sun of Africa, but to not even have so much as a bit of tinsel to deploy ... Hmm, we agreed: Operation Provide Relief should have been renamed Operation Cancel Christmas.

With no time to find a solution we all accepted we would just have to grin and bear it. That was until a trip to the toilet suggested one to me, in the form of a huge Christmas tree – a *real* tree, which must have been brought from the UK – gaily twinkling in the sergeants' mess foyer. Surely our need was greater than theirs? Plus, I decided, in the tradition of heartless felons everywhere, they would have the opportunity in the next week or so to replace it, whereas we pour souls, being off to Africa in the morning, wouldn't.

Sometime later, a certain tree, along with (most of) its decorations and fairy lights, had made its way out of the front door of the mess and, after a night spent covertly in the corner of my room, found itself on the list the following morning to board a certain C-130 bound for Kenya.

Though slightly the worse for wear, I continued to have my wits about me. As the extra ALM on the trip, it was my job to help load all the additional bags on the ramp while the other loadies did their pre-flight. So to help me haul the tree aboard and lash it down, I enlisted the help of the RAF Police warrant officer who was travelling with us as security. Little did he know he had just become an accessory to a crime, or that the photo I took of him holding the tree was for reasons of posterity *and* blackmail.

It was then off to Mombasa. Which, as I looked out of the windows when we came in to land, was rather a shock. I had had visions of sweeping African plains with zebra and giraffes roaming free, but the reality was somewhat of a let-down. There was nothing to see but ugly scrubland for miles, with the only signs of life a rundown fire station and a small, single-storey terminal building. This was definitely not the Africa of my imaginings.

We set about unloading the elements of the detachment that we needed to set up before operations could begin. This obviously included the stolen tree (happily not too much the worse for wear), which we placed outside the detachment tent; it brought smiles to our faces, and a laugh or two as well. Despite adding fuel to the fire by sending a picture of it wearing sunglasses to the chairman of the sergeants' mess committee (himself an RAF policeman), we expected no more than a mild telling off.

We expected wrong. They were absolutely furious. The tree (which after a few days in the scorching sun ended up closer to firewood, in any case) was apparently one of great significance; it had been a tradition in the mess at Christmas for years, imported specially, and at great cost, from the UK. We would have to pay for a replacement, and we should all be in no doubt that There Would Definitely Be Disciplinary Action. That was, until one key bit of photographic evidence 'emerged' – of the tree on the Herc's ramp and, standing grinning beside it, the RAF Police warrant officer.

We paid up anyway, collecting money from all who benefitted, including our soundly duped police colleague, and, safe in the knowledge that we were going to keep both the tree and our jobs, we were in good spirits as we continued to settle in.

As part of operations support, I wouldn't personally be spending much time in Somalia; and after one trip to Mogadishu – essentially to 'protect the detachment commander, should a sniper want to kill him', as it was explained to me – it was something I could be forgiven for being grateful for. But I was young and foolish, and I couldn't help feeling a ripple of excitement when, on Christmas Eve, I was asked to join the crew for one of the daily drops of grain and clean water, as it would be an opportunity to see something of this 'Wild West' myself.

There was no question that the threat of violence was being taken seriously. Since the militias had rockets and, as Brian, the ALM, put it, 'all sorts of shit', our ninety-minute flight to Somalia was routed over the Indian Ocean, only flying over land when we were close to the airstrip we were heading for, just outside Baidoa. Though the strip was rudimentary, we landed without incident, and as the ramp began to lower I got my first taste of rural Somalia, which hit my senses as only a hot, horrible, dusty, desert place can when combined with the stink of burnt aviation fuel.

By the time the ramp was fully opened, there was already a flatbed truck reversing up to it, copious clouds of rust-coloured dust mushrooming around, while ten or so barefoot people milled around. Everyone looked pleased to see us, rather than hostile, which was reassuring, but Brian was taking no chances. As I began unloading sacks of grain alongside the crew and the villagers, he took up a position on watch.

Brian was very experienced, a super-senior loadmaster, and his caution was not misplaced. Word had obviously got out, because we were halfway through unloading the grain sacks when he spotted the unmistakable outline of what we called a 'technical' – a truck with a machine gun mounted on the back – approaching at speed.

'Threat,' Brian called out, getting everyone's attention. This was potentially trouble.

The technical pulled up alongside the truck, creating even more dust, and through the ochre mists we could see there were two men in the front and that the one in the back was very purposefully pointing the machine gun at the truck we were loading.

There were no pleasantries. 'I want that grain,' the machine gunner told the local standing closest to him.

Another villager approached the ramp. 'That guy wants the grain,' he told us.

We had no idea who they were, obviously, or what the situation demanded.

'Should we get involved?' I asked Brian.

Brian shook his head. 'No,' he said firmly. Then, to the villager: 'Shall we leave you to sort it out after we've gone?'

The young man, who looked like he was no stranger to

this sort of thing, thought for a moment. 'I think we should just give it to them now,' he said. He was clearly annoyed, but also philosophical. It just was what it was.

I felt very differently. There was still a consignment of grain and water to be unloaded, but doing it for a bunch of machine-gun toting men seemed unfair.

Despite my keenness to get into a firefight, however, it wasn't my battle, and I had to defer to Brian's wisdom.

Decision made, we closed the ramp, and as we took off I looked down and watched as the daylight robbery commenced. Sometimes, I reflected, in my youthful wisdom, doing the right thing wasn't always the right thing to do.

The next six weeks of my life were a round-the-clock 'work hard, play hard' blur, with a bias towards the 'work hard' part, unfortunately. I was enjoying it, but being in Africa not so much, my pale Scottish skin not being designed for the harsh sun, particularly over some of what were traditionally Kenya's hottest months.

Remarkably, however, I managed to swerve all the bugs. The doctor who'd put the fear of god into us, however, was not quite so lucky. Shortly after Christmas, I spotted him tucking into a lobster dinner with two German military doctors in the restaurant at the detachment hotel. He was also keeping hydrated, via the medium of gin and tonics served on the (local) rocks. It was not a huge surprise when he came down with a fever a few days later. I never found out if it was a bug or malaria, but it was a clear case of do as I say, not as I do.

The constant vigilance against illness and violence notwithstanding, the detachment was exhilarating and challenging, and often both at once. It was also, at moments, pretty petrifying: it seemed that everyone was potentially out to kill you for a bottle of water or a bag of grain, and it was my first time face to face with people who actively wanted to do me ill.

I felt enormous pride too. I was just twenty-one years old, and while my peers from school were mostly enjoying the distractions of university life, I had actually been in the middle of an airfield in Mogadishu, surrounded by dodgy characters toting weapons.

It was great to feel I was doing something so useful, but I was really missing Sharon. In the days before FaceTime, we had to send each other letters. Once I had written mine, I had to fax them to the squadron, where they would be put into envelopes and mailed for delivery; in response, Sharon had to mail hers to the squadron to be faxed out to me. Not ideal for the kind of message that one might want to share with one's new fiancée . . .

We all rotated out in February and flew back through Akrotiri, this time for a slightly more low-key overnighter – I thought it would be prudent to avoid the sergeants' mess, anyway. I also felt changed. Though my role on this occasion had felt more 'sideline' than 'front line', I had learned a lot about the bigger picture and, potentially, my place in it. A place where I felt increasingly at home.

Little did I know that, in just a few weeks, I would experience another rite of passage. And this time it really would shock me to my core.

12. There Are Always Risks

It was May 1993, and I'd been at home pottering around when I received an odd text from an old Air Cadets friend in Scotland who was now a police officer on Tayside.

Do Hercules have ejection seats? it read. *How many crew do they normally carry?* And finally: *Can you call me urgently?*

I immediately rang him and could hear the siren of a police vehicle in the background. He explained that he was responding as part of the police mountain rescue team to reports of a large military transport plane, believed to be a Hercules, having crashed in an area near Blair Atholl, on the edge of the Highlands. I answered his questions, but stressed it was unlikely to be a Hercules as they were so robust, and had four engines. I then remembered that my friend Trevor had left only that morning, as part of a three-ship exercise to be based at RAF Lossiemouth in northeast Scotland. Perhaps I'd give them a quick call.

There was no answer from the squadron operations desk, which wasn't unusual, but when I flicked on the TV and went onto Ceefax there it was . . . unconfirmed reports that an RAF aircraft had crashed in Scotland.

It was later confirmed on the radio that one of the three Hercules aircraft comprising Star Trek Formation had been lost while conducting a combined training sortie, killing all nine on board.

*

For Garry 'GBo' Brown, then a 34-year-old flight lieutenant, the tragic events of that day had felt even closer to home.

Garry had recently joined Support Training Flight – part of 57 (Reserve) Squadron – which had responsibility for the instructors on all three aircraft, and was learning how to become a low-level flying instructor. That morning, Garry was authorized to fly as part of the crew of XV193, where he would be under the guidance of Squadron Leader Stan Muir. They were already on the aircraft, engines running, when Stan suggested that, as Garry was an instructor under training, he would gain more from flying to Lossiemouth on one of the other Hercules and then returning on XV193 the next day. With the agreement of his captain, Squadron Leader Graeme Young AFC (a much-respected pioneer of the use of night vision goggles and formation flying), Garry did as suggested.

It was a perfect sunny day for flying through Scotland at low level and, en route from Lyneham to their nightstop at Lossiemouth, the three aircraft were engaged in formation and low-level navigation flying as part of a reinforcement flying training course. After the formation element of the sortie, the three aircraft split for individual missions and routes, which, for the crew of XV193 (Star Trek 3), included the simulated drop of a harness pack onto a dummy drop zone to the south of Glen Tilt.

As per the planned task, once the individual missions had been completed, the first two aircraft landed ten minutes apart at RAF Lossiemouth at around 1530. However, XV193, due in last, failed to arrive. The two crews had just parked on the dispersal and were waiting for the bus to take them to their accommodation on the base, when the station crash alarm sounded. The siren/tannoy system sounded both indoors and outside, and was also very loud, so everyone on the base would have heard it, together with the verbal message that the crash team report for duty.

Something serious had clearly happened and everyone feared the worst. Moments later, those fears were confirmed: they were informed that one of their Hercules aircraft had crashed and that there were no signs of survivors.

Once the crews had been transported to their accommodation for the night, they were met by the station commander, Group Captain Nigel Day, who urged all the crew and support personnel of the two remaining aircraft from Star Trek Formation to assemble in the Bothy Bar of the officers' mess. They would then be able to identify all who were present, and send an accurate account to Lyneham of who was alive, to avoid any confusion when informing next of kin.

It was Garry who was given this responsibility, and it was at that point that he spotted his name on the authorization sheet for the crew of Star Trek 3 and hastily scored it out. He also noticed that he wasn't the only one to be affected by the hand of fate. Two further crew members had also been moved around during the planning stage: Senior Aircraftsman Fletcher had gone from XV193 to XV176, and thus had also been spared, but Ground Engineer Sergeant Al King hadn't been so lucky. He had been switched from the crew on XV217 to XV193.

Garry was then able to make the call to Station Operations at RAF Lyneham with a list of names they had positively identified. He then had another important call to make. He knew that the Scottish television and radio news would be quick off the mark to report that a military transport aircraft had crashed in Glen Loch, and also that his mum was aware he was flying there that day, so his next action was to call and reassure her.

At around 1700, several squadron commanders from RAF Lossiemouth came to the Bothy Bar to share their sympathy, and extend their condolences. A barrel of beer and a bottle of port were kindly offered and accepted, though neither had much effect on the men's moods. Nevertheless, they followed drinks by heading off to Elgin for a curry; the same thing they always did on these land-aways, seeking comfort in familiarity.

Due to the extreme circumstances, none of them were permitted to fly their aircraft home, so the following day they were flown back to RAF Lyneham by relief crews sent to collect both them and the two remaining Hercules aircraft. They were greeted at Lyneham by the station commander, Group Captain David Adams. Looking drawn and shocked, he spoke quietly with them in private, before they were met by grieving RAF aviators and their own families, everyone stunned that something like this could happen on a training sortie.

Like other iconic aircraft, such as the Spitfire, the Hercules has its own unique sound signature. This is particularly true if it's flying ultra-low and you happen to be standing underneath it. For me, it's even more intense every time I hear it from the ground, because it always takes me back to a funeral on a barren, windswept Scottish hillside – that of my friend and colleague Sergeant Craig Hilliard; though my friend Trevor was not on that fated aircraft, it turned out that Craig had been.

Just as Garry did, I travelled north with colleagues and partners to attend Craig's funeral, in a stream of three Hercules aircraft that delivered us to RAF Kinloss on a typically damp morning on the Moray Firth. We bussed to the church in Inverness for the service, none of us quite believing that we were about to lay to rest this larger-than-life Scotsman and mischievous friend. It was almost impossible to reconcile it with the fact that just a few weekends earlier we had all been drinking together in Route 66, a well-known RAF haunt in Swindon. This, I suppose, is the nature of grief for everyone.

So many of us young aircrew, including myself and Craig, thought we were invincible. We were flying an aircraft that had survived the rigours of the Falklands and the first Gulf War, and which had proven itself – was still proving itself – to be uncommonly forgiving. Our training for a new era of tactical transport couldn't be more exciting or safer. Yet here we were, standing on a windswept hillside overlooking Loch Ness, watching Craig's coffin being lowered into its final resting place.

It was at Craig's funeral that I think it finally hit home for me that we were, in fact, very far from invincible. That we were doing a dangerous job. One with ever-present risks. Also a job that, despite our grief, and while mourning the loss of our friends, we would pick ourselves up for and be ready to do again tomorrow. And for all those tomorrows. It was while lost in such thoughts that I found myself ducking, shocked by the sound of that C-130, ear-splittingly loud, as it roared past us at a scant 100 feet. I looked up then to see the ramp and door open, and the lone figure of the loadie up there, standing to attention; a fitting tribute that, as I write, still brings a tear to my eye. Squadron Leader Al Hill and his crew from 30 Squadron did us all proud that day, fighting appalling weather and driving winds to make it happen.

It is said that advances in aviation safety are written in the blood of those who have gone before, and this tragic accident was a cruel reminder of exactly that. It is rarely true that a single thing causes an accident; it's always a chain of events that leads to the critical moment. James Reason, an eminent professor of psychology, likened this to having several slices of Swiss cheese stacked together. Each individual slice of cheese is part of a layered system of defence, put in place to prevent an accident. If the hazard manages to get through a hole in one slice of cheese, it's unlikely that a hole in the next slice will align in such a way that also lets the hazard slip through. It is only when the holes in every layer align – a rare scenario – that an incident can occur.

Though no one will know the precise circumstances of the crash of Star Trek 3, it is assumed that once XV193 had finished its dummy low-level drop it turned left, to head north from the drop zone, but that a rocky outcrop may have forced the crew to continue turning further left still. After avoiding considerable terrain, they probably chose to reverse the turn in order to enter the valley of Glen Loch and regain the planned route. During this manoeuvre, at low level and low speed, the aircraft appears to have stalled and crashed onto the moorland to the South of Loch Loch, at the bottom of the easterly slopes of

Beinn a' Ghlò. There were no eyewitnesses to the final moments of the flight, and the aircraft was not fitted with either an accident data recorder or a cockpit voice recorder. The board of inquiry's investigation found that the cause of the accident was consistent with the aircraft having stalled at an altitude from which recovery was impossible.

This stall is not like stalling your car – an embarrassing pause, red-faced at a green traffic light. The aerodynamic stall is sudden and brutal, as the wing, when under twice normal gravitational load – 2G – simply cannot claw more lift from the air. What immediately transpires is a jumble of airflow across the wing's upper surface which not even four engines can overcome, even if roaring out full power.

Large aircraft are vulnerable when heavy and operating at low speeds, as was the case in this accident. XV193 was loaded with a single medium stressed platform that it was planned would be dropped the next day, making the air-craft relatively heavy for a training mission like this.

Because the crew were practising procedures for drop-ping, they were flying low and slow in the valley. When flying straight and level, the aircraft is subject to normal gravity of 1G, and it will have a stall speed that relates to the plane's weight and configuration. This stall speed will not increase unless the wing is put under extra loading, such as a tight turn, which increases its G-load. The C-130 was authorized up to a maximum of sixty degrees of bank at low level, and this would have had the effect of doubling the loading on the wing to 2G.

As an example, if a level sixty-degree bank turn were done in a light aircraft, the stall speed of fifty-five knots in straight and level flight increases to seventy-eight knots – an increase of 42 per cent in almost an instant. Although the speeds are different in a C-130, the physics is the same. As XV193 made that turn to avoid the rocky outcrop, and the subsequent turn to regain the planned route, it is likely that the stall speed very quickly exceeded the flying speed, causing the wings to aerodynamically stall.

In straight and level flight, there is a warning of the onset of stall with buffet, but this type of manoeuvre stall is different: the onset can come with little or no warning, which prevents remedial action from the pilot until it occurs. The board of inquiry surmised that this was the case on this flight and, as such, the aircraft was not recoverable in the height available.

All pilots go through stall training, and the C-130 is no different, with actual straight and level stalls being practised in various configurations, at high level, during the conversion course. This accident highlighted that greater awareness of the dangers of manoeuvre stall would be needed to avoid it happening again, with all Hercules crew members subsequently undergoing a comprehensive training package of recognition and mitigation in order to prevent it.

The loss of the of XV193 hit the Hercules community hard, me included, but their loss was not in vain. It contributed to the improved safety of the fleet, and potentially the saving of other lives. For that, and for so many other reasons, they will never be forgotten.

Squadron Leader Graeme Paul Young AFC –
    Training Captain
Squadron Leader Stanley Duncan Muir –
    Training Navigator

Flight Lieutenant Graham Robert John
    Southard – Captain
Flight Lieutenant Stephen Paul
    McNally – Navigator
Flying Officer Jonathan Huw Owen – Co-Pilot
Master Aircrew Terence John William Gilmore –
    Flight Engineer
Sergeant Craig Thomas Hilliard – Air Loadmaster
Sergeant Alan Keith King – Ground Engineer
Lance Corporal Gary Reginald Manning – Air
    Despatcher
RIP

I could not sum this chapter up any better than someone who was there on the day, so I will leave the final words to Squadron Leader Garry Brown:

'When you remember those who have departed and lost their lives in Service of the Crown, remember those who live on and carry their thoughts into the night. May they sleep well, and find solace in fond memories.'

13. War in the Balkans: Sarajevo

The tannoy bellowed. 'Scottie Bateman, call at reception!'

I was in the RAF Lyneham mess anteroom reading the papers when the call came. It was August 1993 and one of those glorious English high-summer mornings when everything seemed right with the world. It certainly did for me; I had just started a period on standby. Colloquially known as '6A', this was a twenty-four-hour period, usually fitted around everyone's schedules, during which a crew would be on six-hour readiness to deploy anywhere in the world to support British forces or other national interests. In reality, it more often than not ended up being a day spent mooching pleasurably in and around the sergeants' mess.

Knowing this was likely to be a call-out, I went to the mess reception to answer the phone.

'Hey, Scottie,' came the loadie leader's voice. 'We need you to come in for a task. An aeromed to Ancona.'

We did aeromeds all the time so this was nothing unusual. And as I got my kit on, it occurred to me that it might be quite pleasant. I had no idea about the whys or the wherefores of this one, but what I did know was that there was definitely a strong possibility that we'd have to spend the night in Italy, which would not be disagreeable.

Having packed a bag, I drove across the airfield to the squadron building, where I and the hastily scrambled crew were quickly briefed. We were to fly to Edinburgh to pick up a specialist team of paediatric doctors and nurses from the Royal Infirmary, and then head on to Ancona, where the medical team would transfer to another Herc, one with the specialist self-protection equipment it needed for flying into Sarajevo. They would then fly in, pick up several casualties, and return to us waiting in Ancona ready to fly them back to the UK for treatment.

We were airborne within two hours for the short hop to Edinburgh, during which all that was on our minds was the fact that my suspicion had been confirmed shortly after take-off – that a specialist crew would fly our aircraft back to the UK with the casualties, leaving us effectively marooned in Ancona and forced to spend the night there, with only handmade Italian pizza and red wine to console us.

As we landed in Edinburgh still with zero intelligence about the patients in question, it was somewhat surprising to find ourselves in the middle of a sea of blue flashing lights; those of the police cars that were escorting some five or six ambulances, all, it transpired, packed with doctors and nurses and every conceivable medical device.

This is going to take a while to load, I thought.

The passengers were all full of nervous excitement as they walked onto the C-130. This was the first time for them all, and many were surprised at how spartan it was inside. Also, that they would have to sit facing sideways! I took the time to explain all the exits, the noise challenges, and, of course, the delicacies the RAF had loaded for them to eat on the way. As in, a white plastic lunchbox containing a few slices of Ryvita and some pâté with an expiry date in 2050, plus a carton of blackcurrant squash to wash it down. British Airways this was not.

As the noise of the starting engines increased, so did the size of our passengers' eyes, and many who had previously declined hearing protection were shouting to ask where they could get some. Comfort established (as far as was achievable), we closed the doors and were off, with no idea that we were about to fly into the epicentre of a political storm, one of the patients being a young girl called Irma Hadžimuratović.

Unbeknown to any of us at that time, she was about to become globally famous; a victim of the terrible war that was raging in the Balkans and the grim poster-child of the infamous siege of Sarajevo.

The fall of the Berlin Wall in 1989 and the break-up of the Soviet Union resulted in a change of the world order, particularly in Europe. It seemed to lift the lid on a number of historic simmering hatreds and conflicts that had been contained by the pressures of the Cold War. The Balkans had always been an area of concern; and, sure enough, the situation in Bosnia and Herzegovina, with its uncomfortable mix of Bosniaks, Serbs and Croats – and the various troublesome factions within each of them – soon boiled over. Throw in some highly dodgy and bellicose local leadership – very violent men with genocidal thoughts and ambitions – and the outlook was ugly. The whole region was a tinderbox, and it took little time for a very unpleasant and complicated civil war to develop, with the Bosnian capital, Sarajevo, at its epicentre.

The increasingly aggressive actions of Bosnian Serbs and Croats meant that, by the end of 1991, Sarajevo's road and rail connections had effectively been severed, placing the city under a virtual state of siege. This prompted the creation of a multinational United Nations peacekeeping force, tasked with the impossible job of keeping Bosnia's warring factions apart. When widespread fighting erupted in April 1992, Sarajevo was cut off completely by Serbian forces, who began to bombard it. With the city's essential infrastructure largely destroyed, and food supplies unable to breach the Serbian blockade, the Sarajevans were soon going to starve.

Operation Cheshire was set up by the RAF in July 1992 to help provide a continuous airlift of humanitarian aid into Sarajevo. It formed part of the effort overseen by the United Nations High Commission for Refugees, which primarily also involved the US, Canadian, Norwegian and German air forces – along with a civilian Ukrainian Il-76, chartered by the UK's Overseas Development Agency – delivering supplies on its behalf. With the exception of the USAF, who operated out of Ramstein Airbase in Germany, the airlift was initially based in Zagreb in Croatia, but then moved to Ancona in Italy later in 1992. The UN compound at Ancona Airport was a secure area, guarded by the RAF Police. The UK forces detachment consisted of approximately 200 personnel, and everyone worked very closely together, both professionally and socially.

It was an enormous and, of necessity, a quickly streamlined operation. Every thirty minutes, one aircraft flew into Sarajevo Airport and then out again. RAF Hercules from 47 Squadron flew to Sarajevo up to three times a day, six days a week, with one day off in the middle to rest both aircraft and crews. All flying had to be undertaken during daylight hours; a requirement set by the Bosnian Serb besiegers in return for allowing the airlift to occur. Even so, flights were carried out under constant threat from ill-disciplined factions who didn't want the United Nations there. Had things turned even nastier in Sarajevo, the RAF Hercules would have fulfilled their secondary role of evacuating UN personnel at night, utilizing their NVGs.

In a theatre that posed ever-present threats, both natural and man-made, the sharing of both experiences and tactics by aircrews was vital. The natural hazards were the unpredictable wind and weather in the mountainous terrain, plus the early morning fogs that prevailed below the 'horseshoe' of hills within which Sarajevo was located. The man-made consisted of weaponry of all sorts, the highest threats deemed to be small- to medium-calibre guns, infra-red man-portable air-defence systems and, lastly, radar-guided missiles. Furthermore, the airfield was randomly attacked by mortars from time to time and the threat from snipers was constant, so much so that the southeastern end of the runway was known as 'Sniper Alley'. Most aircraft therefore tried to avoid using that part of the runway and taxiway.

All the aircraft apart from the Il-76 were equipped with defensive aids suites to counter infra-red and radar missile threat. However, there wasn't really anything that could be done about the small arms fire, which was demonstrated when a USAF Hercules from Ramstein was targeted by a medium-calibre weapon while on short finals into Sarajevo (snipers would position themselves in the apartment blocks about two miles on the extended centreline for exactly this purpose), resulting in several hits on the flight-deck windscreen and damage to one of the hydraulic systems.

Fortunately, on that occasion, there were no injuries and the aircraft diverted to Ancona without further incident. But when an incident did occur, either in the air or on the ground, the airlift would be suspended until the guilty party (the Serbs and Bosnian Muslims were equally guilty) 'promised' not to do it again . . . until the next time.

For Herc skipper Dave Cranstoun, who at twenty-seven had already flown missions in Colombia and the Gulf War, the constant threat from small arms fire was simply one of the inherent risks of flying aid into Sarajevo. That it didn't necessarily *have* to be the case was something he only discovered by chance.

While the USAF mounted all their missions from Ramstein, they had a liaison pilot based in Ancona who would spend a month at a time there before being replaced by another. They were generally great guys and would fly into Sarajevo with the RAF at least once a month to observe their operations. The added bonus for them was that as long as they flew one mission in thirty days they qualified for 'combat pay' of $600 per month. The RAF crews, of course, never got such an allowance, but most of the USAF pilots, perhaps understanding this relative penury, bought more than their fair share of drinks at the bar, which the RAF crews gladly drank for them.

One day, Dave and his crew were flying into Sarajevo with one of the USAF pilots, during which they discussed the threats, and the tactics they employed to negate them. The American happened to be the 'chief of tactics' at Ramstein, and digressed into talking about a video he'd seen of the effects of ballistics penetration of fuel tanks with and without ESF, or explosion suppressant foam.

Simply put, ESF suppresses the vapour in a fuel tank as the fuel is depleted, thereby preventing it igniting if penetrated by an explosive projectile, such as a bullet or cannon shell. In tanks fitted with ESF there was no detonation, the pilot explained, but, in those without, there was a catastrophic explosion. 'So it's just as well we all have foam, eh?' he finished.

Perplexed, Dave turned to the flight engineer. 'Foam?' they asked the US pilot in unison. 'What foam?'

They could see the colour begin draining from their American colleague's face. Indeed, he was oddly quiet for the rest of the flight. Only on landing safely back at Ancona did he provide an explanation. Well, not so much an explanation as a heartfelt declaration.

'I'm sorry,' he told them, 'but combat pay or not, the USAF will no longer be flying into Sarajevo with the RAF.'

They didn't.

ESF or not, with both man-made and natural threats to take account of, flying in and out of Sarajevo Airport was always a risky business. At the time, one end of the runway was designated 12 and the other 30; with the mountainous terrain to consider – as well as all the other perceived and actual hazards – all landings took place on 12, with departures in the opposite direction, on 30. This was irrespective of the breeze which, at times, caused severe turbulence, especially from the direction of Mount Igman to the southwest. And though the runway was 8,500 feet long, only 6,000 feet of it was usable, due to the infamous Sniper Alley, at the southeastern end of the strip.

Lying to the south of the airfield were several Muslim

settlements, connected to the city to the north by 'the Sarajevo Tunnel', which went under the runway just to the east of the ramp. Serb snipers in the buildings to the north-east of the airfield perimeter would keep a lookout day and night for any suspected Bosnian Muslims either exiting the southern end of the tunnel or occasionally running over the airfield, hoping to climb over the perimeter barbed wire before being seen. It wasn't unusual for crews doing their first resupply missions of the day to see bodies slumped over the wire, sometimes surrounded by packs of feral dogs. It was all too easy to imagine what the starving dogs were doing. Much harder to believe this was occurring in Europe in the 1990s.

As the airlift continued and the ground operation became more slick, the crews would leave at least one of the engines running while being unloaded, minimizing ground time and exposure, which was clearly a good thing. Another advantage was that they couldn't hear the crack of the bullets overhead. But just because they couldn't hear them didn't mean they weren't there – as a search on YouTube for 'RAF C130 over Sarajevo' will confirm.

After landing, the preferred option was to exit the runway using the westerly taxiway, offload humanitarian aid on the ramp, then to re-enter the runway via the easterly taxiway. This one-way system ensured that aircraft didn't block each other as they came and went.

The RAF crews mainly flew two distinct types of approach into Sarajevo. During bad weather, or when there was early morning fog (mainly during the summer months), they would use the logical choice in such circumstances – an internal aids approach.

There were no ground-based approach aids at Sarajevo, apart from a mobile precision approach radar, operated by the French – who controlled the airport – which was very useful in getting the aircraft into the best position for a successful landing. Since it couldn't be verified by a dedicated checker aircraft, it hadn't been properly calibrated or certified, so it was backed up by the RAF navigators using their Skins (SCNS) equipment that had been pioneered during the first Gulf War, and giving the crew an 'internal aids' talkdown.

Only the six aircraft in 47 Squadron's mini-fleet were fitted with Skins, and while internal aids approaches were in their infancy at that time, it's fair to say those Herc crews led the way in developing them within the RAF.

A conventional civilian instrument approach would have a 'decision height' of 200 feet above the ground; but at Sarajevo the infrastructure for these approaches had been destroyed, so the Herc crews had no choice but to trust their own judgement. They regularly found themselves entering fog at exactly the moment when, in normal circumstances, they would decide whether to land or go around. Since the default decision was always to land, it was technically a moot point – but it certainly focused the mind. Each captain had his own preferred radar altimeter (radalt) setting, and if the crew weren't visual with the runway by the time the radalt aural warning was triggered, they would go around and either set up for another approach or return to Ancona or Split, to get more fuel.

If the weather was generally clear, however, crews used what was known as the 'Khe Sanh' approach, which had been developed by the USAF in 1968 during the siege of Khe Sanh, in the Vietnam War.

The US marine base at Khe Sanh occupied a strategically important position about ten miles from the Laotian border. Its encirclement by North Vietnamese forces meant there was no safe corridor for transport aircraft resupplying the base to use for their approach; any descent towards the airstrip attracted heavy fire from enemy weapons. In order to minimize the risks posed by these hazardous conditions, the transport crews perfected a manoeuvre to get within the relatively safe confines of the airfield.

This procedure was designed to keep an aircraft as high as practicable until as late as possible in order, hopefully, to negate the threat from small- to medium-calibre guns. The other benefit was that if this approach was flown correctly, the engines would be at idle power all the way from the top of descent until taxiing off the runway after landing, greatly reducing the infra-red signature of the engines compared to a conventional approach, and thus the threat from heat-seeking missiles. The downside was that if the Khe Sanh was misjudged you ran the risk of overstressing the flap as the aircraft accelerated during the steep pitch down, and/ or touching down much further along the runway than planned and rolling into Sniper Alley.

Nevertheless, the Khe Sanh proved a very effective way to minimize the threat from snipers in Sarajevo, just as it had done in Vietnam. Though, like so many of the aeronautical manoeuvres the RAF crews were forced to adopt in such challenging circumstances, both the Khe Sanh approach and the similarly hair-raising tactical take-off used to depart carried significant jeopardy; they were definitely not for the faint-hearted.

One of the quotes often wrongly attributed to Winston Churchill is: 'All that is necessary for the triumph of evil is for good men to do nothing.' At least in this respect, the attention given to the rush to rescue Irma Hadžimuratović was a sign that good men, and women, were inspired to step up in the Balkans conflict.

Though my own involvement ended the day we landed in Ancona, others picked up the baton in terms of trying to save Irma's life in London. The 'story' of her rescue soon became global news, with some welcoming Britain's intervention, and others not so much, to put it mildly. Either way, once the dust settled, few could ignore the humanitarian tragedy that was playing out so close to home.

A few months afterwards, with the signing of the Washington Agreement in February 1994, which ended hostilities between Croats and Bosnian Muslims, it was beginning to feel safe enough for global leaders to visit Sarajevo, and thus show the warring parties that the world would not stand by and allow the evil of the city's siege to prevail.

The proverbial floodgates now opened. Many politicians were clamouring to be in the spotlight and be seen to be doing good; from world leaders to UN ambassadors, everyone wanted to make their presence felt.

The then UK Prime Minister, John Major, already had skin in the game. It had been his intervention that had led to my being scrambled on the first day of my 6A the previous summer. Though the mission he'd ordered us to undertake had ultimately been cancelled, due to the UN stepping in and bringing Irma to Great Ormond Street Hospital themselves, his refusal to stand by and do nothing had, arguably, been pivotal in highlighting the humanitarian crisis of Sarajevo.

So it was no surprise when, on 17 March 1994, Dave Cranstoun and his crew were advised that on one of their aid runs of the following day they would be picking up the PM and two other British dignitaries following the trio's tour of Sarajevo and flying them back to Ancona. Once they arrived in Italy, the PM and the Defence Secretary, Malcolm Rifkind, would get off the Hercules and immediately board a Queen's Flight BAE146 in order to be flown home to RAF Northolt, while Baroness Chalker, the Minister for Overseas Development, would fly back to the UK on one of Flight Refuelling Aviation's corporate jets.

With no sign of the PM during the crew's first two flights into Sarajevo, they were on high alert for their special guests as they approached the Bosnian capital for the last shuttle of the day. When they landed, they were indeed advised that their VIP passengers would soon be joining them for the return trip to Ancona.

Dave taxied to the ramp to offload the five pallets of aid and, once that was complete, the loadmaster, 'Edd the Duck', said the PM, Defence Secretary and the Baroness were on board, so Dave asked him to send them up to the flight deck. Though Baroness Chalker elected to remain in the freight bay, the PM (wearing flak vest and helmet) came up and stood to Dave's left, while the Defence Secretary stood to the right of the co-pilot, 'Helmy'. Each was given a headset, and after pleasantries were exchanged,

Dave briefed them on what to expect, taking care to direct them to the grab handles positioned on either side of the flight deck.

'And just a heads up,' he finished. 'You might want to hold on just here for departure, as this kind of take-off can be quite, er, bracing.'

The Prime Minister having nodded his acknowledgement, Dave turned his attention back to the matter in hand: getting the aircraft safely back up in the sky via the hell-for-leather departure that was the tactical take-off.

Dave then released the parking brake, and the Herc trundled towards the end of the runway. Dave glanced to his left and, seeing that the PM was indeed holding on, gave him a nod, which was reciprocated.

'Everybody ready?' he asked, and, with four affirmatives from the rest of the flight deck, he pressed down on the brakes and advanced the throttles to take-off power, under the wary eye of the engineer. The noise was now deafening, and the aircraft was shaking like a rickety tube train. 'Engines stable,' Dave called, and released the brakes.

The Herc now felt like a caged predator that had just seen its prey. It was raring to go again. And once the cage door was open they were off at a fair tilt; so much so that the aircraft almost felt like it had been catapulted, the ground speed at maximum in a matter of moments. Given the ever-present threat of small arms fire, and particularly with VIPs on board, on the ground was exactly where they were going to stay too, at least until they reached the tyre-limit speed of 136 knots (about twenty knots above normal take-off speed), which would allow for a climb steep enough to avoid getting shot at.

Once through 100 knots, the aircraft was really beginning to want to fly, and as they approached normal take-off
speed it definitely wanted to, which meant quite an effort
was required to prevent it.

Finally, the call from the co-pilot came to rotate. When
Dave did so, the aircraft came off the ground like an express
elevator going for the forty-seventh floor. He pitched to
twenty degrees nose up, and, from behind, heard a loud
thump. Unable to look around, though, he had to wait till
the flight engineer enlightened him. 'Dave,' he quipped,
'you just floored the Prime Minister!'

The Prime Minister himself, thankfully, was very gracious
about it. Once they were able to push the nose forward, at a
safe-enough-from-small-arms-threat 1,500 feet, he simply
pulled himself upright and dusted himself off.

'Well,' he admitted, 'you did warn me!'

Dave was, however, still slightly mortified to think that
the G-forces he'd pulled, of necessity, had brought the
UK premier to his knees. But he consoled himself that,
once they were back at Ancona, he would have another
kind of G-force to offer him by way of apology.

He smiled and nodded. 'Fancy a post-flight Guinness, sir?'

To which the answer, of course, is strictly classified . . .

14. Eight Lives Remaining

As civil wars tend to, the one in the Balkans rumbled on, creating misery for the civilians living in such desperate conditions, pulling forces from both neighbouring and distant countries into its violent and destructive embrace, and testing the best military and political minds to the limit. A way had to be found to end the siege of Sarajevo.

With that goal very much in mind, on 12 April 1993 NATO's Operation Deny Flight began to enforce a UN no-fly zone over Bosnia and Herzegovina; later, the mission was expanded to include close air support for UN troops and coercive air strikes against Bosnian Serb forces. The operation would play an important role in both the Bosnian War and in the history of NATO itself, as it led to the alliance's first combat engagement.

Following the international uproar caused by the wounding of Irma Hadžimuratović, the first air strikes as part of the plan to end the siege of Sarajevo were prepared for August 1993, only to be called off after diplomatic negotiations. Then, in February 1994, the Serb shelling of a crowded Sarajevan marketplace caused NATO to issue an ultimatum ordering Serbian forces to place their heavy weapons near the city within UN-controlled collection sites. The Bosnian Serbs complied before the deadline for the start of NATO airstrikes passed, but went on to violate the agreement in August by seizing back weapons from one of the sites, injuring a Ukrainian peacekeeper in the process. The UN requested NATO air support in response, and two USAF A-10 'Tankbusters' repeatedly strafed Serb targets before the weapons were returned to UN control. The following month, when the armoured personnel carrier of some French peacekeepers came under attack near Sarajevo, two RAF Jaguars struck a Serb tank and destroyed it.

For the 47 Squadron aircrews in theatre, trying to carry out their humanitarian work, every day brought the prospect of mortal danger. While the heads of NATO concentrated on the bigger picture, and on making the skies over the war zone safe and free from enemy aircraft, RAF Hercules continued to be an air bridge to the besieged city.

On 26 January 1995, Dave Cranstoun and his crew had just landed in Sarajevo on their third resupply mission of the day. As they taxied in towards the ramp, it became apparent that all was not well. On closer inspection, they could see what appeared to be the fin of an RAF Jaguar from 54 Squadron sticking up behind several UN fire engines, in what must have been an attempt to hide it from the view of the Bosnian Serb troops who occupied the high ground overlooking the airfield.

Bearing in mind that the Jaguar's sole mission, if called upon, was to attack the Bosnian Serb Army, there was obviously a huge risk to the airport and the UN contingent in the fully armed jet (two 1,000 lb freefall bombs, a 30 mm internal cannon, and two Sidewinder air-to-air missiles) even being there. The term 'sitting duck' sprang to mind; it was extremely juicy prey for the Bosnian Serbs, who had been attacked just five months previously by the same type of aircraft. The one saving grace was that the weather wasn't particularly good, with a low cloud base and poor visibility making observation from the surrounding hills very difficult. But what on earth, Dave wondered, was it doing there?

He soon found out. While Dave and his crew were off-loading their five pallets of humanitarian aid, a lieutenant from the French Foreign Legion, which was defending the airport on behalf of the UN, came up to the flight deck to give them a brief synopsis of the situation. The 54 Squadron Jaguar was based in Gioia del Colle in southern Italy, and was conducting a combat air patrol over Sarajevo as part of Op Deny Flight. At some point, the pilot realized that a shut-off valve within the fuel system had failed to close, which meant he was unable to use any of the wing-tank fuel. The external tank was almost depleted by that time, so he wouldn't have enough to make it back to Split – the closest 'friendly' territory en route – let alone to his base in Italy.

The NATO Special Instructions stated that no combat aircraft was to land in Sarajevo unless in the event of a dire emergency, and the pilot decided this was one such. Despite the Special Instructions, he felt he'd be safer landing at Sarajevo rather than potentially ejecting over the hostile territory surrounding it, and then more than likely being captured by vengeful Bosnian Serbs.

By the time Dave and his crew had landed, the Jaguar pilot had been taken to the UN HQ in the middle of Sarajevo, to enable him to communicate with his squadron in Italy and NATO HQ in Vicenza.

By coincidence, Dave's co-pilot, Paul Atkinson ('Akers'),

and one of their ground engineers, 'Ginge' McCue, had both served on Jaguars at RAF Coltishall in a previous life and understood the technical issue. Ginge, being an expert on the Jaguar fuel system, opined that the solution was simply to pressurize the fuel manifold, which should force the stuck valve closed, and the wing-tank fuel would be accessible. However, the fault could obviously recur en route back to Italy, which would once again leave the pilot up the proverbial creek without a paddle – or, indeed, fuel – so they needed to refuel the external tank as a contingency. The problem was that there had been no aviation fuel available at Sarajevo since the conflict began, and all the fuel bowsers had long ago disappeared or been destroyed. The only other option would be to use the Hercules' fuel system via a FARP kit.

'FARP' stands for 'Forward Arming and Refuelling Point' and, in the case of the Hercules, involved the aircraft landing at an airfield or natural-surface strip and refuelling up to two helicopters simultaneously (while also cross-loading troops and equipment), thereby significantly increasing their radius of action and operational flexibility. On one occasion, the Flight had proved the procedure could be done with a Harrier GR7 as well.

The FARP kit consisted of a standard fuel-bowser semi-rigid hose, which was connected to the Hercules' refuelling panel on the starboard side beneath the wing. This was then attached to a portable DC electric scavenge pump, which could feed two 200-foot flexible hoses whose other ends were positioned outboard of the wing-tips, and in line with the tailplane. Up to two receivers would then taxi into position and refuel either via direct connection to their refuelling panels or by using a hand-held petrol pump which could be fitted to the end of the hose. This was done 'rotors running', as the Hercules had to have one engine running to power the necessary electrics and fuel pumps. After the refuelling was completed, the scavenge pump was used to suck any remaining fuel out of the hoses and back into the Hercules.

The FARP kit could be laid out in about ten minutes, and once any excess fuel had been sucked out of the flexible hoses, packed away in about fifteen. There was only one snag, however; all of the FARP kits were stored back at RAF Lyneham, since this sort of contingency hadn't been envisaged for Op Cheshire.

Now appraised of the situation, and once their C-130s pallets had been offloaded, the crew then got airborne for Ancona, and on the hour-long flight back discussed various potential scenarios and options. By the time they landed, plans were already being formulated to recover the stricken Jaguar: NATO and the UN desperately wanted it out of Sarajevo at the earliest opportunity, and a FARP kit was now scheduled to arrive the following afternoon on the fortnightly changeover flight, along with the replacement crew for Dave's Hercules.

Dave's crew were programmed to do two missions prior to flying the changeover aircraft back to RAF Lyneham in the evening. However, the weather forecast for the next day was looking particularly bad, with thunderstorms and snow showers expected to get worse as the day progressed, and predicted to continue throughout the weekend. At this stage, it was planned that the changeover crew would do the FARP on their first mission on Saturday morning, but the inclement weather could potentially hamper the chances of this for several days, prolonging the risk to the airport and personnel while the Jaguar sat there.

Ginge had in fact pointed out earlier to the rest of the crew that all that was actually required from the FARP kit was the Black Mamba hose that connected the Hercules' refuelling panel to the scavenge pump; this would then be attached directly to the Jaguar's refuelling panel, and once the appropriate pump in the aircraft was switched on the manifold would pressurize and close the dodgy valve. Since the Mamba was actually a universal bit of refuelling equipment, they decided it might be worth trying to borrow one from the Alitalia refuellers at Ancona, just in case the weather was going to end up as bad as forecast; if successful, they would carry out the FARP on the first mission the next morning.

Ginge and the other ground engineer approached the Alitalia refuellers and, after much gesticulating, the loan of a Mamba – suitably renamed Mambino – was obtained. Dave and the crew all then returned to their accommodation – the Palace Hotel in Senigallia – and discussed the following day's plan over a few beers in the bar. Since it was also the last night of their two-week detachment, Carlos, their favourite grandfatherly Italian barman, forced one or three 'Catastrophes' upon them as well. The Catastrophe – Carlos's pride and joy – was a vile concoction of grappa and whatever other spirit, or spirits, took his fancy. Many a sore head and dodgy stomach was had thanks to him.

The following morning, they bade Carlos and the hotel staff *arrivederci* until the next time and arrived at the airport to carry out the first airlift mission of the day. The weather forecast had, in fact, worsened even further, and they set off into the impending gloom with their usual five pallets, and Mambino coiled up in the freight bay. By the time they neared the initial approach point, Vrana on the Croatian coast, they were avoiding thunderstorms on the weather radar, and the French Air Force controller at Sarajevo reported they were experiencing continuous sleet with very poor visibility. The decision was then made that they would carry out the FARP on that mission, and they told the controller to inform the Jaguar pilot, still holed up in the well-defended UN HQ, to get to the airport ASAP.

They commenced the approach to the airfield under the guidance of the French mobile precision approach radar, backed up by the navigator's Skins, and landed without any problems. Taxiing on to the ramp, they spotted the Jaguar, which had been pushed into a revetment constructed of shipping containers, affording it better protection than the previous day. They came to a halt and commenced the off-load of their pallets, during which time the French lieutenant and the Jaguar pilot came up to the flight deck to discuss *le plan* for the FARP.

After pleasantries had been exchanged, Ginge explained what switch settings were required in the Jaguar cockpit and Akers briefed him on the airfield restrictions and safest departure routing. Pallets by now offloaded, Dave proceeded to reverse the Hercules as close to the revetment as was deemed safe, and then the Jaguar was manhandled into a position on the Herc's starboard side, near enough to allow Mambino to connect the two aircraft. Once the Jaguar pilot had set up his cockpit as briefed, and Mambino had been attached, Ginge asked for the pump to be switched on in the Hercules. Just as he'd predicted, the dodgy fuel valve closed. Having spoken with the Jaguar pilot further, it was then decided to transfer 6,000 pounds of fuel to his aircraft to ensure that he could return to Italy should the previous fault resurface. Fuel transfer complete, the hose was disconnected, loaded back into the freight bay and both aircraft prepared for departure.

By now, though, the weather had worsened. The sleet had turned to snow and was beginning to lie on the cold upper surfaces of the two aircraft and the ramp, and the taxiways and runway were now showing signs of contamination. It was also very wet, sticky snow, the worst sort to adhere to an aircraft's surfaces, since it does not move freely off as the aircraft speed increases. During normal peacetime operations, it is prohibited to get airborne with contamination on the aircraft; the findings from the Munich Air Disaster in 1958 led to that requirement, and the associated regulations continue to evolve to this day. Both aircraft would therefore have to be de-iced, and if precipitation was still falling, then anti-iced as well. However, just like the lack of fuel bowsers, there was no de-icing available at Sarajevo.

Both the Hercules and Jaguar probably had about half an inch of snow on their flying surfaces now, which couldn't be removed, making their options limited. Basically, they either had to stay on the ground and hope the snow would melt when it stopped falling, or depart ASAP to prevent further accumulation. However, if they did remain on the ground and the cold spell continued, they could be stranded for days to come, the risk of attack from the Serbs increasing all the time.

The Hercules has a high-lift wing, which means it is potentially less affected by contamination than a fighter-type wing. Furthermore, the propeller wash flowing over the top of the wing creates high-velocity 'blown' lift in itself. Dave and the crew discussed this and, based on all their previous experiences, decided they would be comfortable departing, but with the following caveat. The six mini-fleet airframes were equipped with a flight-deck cupola just left of centre of the top of the fuselage, which gave an observer an almost unlimited view behind the aircraft and of the top surfaces – something that was particularly useful during fighter evasion training. They decided that John Bush ('Bushy'), their air electronics operator (AEO), would look out of the cupola at the beginning of the take-off roll and make sure that, as full power was applied, the propeller wash was blowing the snow off the top of the affected portions of the wings. This would then confirm whether the snow was likely to blow completely off the top surfaces as the aircraft accelerated down the runway. If not, they would not depart.

As usual, they would also wait to rotate till they reached a speed of 137 knots, which would further mitigate the effect of any contamination on the flying surfaces. The flip side to this was that a lot of slush would be thrown up into the wheel wells as the speed increased. Once the gear was raised and the aircraft climbed into the much colder air, the contaminant could freeze onto the landing gear screw-jacks, preventing the gear being lowered prior to landing. They would then have to descend into warmer air and fly around until either it melted or they ran out of fuel. This was obviously not ideal. To prevent the screw-jacks freezing, any time a Hercules took off from a contamin-ated runway the landing gear would be recycled once airborne in the hope that the repeated raising, lowering and raising would loosen and remove any significant build-up, aided by the turbulent air within the wheel wells. They therefore decided the potential contamination was bad enough to warrant three recycles.

Unfortunately, the Jaguar pilot was in a totally different situation to the Herc crew. He was flying a fighter, which was renowned for its less than impressive take-off per-formance, even in benign conditions. It had heavy contamination on its low-loft, swept-wing flying surfaces and was also fully loaded with weapons. Furthermore, it could only use two thirds of the available runway for take-off since the last third of the southeastern end was, of course, Sniper Alley and he, of all people, would be a prime target to be shot at. All these things considered, he decided to remain on the ground until the snow fully melted – a wise decision, despite the pressure on him from the grown-ups to get the hell out of Dodge.

Dave and the Herc crew wished him luck, bade him farewell and taxied out to the runway, with the snow still falling heavily. Dave then lined the aircraft up on the runway, checked Bushy was in place and set full power. Bushy confirmed that the snow had blown off the affected surfaces and returned to his 'nest' on the bottom bunk to monitor the radar chirps and tweets that were processed by the MAROC electronic support measures (ESM) pods fitted to the wingtips. MAROC ESM was a poor man's radar warning receiver in that it required a dedicated AEO to analyse the chirps and tweets and then relay any potential threats to the flight crew – not ideal in a high-threat environment where early reaction was critical. (Which is in no way to denigrate the essential task Bushy and the other AEOs carried out, of course.)

Happy with Bushy's 'Go for it', or words to that effect, Dave released the brakes and they accelerated on the runway until 137 knots. Rotating very slowly, the aircraft climbed away with no noticeable performance degradation. As planned, they recycled the gear three times and headed back to Ancona, avoiding the numerous thunderstorms on the way.

When it came to lowering the gear on approach back into Ancona, it went down with no problems and locked with a satisfying clunk. About an hour after landing, though, one of the ground engineers asked the crew to accompany him back to the aircraft. Once there, everyone was amazed to see that two massive lumps of ice had fallen out of each main wheel well – they must have weighed at least twenty kilograms each. Just as well they had recycled the gear. Ginge returned Mambino to the Alitalia refuellers, and once the replacement crew arrived they did a brief handover, took control of their 'slick' aircraft (one that didn't have self-defence aids on it) and flew back to Lyneham, loaded with the FARP kit that they hadn't needed and the usual pallet or two of Italian wine . . .

The wine for my own wedding, from a vineyard near Ancona, was brought home for me by Dave and the crew after that very mission, so I have a particularly good reason to remember it. But the Sarajevo memory that most endures is of a trip I made myself, just before hostilities ceased completely.

It was mid-December 1995, and the harsh winter was already settling in. The siege had by now almost ceased, but the city was still in dire need of help, some of which we were bringing, flying into the city just as the sun was setting and delivering vital supplies to those in need.

This mission was a round robin, departing RAF Lyneham and returning later that evening, having first taken in two Italian airfields and Sarajevo itself. We loaded five pallets of food and blankets and began our 2.5-hour journey to a city that was still very much part of an ongoing conflict, crossing over the Croatian coast above the former tourist centre of Dubrovnik on the way. It was dangerous, but we could only cross our fingers. We hadn't much to protect us against small arms fire – only the aircraft skin, essentially – and should anyone have infra-red missiles, we had an unreliable countermeasures system (primarily designed for the threat in Northern Ireland) which often didn't work, or overheated.

But it wasn't the thought of enemy attack that would assault my senses that night. The last vestiges of the light were making the clear winter sky a sea of warm colours, but the ground below was white and cold, and littered with half-demolished buildings, the stark signs of a horrible war. There were no artificial lights visible either; evidence of a city hollowed out, so many of its people having fled, and those who'd stayed having no access to power or heat.

I was still only twenty-four, and I had never seen devastation like this – not outside World War II movies, anyway. It was horrific, and I couldn't understand why people would not just flee. (Some years on, I reflect on this and totally understand why you wouldn't want to leave your home; it was not unlike those fighting to save Ukraine.)

We landed firmly, and got set to offload our cargo, as we definitely didn't wish to get stuck in this dangerous place. But we were then told that the airport's condec for offloading the aircraft had broken down and the nearest forklift was twenty minutes away. As you should never trust an RAF minute (twenty could easily mean thirty or forty), we took the same approach with the French military running the airport, and decided to deploy DIY and 'tactically' offload the pallets.

We laid some wooden battens down on the ground and taxied so they were positioned behind the aircraft, then I sloped the ramp down and the entire crew launched the first pallet off the back of the Herc . . . Genius. The captain then taxied forward and we did it again, five times in all, before closing up and taxiing for departure.

Job done. We had hopefully helped make life there a little better.

But as our now empty aircraft roared back into the sky, I couldn't help but feel a great sadness washing over me. Back in southern England, a mere two and a half hours away across Europe, my young wife was safe at home with our seven-week-old son. I couldn't help but think of Irma, the injured child we'd set off to bring to the UK two and a half years earlier, and how she'd lost her life anyway, to septicaemia, twenty months later. I thought of all Sarajevo's children. Of all that senseless death and destruction. That was war. It was a seminal moment.

*

The Hercules of 47 Squadron flew over 2,000 missions into Sarajevo without losing either aircraft or any crew, and I don't think anyone would argue about the scale of that achievement. It wasn't just about the courage and expertise of the aircrews. The contribution made by ground engineers during the siege of Sarajevo was enormous. Along with his fellow GEs, Ginge's ingenuity and can-do attitude were superlative – without him, who knows what might have happened if the Serbs had decided to take action against the Jaguar? As it was, it reached home safely.

Ginge epitomized the highest qualities of the GE fraternity, and, during the course of the four years of the civil war in the Balkans, he flew in excess of 1,000 missions. Thoroughly professional and flexible, the GEs worked day and night, in all weathers and, while never breaking any engineering rules, they certainly explored all the boundaries in order to ensure the aircrews' steeds were ready for action. That few can ever recall cancelling a sortie due to technical issues is a testament to them all.

It was a long haul for everyone concerned. The siege of Sarajevo lasted from 5 April 1992 to 29 February 1996, a total of 1,425 days. This meant it was three times longer than the World War II siege of Stalingrad, and a year longer than that of Leningrad – the longest siege of any major city in modern warfare. It was estimated that just over half a million people were living in Sarajevo at the start of the siege, and that just over 300,000 remained by the end. A total of 13,952 people lost their lives during that period, including 5,434 civilians. On more than one occasion, Sarajevans endured months without gas, electricity, or fresh water supply, which were deliberately targeted by the Serbs.

The international criminal tribunal set up by the United Nations in 1993 to prosecute war crimes committed during the conflict later held the Bosnian Serb commanders Stanislav Galić and Dragomir Milošević to account for these heinous crimes against humanity, sentencing them to life and twenty-nine years in prison respectively. Their superiors, Bosnian Serb president Radovan Karadžić and army commander Ratko Mladić, were also convicted, and given whole life sentences.

We hoped never again to see this type of war in Europe, and then Russia invaded Ukraine. The politics may be different, but the current war raging in Ukraine has many humanitarian and political parallels with Bosnia. War is an awful thing, and seeing the pictures on television of cities such as Kharkiv takes me back to those images of Sarajevo, almost three decades ago, the suffering, the total disregard for humanity, and, set against it, just the sheer will of the people to survive through it, at all costs.

While this is happening in Europe, it's scarily easy to almost feel detached from it; if it is not in the headlines, is it even really happening? Yet, once again, people are needlessly suffering and, yet again, in time, someone will pay their dues for these crimes.

However, good will usually win out over evil, especially when good people do decide to act. During that bleak period in the early 1990s, while much of the rest of the world went about its business, countries stepped up and worked together to support the beleaguered people of Sarajevo. Canadians, Americans, Norwegians, Italians and Ukrainians – to name just a few – and, of course, the RAF. It was an example not only of the power of being allies, but of professionalism and teamwork at their very best.

15. Parachutes

It is 17 September 1986, and the head of the UK's Secret Intelligence Service, colloquially known as M, is in an office briefing three of his most trusted agents on a forthcoming infiltration exercise on the UK base on Gibraltar. The exercise will start with a high altitude low opening parachute insertion that will see the Rock, and elite troops, succumb to the covert service's skill. The meeting ends and, as the door is opened, the office is flooded with sound, to which absolutely nobody reacts; this 'office' is in the forward area of a Hercules.

We now see the loadmaster, as the parachute jump lights change from red to green. The agents then stroll to the back of the aircraft and, as the ramp opens, with the Rock of Gibraltar clearly visible in the distance, one by one they jump into the abyss.

One of the freefallers on this day is a sailor; one who wears the coveted upside down 'HALO' wings of a special forces operator. It may by now be obvious, at least to the eagle-eyed reader: the parachutist in question is one Commander James Bond, 007.

Iconic scenes like the opening to *The Living Daylights* don't come out of thin air. They are fashioned around real people, real missions, real Hercules aircraft; the capability to drop parachutists having been key for the C-130 from day one.

Much as I like the idea of being the inspiration behind a blockbuster action movie, my own parachuting exploits probably preclude it. In fact, I'd go so far as to say that if anyone did consider doing that, it would more likely take the form of a tragicomedy.

I am a big guy. I am not, and never have been, built for parachuting. Something that was already obvious to me as an aspirational fifteen-year-old on the day I was privileged, along with five of my fellow air cadets, to have my first ever flight in an RAF aircraft – a De Havilland Chipmunk, at RAF Turnhouse in Edinburgh.

I was as excited at the prospect as any fifteen-year-old would be: I was about to join the realms of all those World War II fighter aces that had also flown taildragger aircraft. This was going to be my personal Spitfire.

How wrong I was. As I trudged out with the pilot to the waiting aircraft, I was already uncomfortable; hunched over, trussed up, much too heavily laden, weighed down by a parachute I was assured that I wouldn't need, but was there just in case I *did* need it – go figure. The pilot, clearly a man whose parachute-jumping love had long since waned, remarked, 'Nobody in their right mind jumps out of a serviceable aircraft.'

Those wise words have stayed with me ever since. Although it's slightly odd that, just under a decade later, they were nowhere to be found – at least, not till the moment of absolutely no return. I was about to jump out of a perfectly serviceable aircraft, and of my own volition too.

I had spent many a day, over the years, flying at The Parachute Training School at RAF Brize Norton, taking those aspiring airborne soldiers on a short hop to the

Weston-on-the-Green drop zone so that they could chalk up another jump towards gaining their coveted parachute wings. Turning endless circles at 800 feet above the Peartree Roundabout on the A34, on some days we dropped enough troops to invade a small country, let alone a small patch of rural Oxfordshire.

In truth, I was always as parachute-curious as the next person, wondering what it must feel like to jump out of an aircraft, to feel that rush of air and adrenaline as you take what is a massive leap of faith, with nothing more than a handkerchief to arrest your fall. Although curious, it wasn't the jumping that kept me from attempting it. No, it was the bit at the other end, the landing. I had heard of too many others being badly injured during awkward landings for the prospect of becoming one of their number to really appeal.

That was until the day when the offer of a jump into water was circulated around the squadron and my right mind went absent without leave. *Why not?* Or so my thinking went. *Let's give it a go.* Jumping into water was obviously a far safer option – how could it be otherwise, if no hard, painful ground was involved?

The drop was to be part of an exercise with frogmen off the south coast of England. After the crew spent the day dropping the professionals, me and five aircrew buddies would get the opportunity to have a go as well. So it was off to Brize Norton, for what was to be two days of intense training.

The training was not as intense as we all had imagined. In fact, it could probably be summed up in three sentences. This is how you put it on. It'll open itself. If it doesn't open itself, pull this. There was also a contraption to the side of a large hangar. A row of mocked-up aircraft doors at the top of a tall tower, each accessorized by a kind of pneumatic spring – rather like the kind of contraption you might find on a rowing machine in a gym; the harder it was pulled on, the more it resisted. This was obviously to simulate the action of a parachute arresting a person's fall, and though it ensured we didn't plummet to certain death off the tower (just made an ungainly and crumpled reacquaintance with the crash mats) for me, at least, it didn't inspire a lot of confidence.

There was another small detail which also slightly deflated the spirits. We would not be jumping heroically from the ramp, Bond-movie style, as I'd imagined, but instead through the more worrying side door. This, we were informed, was to give the guys at the back of the aircraft a break after a long day, but it also meant an extra element of jeopardy. Going straight out of the back means your canopy can open unhindered, whereas from the side means you are subject to the forces of the aircraft's slipstream, leading to a higher probability of getting twists in your parachute. Now, while this doesn't seem like a big game-changer – parachutists jump from the sides of planes all the time – psychologically it felt like a mountain of a difference, because I couldn't help thinking that at any moment I was going to die.

The training naturally focused on the emergency procedures: basically, how to reduce the chance of expiring while parachuting, due to twisted rigging lines, or from having no main parachute at all. We rehearsed these until the drills had become second nature. By lunchtime on day two, the instructor had seen enough, and decided that we were good to go for tomorrow's sortie from RAF Lyneham. His final comments were, 'Whatever happens, don't get caught in the water with the parachute lines around you. And anyone who inflates their life jacket buys the beers.' With those rousing words, we were off.

It felt a bit odd not being part of the crew for the drop – as would be the case for me normally – and we were obviously all feeling a bit anxious now too. Banter and bravado it was, then. Important to keep up appearances. We then duly kitted up and were loaded onto the aircraft, and as the noise of the small jet that started the main engines began building, I thought, *This is it. I'm going to jump out of a serviceable aircraft.* It was a thought I did my best to extinguish.

It was only a short flight to the south coast, and the main drops soon commenced. As I watched the professionals disappear, and make everything look so easy, my nerves settled a little, despite the choppy-looking seas below. At least until the ramp closed, and it was our turn.

Jumping from the side door involves your parachute being hooked onto a static line, with each jumper checking the guy in front's parachute. Since I was the last of the six, I had the jump instructor checking mine; once he'd tapped me on the shoulder, I knew we were good for the drop.

The door opened and the calm inside the freight bay of the aircraft was now replaced by the turbulence and noise of a sudden, swirling wind. Then came the shouted words 'Action Stations!' and we shuffled up towards the exit. I watched the lights next to the door, saw the red one illuminate then, after what seemed an age, the green. Green for 'Go!' It was at this point that I was hit by the largest shot of adrenaline that I had ever (and *have* ever) got. Then the shuffle into the doorway. Then silence.

The first sensation I felt was a hard tug to my crotch. I looked upwards instinctively and thought, *Thank fuck for that*. The canopy was open. Everything seemed to be okay. I could now enjoy the short ride to the water. Which I did for a while, picking out the five RIBs bobbing on the surface below, each ready to follow one of the parachutists to their splashdown zone. I noticed my own team – there were three men per RIB – coming towards me, and something else too: despite being the last out of the aircraft, I seemed to be falling a little more quickly than everyone else. I was going to be first in, it seemed, and by some margin. Such are the laws of gravity, mass and motion.

I was getting close to the water now and had to concentrate. I knew from the drills that I must not release my chute until my feet touched the water. The trouble was that it was proving difficult to judge my height above it. I also knew of someone who'd tried to be clever and release early (perhaps having the same fear of tangled lines I was currently experiencing), only to find they were still quite high in the air and, as a result, had injured themselves quite badly. Not me – I was going to wait. I was just thinking that when – *bang!* – I hit the freezing ocean, causing an involuntary inhalation of both air and a lot of sea water. In my panic, I was late in releasing my chute, which was now wafting gently down on top of me.

Spluttering back to the surface, and now furiously treading water, I couldn't find the edge of the parachute; as it began sinking, I could feel the dreaded lines wrapping around me. I was resolute, however. There was no *way* I was going to inflate my life jacket. (I am Scottish, and buying the beers is an expensive pastime.) Notwithstanding this, I was definitely having a little bit of a panic by the time a friendly Royal Marine popped up beside me, dragged me under the water and out of the chute, before ushering me towards the waiting RIB. The guys inside, having pulled their buddy back in first, then reached for my harness to drag me in too.

Which they failed to. I think my mass must have taken them by surprise, because all I actually did was bounce off the side and plop straight back into the sea. The zero finesse and the humiliation were bad enough, but worse still was the fact that the beaded handle that activates the life jacket got caught on the side of the boat and (*Oh fuck – beers*) it duly inflated. Though *it* did. Not *I* did. Important difference.

I was grabbed a second time and, perhaps mindful of the first failure, they did it with such commitment that I was almost catapulted straight over the other side of the boat. It was then back to the larger vessel and a reunion with the others. I tried to explain about the life jacket – it wasn't me! There were witnesses! – but, unsurprisingly, nobody cared. It was inflated. End of. Rules were rules.

I was just getting dried off, when a familiar sound began to build. It was the Herc doing a fly-past – a 'well done, lads, see you later!' – but the boat was so big, and the aircraft so low, that it looked like a giant green shark's fin was speeding past us: we had to look downwards, rather than up, to see the whole aircraft, because it was flying *lower* than the deck we were standing on. Surreal.

It pulled up then and flew back to Lee-on-Solent to pick up more marines for another go, but we were well and truly done. Anyone that says jumping into water is safer is deluded. No way you should be jumping out of an aeroplane. Not willingly. I decided that this would be both my first and last jump from a serviceable aircraft.

Dropping other people from a serviceable aircraft is much more my thing. During my time on the C-130 fleet, I have been qualified to deliver a broad spectrum of cargoes, 'humans under canopy' being one of them. Parachuting comes in many flavours, and each of these requires a different qualification for the aircrew delivering them to the drop zone, as well as for the person under the canopy. At the simplest level, this includes a static line drop, where a line attached to the aircraft is reeled out as the parachutist falls from the door, and eventually pulls the parachute from its packed bag and deploys it. During training, these parachutists are dropped from 800 feet and carry a reserve chute, in case of main chute failure. But in an operational scenario, you don't want to be drifting down from 800 feet in enemy territory, so the same chute is also designed to be dropped from a mere 250 feet and 'snap open' to give a few swings before ground contact, decreasing the chances of getting shot, but also removing entirely the need for a reserve, as it is a one-time-only deal. This chute is made by Irvin-GQ and is called the 'low-level parachute'. It is the type of chute that most military parachutists will use and be familiar with. As the LLP has limited steerability, and the higher it goes the more it's susceptible to wind, its use is usually kept below 1,500 feet. The next level of parachute is a static line steerable chute, which gives the parachutist some rudimentary steering of the parachute, and thus greater landing accuracy.

We would then graduate on to military freefall parachuting, which is further subdivided into two main categories: those that require oxygen, due to the height of the drop; and those that do not. With the latter, the military freefall operation was very much like civilian sport parachuting, with larger square-type parachutes that allow steering and a modicum of 'flying'. Dropping at the higher altitudes that required oxygen, however, was a specialist role, for specialist units. These evolutions are called HALO (High Altitude Low Opening) or HAHO (High Altitude High Opening). HALO normally involves a drop fairly close to the intended destination but from many miles up, where the air is very thin and cannot sustain life, followed by freefall to an altitude that is just a few seconds from the ground, resulting in a short time under canopy to the target drop zone. HAHO is a stand-off parachuting capability that sees troops 'hop and pop', which means they jump off the jet at, say, airliner altitudes, immediately pop the chute open and then – depending on drop height and other environmental factors, such as high-altitude winds – travel many, many miles before landing.

For both aircrews and parachutists, HALO and HAHO are highly dangerous.

By the summer of 1996, just like many 25-year-olds, I was having a modest quarter-century crisis. I was married now, I had a child, and I was contemplating career matters. Did I give my dream another shot and try to become a pilot?

In the meantime, I was enjoying life as an ALM, which continued to broaden my horizons. I'd recently flown out to California and was now at Imperial County Airport, near the southern border of the United States, as part of a month-long training detachment that allowed specialist troops to practise military freefall and HALO techniques. The clear airspace and great weather of Southern California meant that we could launch four to five sorties a day, allowing the troops to maximize their training opportunities while also enjoying the glorious hospitality of the inhabitants.

As with all military training, there were huge risks. What had happened in Scotland back in 1993 was never far from my thoughts, obviously. But training tragedies never lose their power to bring everyone up short; not long after we'd arrived, one of the soldiers had died when both his main and reserve parachutes malfunctioned during a complex freefall descent carrying military equipment. So although everyone was relaxed as we were about to conduct a night-time HALO practice insertion with equipment – something far from routine – we were still very conscious that there was real life-or-death jeopardy involved.

When I arrived with the flight engineer, it was to an aircraft that had been sitting on the ground since the evening before. Opening the crew door, we were greeted by that familiar smell of oil and hydraulics, forced out in a wave of such heat that it was akin to opening an oven. We both climbed aboard, and while Nige, the eng, went upstairs to start the GTC – the small jet engine used to power the aircraft on the ground – I turned right, into the freight bay, and went straight to the back in order to open the big ramp and door and get some throughput of air to cool the 'oven' down to gas mark 4. The spooling-up noise of the jet outside was getting louder and eventually peaked, there were a few clunks and clanks and then the lights came on. We had power!

Although the ramp and door could be opened using a hand pump, this was not the time for that. With a flick of a switch, the small hydraulic pump whirred into life; two more switch presses and we heard a loud clang as the ramp's locks disengaged and it began to lower, while the door began to lift towards the roof. Another loud, satisfying clunk secured the door, and just before the ramp touched the ground, I ventured down and jumped outside to ensure there was nobody under or near the aircraft, as when it touched it would push the nose down a little. Nobody was there, so I pressed the switch again to bring the ramp all the way to the ground. With a click, the noise of the pump was off, and the dull whine of the small jet was all we could hear.

The difference to the inside temperature was immediate, and when the side parachute doors were also opened, we at least had a decent breeze blowing through the aircraft.

Almost everything in aviation is driven by checklists, and pre-flighting the aircraft for that evening's HALO drop was no different. I started with the normal aircraft checks of the hydraulics, the seats, and so on, then moved on to those specific to the tactical role we were employing on this mission. The stakes of getting something wrong were very high, and this was on the minds of everyone as we worked diligently through the checks. Not long after

I'd started, the parachute jump instructors arrived and started prepping the oxygen consoles for the parachutists. Just before they dropped at 25,000 feet we would depressurize, and they would therefore need oxygen to breathe. But to prevent the bends, a condition that we traditionally link with diving, they would need to purge the nitrogen from their bloodstream by pre-breathing oxygen for about thirty minutes before the drop. The consoles are self-contained pure oxygen delivery systems that allow the troops to purge while the crew are still in a pressurized aircraft environment.

With the jump instructors' and my checks complete, the troops started to arrive and lay out and arrange their equipment at the back of the aircraft. The banter was fierce between the UK and US troops as they started the big willy competition of the evening. A bet was made: the furthest from the touchdown zone (i.e. the least accurate parachutist) would buy the beers for all in the bar later. The game was on.

Rick, the captain, had now arrived with the rest of the flight crew and, after some pleasantries, we dived into the mission briefing. This included the lead PJIs, who in turn would brief the troops and their own teams. The route was outlined for the night's mission, we were to climb out to the east towards Arizona's Chocolate Mountains and Phoenix, levelling off at 25,000 feet before turning west and running in for the drop zone. Rick outlined that he'd had challenges coordinating with air traffic control in LA and he still wasn't sure they understood what we needed in order to accomplish the mission, but Will the co-pilot was going to sort it out in the air. We then went through the sequence of events from take-off to drop, and finally discussed the likely emergencies and how as a team we would handle these, plus some of the contingencies.

With the formalities over, it was time for a pre-flight snack. I'd arranged some bacon rolls and ketchup to be delivered from a local diner, and we all took a few minutes off to eat them. I was wearing shorts and a T-shirt with my flying boots, allowing the evening breeze to wash over and cool me as I watched our 'customers' for this evening getting ready. They were a mix of instructors from the UK parachute training school and some UK military students (all wearing shorts, like me), plus some from the US Navy who were taking the opportunity to jump from a UK aircraft (this would earn them UK wings), and who were kitting up in wetsuits, with attached fins. *We're in the middle of a desert, nowhere near an ocean*, I thought. *So why are they dressed up as frigging frogmen?*

Food and flippers both deployed, we began to board. The troops filed up the ramp in seat order and laid out their kit beside or in front of them. We only had twenty-six of them, so there was loads of space to spread out around the oxygen consoles, which were tied down on the floor of the aircraft. As we were closing the ramp, the first engine started to turn on the right of the aircraft, signalling that we were on our way. Engines running, the ground engineer put the chocks on the aircraft and waved us off as I closed the front door; they would normally fly with us on sorties, but due to the requirement for oxygen, tonight they decided not to.

I checked that both the people and the kit in the freight bay were secure and made my way to a seat at the rear.

After I confirmed to Rick that we were good to go, we were off. We had the large door open at the back to let in some air, and as we accelerated down the runway I could see the amount of dust we are kicking up. It was the beginning of another mission, and we were ready.

As we passed through a few thousand feet, I closed the large door and the aircraft began to pressurize while the British PJIs and troops started to put their kit on, changing from shorts and T-shirts into their black suits, complete with helmets and masks. I provided the US jumpers with plenty of water; by now, in their frogman get-ups, they were really feeling the heat.

The troops were all pre-breathing oxygen from the consoles as we approached 20,000 feet, and I could hear Will asking LA Center for a westerly heading back towards the area of the drop zone. This seemed to confuse them, and they asked for our destination. Will told them we were going back to Imperial County Airport after a parachute drop. This was met with a 'Roger', then, 'Proceed as requested to the airport.' This was not a good sign.

Ten minutes from the drop, now at 25,000 feet, it was time to depressurize the aircraft. Everyone was on oxygen now, myself included. Though in my case it was via a long caterpillar-like tube attached to an oxygen regulator at the back of the aircraft, which allowed me to move around freely. With our rubber masks on, we were all sounding a bit like Darth Vader; and with the aircraft depressurized, it was now becoming chilly, and I was beginning to regret how little I had on under my flying suit. (*Touché!* the US guys were possibly thinking . . .) It was now time to go to red light in the freight bay.

The troops were off the consoles now; from here on, they would breathe their own bottled air supply from a small canister attached to the front of their body, which would give them about thirty minutes' oxygen, should they need it. Time to open the ramp and door. I stared out into the black abyss of the desert far beneath us, with the lights of Phoenix some 100 miles distant. It was a surreal feeling, standing on the ramp at 25,000 feet with a bird's eye view of the world, in an environment that, without oxygen, would instantly kill you.

'Two minutes,' the nav called, so I held up two fingers to the troops – their signal to shuffle towards the lip of the ramp and face that abyss, while they broke the chemical light sticks on the backs of their feet and hands; a measure to prevent them from crashing into each other in freefall.

Will spoke again with LA Center. 'Two minutes to the drop zone.'

There was a pause, and then, rather than an acknowledgement, a question. *Are we dropping troops from 25,000 feet?* Our concern about their response minutes earlier was clearly justified. Parachutists usually jump at 12,000 feet in that area, so it probably didn't compute that we were dropping troops from around five miles high. Will answered yes, and that we were only moments away from doing so. They immediately issued a few vectors to other aircraft nearby, to clear the skies below us. Then replied, reassuringly, with, 'No traffic to affect.' Phew.

I was now in position on the right edge of the ramp, with a clenched fist held out horizontally across it – the visual signal for action stations. The troops were huddled together near the edge, when the navigator said, 'Red on.'

As I lifted my hand in a chopping motion, the red lights bathed the ramp area in a devilish glow.

'Green on!' I chopped my hand down, and the troops began jumping, in groups, as per the prearranged formation. 'One, two, five, seven, twelve, fourteen, sixteen, nineteen despatched,' I called over the intercom.

'Red on,' from the navigator and, just like that, they were disappearing; the glow of dozens of chemlight sticks quickly fading. It's a weird thing to watch human bodies falling like that; tumbling away, disappearing into complete inky blackness, the desert still so far, far away. They'd reach terminal velocity – some 120 miles per hour – in as little as fifty seconds, and would continue to fall, albeit more sedately for the last part, for some two and a half minutes.

We were already descending as we closed the ramp and door, and negotiating with LA Center to get down on the ground ASAP. We were descending quickly now, and one of the PJIs was struggling to clear his ears, so once we were down below 12,000 feet we slowed, meaning that the rear crew could take their masks off, which always helps. Below 8,000 and everyone was off oxygen.

We were on approach to the runway when we got the message that everyone was down safely and – music to my ears – one of the frogmen was buying.

Much as we enjoyed celebrating with our frogman colleagues, it's important to mention that dropping stores and equipment is one thing, and dropping humans quite another. Despite a great safety record, particularly with modern parachute design technology,[2] military parachuting presents significant risks to those who carry it out, from the complexity of the parachuting equipment itself, and the fact that they are jumping in environmental extremes (there is no air to breathe, and the outside temperature would cause instant frostbite on exposed skin), to the vagaries of dropping into a military scenario, which requires equipment and weapons to be carried. Inevitably, there will be tragedies.

RIP the fallen Royal Marine, whose memorial stands at a desert strip a few miles east of the town of Holtville, California. By Strength and Guile. He will not be forgotten.

16. An Officer and (Hopefully) a Gentleman

New Year's resolutions are generally a fine thing to make. No, you might not always stick to them, but it's always good to aspire. Or so my thinking went when, encouraged by Sharon, I resolved to have another stab at getting a commission as a pilot. My last stab, in fact. On that point I'd been clear. It was 1997 now and, at twenty-six, I was on the cusp of being too old to commence training anyway. It really was a case of now or never.

By February, I was feeling rather differently. Six weeks had already passed, and I still hadn't heard anything from the selection board; and, since the boss had now disappeared to go skiing with his family, it was pretty clear that I wouldn't be either. At least, not any time soon. So, once again, I was readjusting my expectations.

Having passed the morning at Lyneham, poring over the notices for any courses that might tick the boxes for promotion to flight sergeant and beyond, I spent the afternoon downloading various application forms and filling them in. Before going home, I stopped by the adjutant's office to drop them off, and was greeted by the lovely sergeant admin clerk, Caroline. She took the forms and looked at them, then looked back at me, confused.

'Why have you filled these out?' she asked.

Now it was my turn to look confused. 'Erm . . .' I began.

'Didn't the boss see you before he went away skiing?'

I shook my head. 'No, he didn't. Why?'

'Wait there,' she said, then headed down the corridor, returning a few moments later with one of the flight commanders.

'The boss said nothing to you before he left?' he asked.

I shook my head again. 'Nothing.' I was getting worried now. Was I in trouble? If so, what had I done?

They both disappeared into the boss's office, and through the open doorway I could see them riffling through his in-tray. They found a big Manilla envelope, and I was summoned through by Caroline.

'Grab a seat,' said the flight commander, motioning towards the comfy chairs. Which was a relief. Comfy chairs meant this was unlikely to be a bollocking.

He sat down across from me and handed me a letter – one with the Officer and Aircrew Selection Centre header. My heart sank. It made sense. It was obviously a rejection, which was presumably why the boss couldn't stomach giving it to me before his holiday.

I read it, anyway, my eyes focusing immediately on five words I had not expected: 'We would like to offer . . .' *What?* I read on: '. . . a start date of 6 April 1997 on 167 IOT for commissioning in the branch of General Duties (Pilot).'

I stared at that 'brackets Pilot close brackets' for a very long moment. Unusually for me, I was entirely lost for words.

'Are you okay?' asked the flight commander.

'I think so,' I managed finally.

'Well, congratulations!' he said, extending a hand, which I shook.

I arrived back in the adjutant's office in a complete daze,

to find Caroline brandishing the bunch of applications I'd brought in only ten minutes previously.

'I'm guessing I should bin these?' she said with a smile. 'Hello? Are you with us?'

But I was already airborne. My journey to the flight deck of a Hercules was finally under way.

There was still a bit of travelling to do, however. To become a pilot in the RAF you first need to become an officer, the transformation into which took up the bulk of my time during the spring and summer of that year. Although that kept me away from my wife and young son for many months, it really focused my mind on the value of their support and the ultimate goal of giving them a better life through my efforts.

The course, at RAF College Cranwell, was split into three parts – essentially basic soldiering (which I knew about; I had already done plenty of marching), followed by leadership training, which was mentally and emotionally challenging, and opened my horizons to a new way of thinking. Finally, in order to bring together everything thus far taught, there was the opportunity to put it into practice in the real world, albeit in a managed environment. Only after this would I be allowed to walk up the steps to College Hall, with my new rank on my shoulder. I would then, finally, be let loose at the controls of an actual aircraft – a single-engine Slingsby Firefly – and get my pilot dreams actually, *literally*, off the ground. This would at last allow me to play with the big boys' toys: learning how to fly a multi-engine aircraft. This was the big league. Big aircraft. Big dreams resting on it. More than that, though, shit was suddenly getting serious.

*

According to Military Wiki (yes, there is such an entity), 'The Lockheed C-130 Hercules is a highly reliable aircraft: the Royal Air Force recorded an accident rate of about one aircraft loss per 250,000 flying hours over the last forty years, making it one of the safest aircraft they operate.'

These are reassuring words. But no aircraft is infallible. They can and do crash. And as I contemplated the next stage of my training, at the Multi-Engine Training School (METS) back at Cranwell, I had never been more acutely aware of it.

For any pilot, the route to gaining the coveted RAF flying badge is never an easy one. The training is designed to be tough and to stretch individuals to their personal limits, instilling confidence in them as aviators, and giving them a foundation to take to their operational conversion unit, and then on to the front line, where the learning never stops.

Unlike many that had been on my Joint Elementary Flying Training School course, I was not a natural pilot. I had to work hard to be average. This final course towards my wings would teach me key new skills that would be essential on any of the operational platforms in the RAF – not least, flying safely with asymmetric power following an engine loss. A single-engine aircraft, such as the Firefly I had initially learned on, offers no control issues when that engine is lost, as it effectively just turns it into a glider. A multi-engine aircraft is a very different beast. Losing an engine creates an imbalance of thrust, and needs dextrous handling to correct that asymmetry.

While people generally tend not to dwell on the traged- ies of the past, sometimes it's important to be mindful of

Prime Minister John Major enjoys a Guiness with the 47 Squadron crew that flew him.

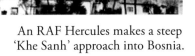

An RAF Hercules makes a steep 'Khe Sanh' approach into Bosnia.

I rejoined my old squadron as a pilot.

In the pilot's seat at last. Or co-pilot's seat, at least.

A Hercules kicks up dust on
operations in Afghanistan.

Downtime in AFG.

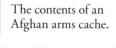

The contents of an
Afghan arms cache.

I'd once wanted to fly
helicopters. Turned out,
I sort of could …

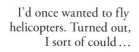

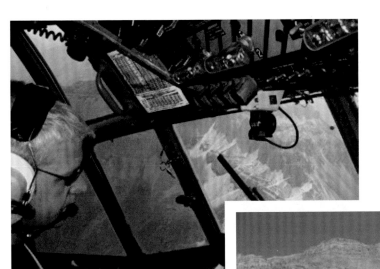

Threading through
the mountains in AFG.

The view from the cockpit.

Chasing shadows in AFG.

There's no AA to help
change a wheel in AFG …

Flare dispensers were fitted to keep us safe from heat-seeking missiles.

But flares couldn't protect the aircraft from IEDs and mines on the ground.

As the song says: cool guys don't look at explosions.

In 1993, the nine crew members were tragically killed when their Hercules stalled and crashed near Pitlochry in Scotland.

The repatriation of the crew of Hilton 22, killed in Iraq when their 47 Squadron Hercules was shot down by groundfire.

Taxiing out for the
coronation flypast in 2023.

The view from the cockpit.

In formation for the coronation flypast.

Beauty is in the
eye of the beholder.

Celebrating the coronation in style...

...with a cream tea.

Departing RAF Akrotiri in May 2023 to evacuate British nationals from Sudan.

Sans Peur. Without fear. The unofficial 47 Squadron badge celebrates the squadron's time in Sudan between the wars. 2023 saw it return after eighty-two years.

The end of an era. The Hercules retires from RAF service after fifty-six years.

them. I was conscious of one notable C-130 loss due to asymmetry (and extremely bad luck) – a crash at RAF Colerne, back in 1973. The Herc, which had been flying a routine training sortie, was lined up on the westerly runway to depart on another circuit. The crew initiated the climb without incident, during which the training captain failed the No. 1 engine by pulling the fire handle. But almost instantly, during the climb away from the runway, the No. 2 engine for some reason also failed. Now double asymmetric (that is, both engines on one side out), and obviously flying at very low speed, the aircraft would have had serious controllability issues. Despite the best efforts of the crew, it rolled slowly to the left and crashed in a wooded area a few hundred yards past the runway's end. The aircraft was destroyed, and all five crew members were killed.

I was in no doubt, then, that getting this bit of my training wrong might not just be embarrassing. It could be deadly.

Because I had to wait for a place at METS, it was January 1999 by the time I made my way back to RAF Cranwell, and without Sharon this time, living in York House Officers' Mess, on the main site away from the college. Although I was missing my family, I knew the opportunity not to have the distraction would allow me to focus on the course and get through it as simply and quickly as possible. Glad as I was to have racked up by now a rare double, Best Recruit in Airman Training and also the Wilkinson Sword for Best Officer Recruit, the one I really didn't want was 'Longest Journey to Become an RAF Pilot, EVER'.

The METS course was split into two phases. The first

was called MELIN (Multi-Engine Lead-In), and it saw me back in the Firefly I'd initially trained on, for a more focused thirty hours devoted to all aspects of instrument flying and multi-crew cooperation. It was then back to ground school, for a further four weeks, to learn about the BAE Jetstream T2, the RAFs main multi-engine trainer.

I settled quickly into flying the Firefly again, it being a joy to practise something I felt proficient at. The tone of the course had changed now and was definitely more relaxed than JEFTS, aided by my living in the mess with the other students, and not having to juggle family life. Yes, the guilt was always present, but the sacrifice paid off. I passed, and joined 45 (Reserve) Squadron to be trained to fly the Jetstream.

While at METS, I really found my pilot mojo. I was never going to set the world on fire, but I was steady and safe, which saw me clear all of the hurdles required of me. That was, at least, until the final test on the course: my trip to qualify for my RAF wings.

My examiner, Squadron Leader Dave Thomas – one of the senior team on the squadron – was known for giving no quarter, and on the day before my wings trip, he had given me a plan of what he would like to do on our sortie. I planned that mission like no other, ran through every scenario in my head, spoke to other students who had flown the test profile with him earlier in the week, and I had every contingency covered. I was 100 per cent ready for this sortie, and went off to bed and slept well.

But it was clearly not to be. I opened the curtains the following morning to find the landscape almost completely obscured by a almost Keatsian 'season of mists' thick fog – the last thing I wanted to be faced with. It was not quite how I'd envisaged starting the day – this day on which my entire future as an RAF pilot would be sealed – but I could only remain optimistic. Perhaps it would lift and all would be well.

Walking across to the squadron building, the aircraft on the flight line majestically silhouetted within the fog, I began to doubt it. My apprehension was further endorsed when I looked at the forecast. After the met brief, Dave Thomas approached me.

'I will let you make all the decisions about today's flight,' he told me. 'This is down to you. Use your limits and tell me what you think.' Nothing like piling on the pressure.

'I think it's too early to call it either way,' I responded. 'I'd like to wait until lunchtime to make a decision, and maybe delay our departure to suit that.'

He nodded, hopefully because he thought it was sensible, said he'd see me in his office at 1230, and with that he was off. The rest of the morning passed painfully slowly, only adding to my jitters. I checked the weather constantly, and even went outside a couple of times to look at the dew on the grass. It wasn't disappearing, so it was unlikely the fog was going to lift any time soon. Time to make another decision, then. At 1230, I went up to Dave's office.

'So,' he said, 'what's the verdict?'

I explained that although the fog might lift later in the day, at around 1500, visibility was unlikely to be brilliant and we definitely wouldn't have time for the whole sortie profile and be able to return to Cranwell by 1700 for the airfield closing.

'So,' I said reluctantly, 'I think we should cancel.'

'Good decision,' came the answer, causing my spirits to lift slightly, even if the fog hadn't.

Back to the mess, then, to wait another twenty-four hours to find out whether I was going to be an RAF pilot or not. Or, indeed, fly at all. Because the next morning the wretched fog *still* hadn't lifted. In fact, as I opened the curtains and peered out, it looked thicker. My heart sank. I had been waiting for this moment ever since that air show at Leuchars, and every time I got close, it kept slipping away. Still, you never knew, so I showered and got dressed in my flying suit, and after a quick breakfast made my way to the briefing room for the met brief. It was basically a busted flush: there would be no flying that morning.

I continued checking the weather throughout the morning on MOMIDS, the Met Office Military Information Distribution System, which had direct feeds from the Met Office and provided a good picture of the weather in the UK. By lunchtime, certain that the fog was finally lifting, I stuck my flag in the sand and told Dave.

He looked out of the window. 'Okay,' he said. 'If you are sure, let's meet in ten in the downstairs briefing room.' We were finally wagons rolling.

Dave had lots of probing questions during the brief, and as well as inquiring about aircraft limitations, asked me about instrument recovery limits too, which seemed a little strange. As a student, I had a limited 'amber' instrument rating, obviously higher (as in a decision height that's higher above the ground) than the instructors, who had green ratings. I duly told him my limits, then, briefing complete, Dave authorized the flight in the operations room. Aircraft duly signed for, we headed out to the apron.

The fog had by now lifted significantly, and the visibility was several miles, so although the cloud base was low, around 1,000 feet, I felt confident that today would be the day.

The Jetstream is a low-winged turboprop aircraft, which was originally designed as a small commuter-style plane for regional use. The biggest versions of the aircraft could carry about forty passengers, but the smaller version that the RAF had was equipped for two pilots plus five in the cabin. It was a lovely multi-engine trainer, with just enough complexity, but also forgiving if you made an error. As we approached it, though, it looked intimidatingly enormous.

I still felt a great affection for it, however. This was possibly the last time I would ever fly it, and, as I did my pilot walkaround, kicking the tyres for no other reason than that I could, I knew I would miss it.

Once back at the door, I looked in to see Dave already in position, setting himself up in the right-hand seat, plugging in his headset, and arranging his maps. As I climbed aboard myself the rear of the aircraft dipped slightly. *I must go on that diet*, I thought, *if I pass. No, Scottie, not if. Once I pass.* This was a big deal, but we were going to be okay.

I moved forward, pulled my headset and maps out of my flight bag, then folded my six foot two inches of body up and slipped into the left seat. It was now time to consult the flight reference cards for the pre-flight checks. These flip cards ensure the correct procedures are followed at all times, and are key to a standard operation.

While the Jetstream could technically be flown by a single pilot, during the latter stages of the METS course we worked as a crew, as this was the type of operation we would all see on our front-line aircraft. Today, Dave was going to act as a competent crew member, but one who lacked initiative, and wouldn't be offering anything much of any use. Unless, of course, I asked him, which I hoped I wouldn't have to.

Once the to and fro between cockpit and tower was complete, I held one finger in the air so the ground crew outside could see it; as the first Turbomeca Astazou engine started to spool up, and the propeller began turning, my gaze was glued to the instruments. Any anomaly, and I would shut it down again. All was well, though, and when it was stable, I held up two fingers at the window and the ground crew shifted their focus to the other engine. 'Starting two,' I announced and moved the start switch to the start detent.

Now it was time for the after-start checklist, so Dave flipped his cards, and we went through the ritual of challenge and response again. That completed, I released the brake and we were off. My day of reckoning was about to get under way.

I deliberately took the taxiing a little slower than normal, buying myself some thinking time to ensure that I had covered all the bases. I noticed that we were the only aircraft moving on the normally busy training airfield, which felt a bit odd, but by the time we'd reached sufficient ground speed for Dave to announce, 'Rotate,' my mind was wholly focused on the task in hand – to fly this thing, fly it well, and bring it safely down again.

I was now entering the second phase of the test: an airways transit to Humberside culminating in a successful approach and departure into low level. The low-level portion was all running to plan too when Dave said, 'Let's divert to RAF Linton-on-Ouse, please.'

This was a surprise. So much so that it took a few moments for me to come up with a plan, and as I started to deliver on it, heading in the new direction I'd plumped for, I became momentarily unsure of my position. Rather than admit this, I pulled up a little and contacted RAF Linton-on-Ouse for a radar service with vectors to their runway in use.

Dave piped up again. 'Okay, that's enough,' he said, in a tone that suggested – oh, dear – that he didn't like my plan after all. 'Take me back to Cranwell,' he added, rather crisply.

I could see him out of the corner of my eye, writing notes on his pad. Did he know I was lost? Had I, for whatever reason, just blown it? I pushed the thought away miserably as we began heading back to Cranwell. Whatever was to come later, I had to focus on the job in hand.

Meanwhile, Dave was busy changing the frequency, and once we'd been identified and cleared, he started taking down the Cranwell weather: 'At 1600 is wind 240 degrees at two knots, 1,200 metres in heavy rain and mist, cloud overcast at 300 feet.'

Bugger. That certainly wasn't forecast. It was also below my operating minima, which meant – horror show of horror shows – that I couldn't get us back to Cranwell on my limits. So I asked Dave if he could also request the RAF Waddington weather – our nominated diversion airfield. Dave got it and, to my surprise, it was even worse than Cranwell.

I was beginning to get the feeling that Dave was enjoying this now and could even hear the cogs in my brain working.

'What's the plan, skipper?' he said, just to add that extra bit of pressure.

I shared it by thinking aloud, saying that it was outside my limits at both destination and diversion, and that I would like him to ask air traffic control to hand us back to Linton so we could go there and land instead. Dave looked at me oddly. Had I missed something?

'Reasonable plan,' he said. 'Use my limits and take me home to Cranwell.'

I had never been so focused on flying an instrument approach in my life; it was scant consolation, but at least I nailed it. We broke out of cloud at 300 feet and although I crossed the threshold of the very damp looking runway a little fast, we touched down nicely. I selected reverse and we exited onto the taxiway at a fast walking pace.

As we taxied back, Dave was already tidying away his stuff. I decided to concentrate on the aircraft. I knew I couldn't change anything, but I still had my standards, and taxiing on the grass would be a bad way to end my regrettably short career. I turned onto the parking spot and the marshaller in front of us crossed his arms above his head, signalling us to stop. I brought us to a halt and applied the parking brake.

Dave was already unstrapped now and out of his seat, and as I shut down the engines, I felt the draught as the rear door opened. Okay. So apparently the debrief was going to have to wait. I shut down the aircraft fully and, as I handed it over to the engineers, I could see the lights of the squadron building reflecting on the wet apron, a bit like tears.

It was a short walk, but also the longest of my life, made even longer, at least in my head, by reminding myself of the mantra I had come to use as my lodestone – that nothing is ever as bad as you think it is, nobody else probably cares, and nothing will change unless you change it yourself. *Really?* If I failed now, it *would* be bad, and Sharon *would* care – I knew she would be heartbroken for me. And as for nothing changing unless I changed it myself – well, how exactly would I change the outcome of this? I couldn't, not unless I had a time machine. I could only suffer the humiliation of having to start all over again.

I entered the crew room to find it almost deserted. The only occupants were Dave and my normal instructor. They were chatting over cups of tea, and stopped when I entered. Once Dave had passed me one – *Get that condemned man some tea!* I thought – he motioned for us to sit down.

'How do you think that went?' he asked.

I duly answered him as best I could, going through each part of the sortie while he nodded and began crossing stuff off a list that I could see ran across several pages. I was honest and, in the true fashion of all military pilots, quite self-deprecating in my assessment. But even given that . . . I knew. I was *not* going to pass this.

Dave then passed me a piece of paper with a forecast of the Cranwell and Waddington weather. 'This is the 1200 forecast,' he said. 'Did you look at this before we walked for the sortie?'

My heart sank even further. I had completely forgotten to get the new forecast. I fessed up. I hadn't. 'It was an oversight, and I should have checked,' I admitted, knowing this was a *big* error.

Dave met my eye, his expression pretty stern. 'Had you just said that you *had* looked at this, which, of course, you should have done,' he said, 'and we had subsequently gone off with a forecast out of limit, I would've failed you today. But it was an oversight,' he continued; 'and, when it became apparent the weather was awful, you had a good plan for a safe outcome. You won't do it again.'

He then stood up and leaned over me with an outstretched hand. 'Congratulations,' he said. 'You won it on the debrief. It's a pass.'

And with that, on a dreary late autumn afternoon in 1999, I became an RAF pilot.

But piloting what? After a couple of weeks off with Sharon and the children, I had the biggest career decision of my life to make. In the process of deciding on my first operational platform, I was allowed to express a preference for three aircraft. This would be taken into account, but other factors would also be considered, including ability, skill set and attitude.

I elected for Hercules, VC-10 tankers and Tristars, and waited for my fate as a newly minted pilot to be revealed – as is traditional in the RAF – in the York House Officers' Mess bar, at 1700 hours on the Friday two weeks later.

For new pilots, this was cruel. For everyone else, it was fun. The junior course, who organized the event, had a wheel with pictures of the various aircraft on it, which each anxious new pilot had to set spinning. In a gladiatorial twist, each time you landed on one, the boss would signal your fate with a thumbs up or a thumbs down. Thumbs up, that was your posting; thumbs down, and it was not – instead, you had to down a pint of lager and take another spin.

I was first up. The wheel stopped on the Nimrod.

Fuck, I thought. *Noooo. Not Scotland! Sharon will kill me.* But it was 'thumbs down and down a pint', which I did extremely willingly. In fact, never had I been so glad to down a pint in my life.

Another spin, and this time it was the BAE146 or HS125, the Queen's Flight. More relief; I already knew I didn't have to worry about that one. Only the best of the best got posted to the Queen's Flight.

Another pint was quickly necked. I needed to score a win soon or I was likely to be sick.

I spun a third time. Again it slowed, and this time stopped on the Herc.

I felt my heart begin to thump. This was it.

Or was it? I couldn't even look at the boss. But when I did finally dare to turn, it was to see his thumb solidly pointing upwards.

I had got my wish. I was going to be a Herc pilot.

Awash with joy and lager, I slipped into the corridor to call Sharon.

'We don't have to move!' I told her. 'I did it! I got Hercs!'

It took her some time to stop shrieking her delight. After which came a stern wifely order: 'Don't get too drunk.'

I may not have taken that advice.

If that had been the icing on the cake, there was a cherry still to top it. We were presented with our RAF wings just before Christmas, at a formal graduation ceremony with our loved ones in attendance. It was a proud day in any case; but, to my utter astonishment, I was also awarded the cup for best all-round METS pilot on the course. So maybe I wasn't that shit after all.

Goodbye, Cranwell. And hello again, RAF Lyneham.

17. Driving the Pickfords Van with Wings

Leaving the training world behind, I was now destined for the Hercules Operational Conversion Unit (OCU), to hone everything I had been taught into practical application on the front line. But first a Christmas at home beckoned, complete with a frisson of anxiety; with the millennium threatening an imminent global meltdown, would any of us survive to see the New Year?

In my three-year absence, 47 Squadron had been kept busy with deployments in Kosovo and the Gulf, as well as detachments in South America. There had also been a very close shave on an operation in Albania – the talk of the crew room and all the Christmas parties, despite having happened back in June. That tends to happen when you crash a plane like the C-130.

The aircraft had been engaged on a mission to land at the disused airstrip at Kukes, in Albania, to recover troops that were operating there. The recce photographs of the airfield had confirmed that the strip was more than sufficient for the C-130 to land and stop, and then to take off without any reversing or backtracking down the runway. So the crew were unconcerned when they landed on the night of 11 June 1999, despite being in total darkness and having to use their NVGs.

While the loadmaster grounded the ramp and loaded

the troops and their Land Rover, the crew at the front prepared for departure, and with all on board, they advanced
the power against the brakes. As the noise peaked, the
brakes came off and the Herc accelerated down the tarmac
to 100 miles per hour. Unbeknown to anyone, they were
barrelling towards disaster.

Not seen in the photographs was a recently built agri-
cultural fence, unhelpfully strung across the airfield. It was
now in the path of the speeding C-130.

The co-pilot gaped as the blurred shape of the obstruction came into view. 'What's that?' he exclaimed.

'A fucking fence!' the captain answered, with feeling.

In a last-ditch attempt to save the aircraft, they pulled
back on the column to try and leapfrog it over the fence,
but their normally forgiving Albert wasn't yet ready to fly.
Though it eased up, it was insufficient to avoid the fence
becoming entangled with the landing gear.

The captain wrestled with the aircraft for what seemed
like an eternity, but their fate had already been sealed when
they hit the fence. Despite his best efforts, the Herc rolled to
the right in a matter of seconds, and the wing struck the
ground. It then detached, causing the aircraft to lurch back to
the left, breaking apart as it scraped along the rough terrain.

There was a moment of silence as the aircraft came to a
stop, but the loadmaster, aware that the Herc was almost
certainly now on fire, marshalled the passengers and led
them to comparative safety, herding them through a hole
that had conveniently appeared in the side of the fuselage.
'Run upwind!' he yelled as they left.

On the flight deck, however, it was a different story. The
ALM made his way forward to find that the crew were

now trapped; on coming to a halt, the aircraft had rolled further to the left, blocking any exit through the crew door, which opened outwards, and now was sitting on the ground with a C-130 on top of it. He could also see that the entrance into the freight bay was blocked by elements of the load that had become unrestrained in the deceleration. The only route available was out through the small window adjacent to the captain, something all Hercules crews knew, theoretically, was an exit, just not one they envisaged they would ever actually use.

They needed to now, however, and they needed to do it quickly, so the captain, who was nearest, opened it and began to push himself through. He immediately became trapped, and realizing his girth might be the problem, urged the crew to use their leverage to try and launch him through the portal; if he failed to get out, they would all be trapped inside. There was no joy, though. Despite their frantic efforts he remained stuck.

'Get him back in,' the navigator suggested, so they started pulling on his legs. The loadmaster was now waving up at them from outside the aircraft. After making a quick assessment, he realized the captain's girth wasn't the problem; his belt had been caught in the window mechanism. He clambered up to the exit and out came his trusty knife, enabling him to cut through the leather, release the trapped captain and allow the rest of the crew to escape the inferno. By now, the fire had really taken hold.

It had been a tragedy in the making, and a very near miss, but though the aircraft was completely destroyed by the fire, all crew and passengers were recovered safely.

*

With the world still turning after the millennium meltdown-that-wasn't, the New Year saw me join the first class of 2000 on the C-130 OCU. Though it was my second Hercules OCU, it was my first as a pilot and officer. It also felt good to be back at RAF Lyneham, surrounded by the buzz of the people around the squadrons and officers' mess. I had always hated the formality of the training stations, where there was a clear line between the staff and the students; here we were all in it together. I liked that.

Since I had last done the course as an air loadmaster, it had moved from the old Nissen huts adjacent to the runway into the quieter environs of a new modern building that was also the home of 24 and 30 Squadrons. These were both the former C-130K route and tanker squadrons, colloquially known as 'trash haulers', which were to be re-equipped with the new C-130J.

The C-130J had entered RAF service in 1997, and was now becoming a familiar sight on the ramp as new aircraft were seemingly delivered almost every week. With the new aircraft also came a new schoolhouse facility, one that encompassed state-of-the-art computer-based training, full-flight simulators, and an entire rear fuselage of the aircraft for loadmaster training.

Lucky C-130J crews. By contrast, the C-130K classrooms in a building next door were still using a lot of 'chalk and talk', and I swear the presentations were just some overhead projector slides from the 1980s that they had digitized to bring them up to date.

The course started with the obligatory ground school and external survival training: eight weeks of mostly eight-till-five classroom work, with the occasional field trip thrown in. Deep in the winter, the relentless drudge of being in the classroom was hard going. Getting up in the dark, going home in the dark, and sitting all day in a dimly lit room in between meant I couldn't wait till it ended. So much so that, uncharacteristically, I was champing at the bit for the day when the exams finally came around. We were tested in all manner of subjects: aircraft operations, performance A (the certified performance of normal civilian airliners), aircraft technical, navigation, global meteorology, dangerous goods and, of course, weight and balance. I was fortunate to have seven years of C-130 ops to fall back on, which made many subjects easy, but to this day I still believe that global meteorology is a dark art that only grand wizards can master.

As is traditional in the RAF, we finished the ground school phase with some beers followed by a curry in a fine establishment serving Indian cuisine in nearby Royal Wootton Bassett. The weekends at home, meanwhile, were no less exciting, filled as they were with the inevitable chores; as has always been the case – and probably always will be – my DIY efforts were invariably followed soon after by a tradesman coming round to sort out the mess. Still, come spring, our new home straight and the classroom work done with, it was at last time to move on to the next stage of training, which coupled simulator learning with training in the aircraft itself.

After a week acquiring the basics in the sim we were considered ready, and on a fine spring morning we were sitting in an office, listening to the instructor brief us on what our first sortie was going to look like.

The plan was that, once on board the aircraft, the

instructor would take the pilot's seat for the initial departure and circuits. We would then land and, while he jumped across to the captain's seat, I would take his place for my first departure and circuits.

All briefed, I got on the crew bus to the aircraft. This felt weird. In my previous role, I would have gone out to pre-flight the aircraft with the flight engineer, but this time it had been done by two of my former colleagues, Flight Engineer Gary Nicholson and ALM Bob Mason, a good friend – I'd done my first OCU with him as a loadie.

The bus stopped at the nose of the aircraft, and as I stepped off, the beaming grin on my face must have made me look ridiculous. But I couldn't stop smiling; this was the fulfilment of such a big dream. Stepping aboard the aircraft, the smells and sights were all familiar, but as I settled in the right-hand pilot's seat, everything felt different. What *did* feel familiar, however, was the harshness of the banter, my former non-commissioned aircrew friends ribbing me so relentlessly about the medics they'd had the good sense to arrange that I didn't have much chance to be genuinely petrified. This was all I had ever wanted to do, and I was up for it. But what if I couldn't fly the damned thing?

'Pre-start checks,' the captain announced, and I was brought back to reality, my hands flashing almost instinctively across the panels, as if to reassure me that they, at least, knew what to do.

Checks complete and we were good to go. The four Allison turboprop engines were started – four, then three, then two and then one – and hearing that oh-so-beloved noise, knowing that *I* had been the one responsible for it, made my anxiety melt away. All those years of wishing and hoping and, at times, losing hope, and I was at the controls of a Herc. It was a moment I knew I'd treasure always.

This was no time for getting emotional, however. There were actually two lots of training being done that spring morning. As is usual, the instructor was training both a student pilot and a student captain together. So once we'd taxied to the holding point, we did another swap around, the student captain, Jamie, taking my place, while I stood behind the instructor, who was now in the co-pilot's seat.

For the next hour, we flew around the airfield at Lyneham, doing the basic circuit pattern. Then all too soon, it seemed – or so my nerves seemed to be telling me – it was time to land and, once again, swap seats. My heart was now hammering, trying to jump into my mouth as we taxied for take-off. The checks were run one more time and Jamie turned to me.

'You good?' he asked, but it was more of a statement than a question, and immediately followed with those three immortal words: 'You have control.'

'I have control,' I agreed, more by instinct than anything. The concept of having it was almost too much to think about, so I didn't – I just pushed forward on the throttles. Although I had flown in a Herc perhaps hundreds of times, it had never felt more powerful than now. *I* had never felt more powerful.

'Rotate,' Jamie called. And with that, I was officially a Hercules pilot – though there was a long way to go to becoming an operational one. For a moment, the usual banter seemed to have been forgotten. Garry Nicholson, the flight engineer, was standing just a little bit behind us pilots, and as we lifted away from Lyneham on that first sortie, he spoke.

'Fuck me,' he observed. 'He *can* fly, after all!'

It was exactly what I needed to hear.

My operational conversion to the C-130 successfully completed, in May 2000, I was posted back to 47 Squadron as a co-pilot. Part of rejoining the squadron is something called an acceptance check, and this was done on my first day at my new-old home by 'Geese', a training captain I had known for many years. We launched into the circuit above RAF Lyneham, and he put me through my paces for an hour with a mix of visual and instrument flying. I obviously was good enough to be 'accepted': when we shut down, the debrief consisted of two words, 'Welcome back.' I was once again where I wanted to be, part of the family on 47 Squadron, three years after I'd left.

The next few months were a blur of training flights and sorties across the globe as I settled into my new role. When you leave the OCU, all new crew members are graded as 'Limited Combat Ready', which essentially means that you have the fundamental skills to operate the aircraft but limited experience in doing so. The squadron then uses its own training staff to expose you to situations and training that will help develop that experience over a period of around six months. You are then tested on those core skills and, if you meet the standard, you are awarded Combat Ready (CR) status.

On the C-130, the award of that status also meant that you now had the capacity to add other elements to your core skills, such as tactical flying. By mid-September 2000,

I had achieved CR status and was looking forward to adding the tactical skills to my portfolio after a period of consolidation. This was a much-coveted course and I had to wait my turn, which meant I started in early 2001, alongside the new USAF exchange captain, John.

The course was challenging; as I've said before, I am not a natural aviator, and have always worked hard (harder than many, at least) to keep on top of my skills. While I loved flying at low level, I was never as truly comfortable there as I knew others were. And while the culture of the unit meant I was outwardly brazen about operating in that environment, in reality I was under-confident flying down low, never stretching my abilities and always staying in my comfort zone, something that persisted throughout my career in both the right- and left-hand seats of the aircraft.

That said, it was the only place to really see what the aircraft was capable of in a tactical environment, and that's what the course taught you to do. We threw an aircraft the size of a Boeing 737 around valleys like it was a fighter, delivered tons of stores and dozens of parachutists, in all manner of configurations, while flying slower than a Cessna 172 in order to do so. If Carlsberg did tactical air transporters, this was the one.

Post 'tac course', my 2001 calendar was filling up with a mix of exercises and route flying in support of operations in Kosovo and the Gulf, both of which showed no let-up in their need for constant resupply. This, combined with my recurrent and simulator training, meant it was always going to be a busy year. I was midway through my recurrent training period, having a coffee in the simulator block on a dreary September afternoon and chatting with the crews in the small tea bar while I awaited my turn in the 'box', when the TV in the corner of the room caught my attention.

A newsflash. On a bright sunny morning in New York, an aircraft had crashed into the twin towers of The World Trade Center. A flight engineer who was nearest to the set had also noticed and had moved across to turn up the volume.

'Look at this, guys,' he said, and the urgency in his voice made us all immediately sit up and take notice. We were all mesmerized, speculating on what type of aircraft could have caused such damage when, from the right of the picture, an airliner appeared and struck the other tower with devastating effect.

'Fucking hell,' said someone in the tea bar, accurately reflecting what we were all thinking.

One of the more experienced pilots, who had been observing further back, added, 'That's a terrorist act, that is. Christmas is fucked.'

Perhaps naively, I had no idea what he meant, but I soon came to understand. In fact, not only was Christmas 'fucked', at least for us, but the acts of a few criminals on that day in New York would affect tens of thousands of lives, and not just for Christmas either, but for decades.

It would start in Afghanistan, and would be followed by some unfinished business in the form of Saddam Hussein. The Iraqi dictator was already in the crosshairs of President George Bush anyway, and with the threat of his capability to use weapons of mass destruction in the region, the US government now had a mandate to invade Iraq.

The 'War on Terror' was about to begin.

18. Gulf War 2: The First Night In

By the early 1990s, it was obvious to the RAF that, though it had a winner in the C-130, its fleet of workhorses was showing signs of wear and tear, so it started to explore its options in terms of augmenting them. There was really nothing in the marketplace to compare with the utility of the C-130, and so a decision was made to procure twenty-five C-130J Super Hercules. This model entered service with the RAF in 1999, and was initially used in a strategic transportation role, but as the tactical capability and crew experience grew, the J became the mainstay of the fleet.

Although the silhouettes of the K and the J are similar, that is just about where the similarities end. The old steam-driven gauges of the K are replaced by flat LCD screens and head up displays. The avionics upgrade and the advancement of systems mean that the flight-deck crew loses the flight engineer and navigator but sees the newly named weapons systems operator (air loadmaster, in old speak) much more involved in the airborne operation of the aircraft, supporting the pilots. The beast is still powered by Allison engines, albeit new, electronically controlled ones, which are attached to six-bladed composite propellers. If we laid the Top Trumps cards for the Super Hercules and the Classic Herc side by side, the new one eclipses its older sibling in every category, apart from the 'size of drinking team' category; with five against three, the K will always win that one. We were on the cusp of a second Gulf War by this time, and though the young pretender, the J, was the new kid on the block, the crews were not yet tactically trained on it enough to enter into the fray. So the K model had to step into the breach once more, despite not having all the shiny new toys.

The RAF did have a few specially decked out C-130s, which were reasonably well equipped, but the majority of the aircraft were very basic, with little or no defensive measures whatsoever. They had no cockpit armour, no directable infra-red countermeasures (DIRCM), no chaff and flare dispensers, and no fuel-tank fire-suppressant foam, which reduces the chances of an explosion should the aircraft be hit in the fuel tanks, igniting the highly flammable fuel vapours within them. The bosses at Lyneham had been asking the MoD for funding for defensive upgrades since the Falklands conflict, but there was apparently no money available for aircraft that, unlike the six mini-fleet airframes, would never go behind enemy lines. Battle-ready they were not. But that's exactly where they were about to go.

When the second Gulf War started in March 2003, Flight Lieutenant Mark 'Merky' Baines was a well-respected Hercules skipper at the top of his game. As a tactical training instructor on 47 Squadron, his primary role was teaching all the tactical aspects of the C-130 to pilots who were already qualified to the fly the aircraft – pilots who included me. He taught low-level flying, both as a single aircraft and in formation, and both day and night; airdropping, which included everything from a small harness pack of supplies up to eighteen tons of equipment at once (think light tanks, Land Rovers, field guns, etc.), as well as paratroopers; night vision goggle (NVG) flying; short-field strip landings; and, finally, air-to-air refuelling.

All of that made Mark particularly well qualified to captain one of the RAF C-130s asked early on to provide support to Operation Shock and Awe, known in the UK as Op Telic. Four days after the start of the war, his aircraft and two other Hercules were tasked with a mission from Lyneham into the danger zone of Southern Iraq.

Mark's Hercules was one of the rather less well-equipped versions, colloquially referred to as a 'slick' aircraft, as it had no 'lumps and bumps' fitted to it. Unlike the American C-130s in Iraq, which were bristling with defensive kit, it was as factory fresh as the day it had rolled off the production line. However, it did at least have one vital upgrade: a 'Have Quick' frequency-agile secure radio, which at least meant they could speak to the AWACS and other better-equipped aircraft in theatre. This would allow the crew to use the eyes and electronic ears of other planes to keep safe and away from any threats. Although it's worth pointing out that this was only a valid strategy if others knew they should be feeding them that information.

The three RAF crews were supposedly despatched to theatre with all they needed for war. Two firearms apiece (an SA-80 rifle and a 9 mm pistol); five gold sovereigns with which they could hopefully bribe any passing goat herders should they be shot down; a waterproof 'we need your help, my friend' letter in multiple versions of Arabic; a gas mask and NBC suit (in case Saddam's WMDs were deployed), a camp bed, plus an Arctic sleeping bag (they were still doling out equipment designed for the USSR, not the desert), and sufficient twenty-four-hour ration packs (rat packs) for the duration of the mission.

The crews were concerned about this less than ideal situation. The very minimum they felt they needed in order to fly into Iraq was the PRC-112 CSAR (Combat Search And Rescue) radio, as this was used by American rescue teams to positively identify their forces and so recover crews when planes were shot down (and it still is, in an updated form). At least during their twenty-four hours off in RAF Akrotiri, they were able to borrow (or, in aircrew terminology, 'reallocate') six Kevlar flak jackets, which should give them some sort of body protection from the anticipated small arms fire.

In the evening of 24 March, the three aircraft left Akrotiri and flew through Jordan and Saudi Arabia into Kuwait International Airport. Their freight bays were full of various supplies, mostly of the explosive kind (collectively called 'Bang'), alongside members of 16 Air Assault Brigade, which provided the lead battalions in theatre at the time.

On board, they also had two VIPs (in this case, British politicians). Halfway across Saudi, as the crew began putting on their flak jackets for the approach into Kuwait, the two VIPs, sitting on the bunk on the flight deck, started to don the two spare ones. The flight engineer turned around and, in the way only a flight engineer can, told them to take them off again, explaining that they were for the two pilots to sit on.

'If the pilots took a bullet up the arse,' he clarified, 'then everyone on the aircraft would die. But if you took the bullet up the arse, sat on that bunk there, we would just scrape what was left of you off the roof, scoop it up and throw it down the back of the aircraft, and carry on.'

It was a moment of levity for them, though perhaps not for the politicians, in what was already a somewhat stressful situation.

On arrival in Kuwait there were no ground personnel to be seen, so they parked the aircraft and were strolling around outside getting some fresh air when they saw all the ground crew hunkered down, with gas masks on, waving at them from an air raid shelter. Apparently, an air raid siren had been sounding as they taxied in, but there was apparently no way of informing them. Shit.

Still, no bombs were forthcoming, so once the politicians (who were now very glad to see the back of the crew), troops and Bang were unloaded, the crews were shown to their tents. They were inside the airport boundary, enclosed by enormous sandbag walls. Mark had been in this type of environment before, during the first Gulf War, the Bosnian War, Afghanistan and several African operations, including Somalia and the Congo, but for some members of the crew it was their first time in a combat zone and was a stark reminder of what was possibly to come. Three times that night they were awoken by air raid sirens and, as they ran to the shelter in only their gas masks and underpants, they could see the Scud missiles being shot down by the US Patriot defensive system. It was reassuring that the Patriots worked as advertised – although, if the Scuds were loaded with chemical weapons, then surely all the toxins would just fall out of the sky onto them anyway. Having reached that cheerful conclusion, they all went back to bed and slept soundly.

The next morning, 25 March, the air tasking order was produced for all the flying on the 26th. The ATO was a massive undertaking, which resulted in a top-secret file as thick as a phone book. It was written each night in order to ensure that every single asset in play the next day was deconflicted and aware of the others, and thus even amid the fog of war there would be no blue-on-blue engagements between friendly forces.

The three Herc crews received a fragment of this document (the frag) outlining their specific mission for the following day. It involved their leaving Kuwait Airport under cover of darkness on the night of the 26th, and flying up to Camp Coyote, a forward operating base (FOB) on the Kuwait–Iraq border, for a landing on a 2,500-foot strip of flat, sandy desert that had been cleared of landmines, rocks and stones, and marked out by five lights down each side. From there, they would fly into Southern Iraq, to land at Jalibah Airfield, which had been captured the day before by coalition forces, unload, then fly back to Kuwait City.

They spent the rest of the 25th digesting the ATO. All the fast-jet sorties, they noticed, had super-aggressive formation callsigns, such as 'Slasher', 'Jedi', 'Evil', 'Killer', and so on. They were 'Albert' formation – slightly embarrassing, but nevertheless appropriate, as it derived from 'Fat Albert', the nickname of the Hercules. However, the RAF navigator from Lyneham who had been posted to Kuwait Airport for the previous two weeks to set up the operation and get flights into the ATO thought it would be quite funny if he named a separate Hercules formation 'Fluffy' – not very punchy, to put it mildly. Still, at least it caused a bit of merriment for the rest of the aircraft flying that day.

The big thing they gleaned from the ATO was that it *was* mandatory for every aircraft in theatre to carry the PRC-112 CSAR radio. Without it to identify them as friendly forces, they would be deemed hostile, i.e. Iraqi, and it would be a case of 'shoot first, worry later'. They'd been told the RAF 'only had enough for the fast-jet crews'. But as things didn't tend to be mandatory without reason, there was a lot of discussion, among people both senior and junior, about whether, without this vital bit of kit, they should even enter Iraq.

Despite all three crews questioning this decision several times, the detachment commander was very keen for them to go; he was obviously under a lot of pressure from his superiors to make sure the mission happened. They weren't sure who was the driver of this, but somebody somewhere high-up wanted them involved . . . perhaps in order to have a UK presence in the push forward. Although they weren't directly ordered to go, and had told their boss in Kuwait several times how unhappy they were, they took it on the chin, on the basis that if they'd refused they would simply have been ordered to go anyway. (It would have been quite an embarrassment for the RAF to have got as far as Kuwait and then just turned round and come home because its crews didn't have the correct kit to go sausage side.)

Mark and the crews left Kuwait Airport on the night of 26 March, flying at extremely low level on night vision goggles to the forward operating base at Camp Coyote, speaking to the AWACS aircraft on their Have Quick radio. The visibility wasn't very good, due to a sandstorm blowing in, and Mark did a fairly heavy landing at Coyote.

(That is actually a good thing when making a short-field strip landing, as it means you will most likely stop before the end of the marked out 'sterile runway', rather than floating just above it and going off the end, but it did keep the engineer busy, making sure they hadn't bent anything . . .)

On landing, they saw four US Marine Corps C-130s parked up on the sand, so they positioned their Herc next to them and went into the ops tent to have a briefing. These four C-130s were fully fitted with every single defence system but, to the RAF crews' amazement, they were crewed by the Air National Guard, the equivalent of the UK Territorial Army; among them were even a butcher, a baker and a banker. They seemed surprised to see the RAF, as they obviously hadn't studied the ATO quite as deeply as they should, but were nonetheless happy; as they freely admitted, having Brits doing some of their work for them meant they would have less to do themselves.

As they had been to Jalibah the previous night, they briefed the three RAF crews. It quickly became apparent there was only room for one C-130 at a time to park at Jalibah, so the UK crews decided to go at 'thirty-minute stream', i.e. with thirty minutes in between each aircraft so that the preceding aircraft had time to land, park, offload and depart before the next one arrived. Mark was tasked to be the No. 2 aircraft in the stream. On their way back to the Hercs before they departed the FOB, they walked past a tent that was stacked full of boxes of American MREs (Meals Ready to Eat), which were a million times tastier than the rat packs given out at Lyneham. They helped themselves to as many boxes as they could possibly carry and hurried back to the aircraft before anyone realized they had 'reallocated' them for internal storage at some later date.

Copying what the Air National Guard had done the night before, Mark's Herc flew at between 50 and 100 feet across the desert on NVGs to avoid being shot down. Visibility was fairly poor, so they couldn't see much in their goggles – other than an occasional, petrifying glimpse of a high sand dune when the air cleared for a moment. This was what they had trained for, but it was patently bonkers, and they weren't sure if it was the enemy or flying in this appalling weather that was the greater risk at this point.

Approaching Jalibah, they were told that one of the pallets of Bang in the first C-130 on the ground had twisted and was stuck in the back of the aircraft, and so they couldn't offload its cargo. This meant they now had to hold off in enemy territory for twenty-five minutes before they could land. This was not in the plan, or indeed good news of any sort. They held at low level over the desert, trying not to overfly the same point more than once as they didn't want Iraqi soldiers to know where they were or what they were doing.

As the captain, Mark was sitting on the left-hand side, with the navigator and co-pilot on the right. At one stage, at about eighty feet above the ground and 240 knots, Mark was told they had just flown past a 'mast, or something with lights on', very close by the right-hand side – something, at any rate, that was higher than the aircraft. They hadn't seen it until the last minute, it wasn't on any maps and the Americans hadn't mentioned it in the briefing, but the nav and the co-pilot both confirmed it was there and they would have been very poorly placed had they hit it.

They eased up just a little after that, as it was quite a big shock, and they now wondered what else could be out there.

They eventually landed at Jalibah, only to be told by the American troops on the ground that while their Herc was making its approach about three miles out from the runway, they had seen a missile, flare or grenade fired at the aircraft from the ground. It had obviously missed as they were still alive. And, thankfully, they'd been completely unaware of it either, having no systems on board that would have warned them of its approach.

If they'd had those systems, obviously it would have massively increased the stress and workload of the flight, but ignorance really had proved to be bliss in that situation. Being none the wiser, they had just carried on with the task.

As it had passed midnight while they were flying, they suddenly realized on landing that it was now their loadmaster's birthday. So they all sang a very out-of-tune rendition of 'Happy Birthday' before unloading the cargo. The Americans thought they were all mad.

On starting up to go back to Kuwait, they were approached by six rough-looking American soldiers who were fully tooled up with more guns, mortars, grenades and ammunition than you could shake a stick at. Their commander asked if they could have a lift back to Ali Al Salem Airbase in Kuwait as that was where the rest of their comrades were. They had obviously had a bit of a busy night themselves, as they looked absolutely shattered.

To do everyone a favour, the Herc crew asked no questions and just said yes. It meant they were now 'off frag', though, as according to the ATO they were only supposed to go from Jalibah back to Kuwait Airport.

They departed about ten minutes later, flying very low – between twenty to fifty feet – for the first few miles, as they didn't want a repeat of what had happened on the way in: the lower and faster you fly, the less likely you are to be shot down, as you are out of range before the enemy have time to react to your presence. Flying at that height gives you a new appreciation of the speed of the Hercules; for a short period, the US soldiers thought they were in a fast jet.

The crew spoke to the AWACS using Have Quick in order to arrange a 're-frag' to drop off the six Americans and reunite them with the rest of their platoon. The new routing took them past lots of the burning oil wells that the Iraqis had set on fire before fleeing. The flames were leaping into the night sky, higher than the aircraft, and thick black smoke was billowing everywhere. Through the NVGs, it looked completely unearthly.

The smoke was so thick that they were forced to fly higher and off their intended track; not only could they not see through it, there was also ash to consider, which would have been bad news for both the aircraft and their own health. They soon dropped the Americans off at Ali Al Salem Airbase, and with no further excitement or drama proceeded to Kuwait Airport, mission accomplished.

Back at their tent after a debrief, with no alcohol in camp to drink, they gorged themselves on the 'reallocated' MREs, and, as was tradition, some amazing-tasting fresh oranges.

The 27th and 28th were spent on standby but, with no frag in the ATO, the three crews knew they wouldn't be used for anything else, which left them free to enjoy a bit of Kuwaiti-style downtime during the day, including an obligatory visit to the souk, to buy that camel clock that no one ever really needs, and, at night, watching the Patriots shoot down Scud missiles; having rationalized that (a) a few sandbags and some corrugated iron were not even remotely bombproof, and (b) the chemical weapons would likely get them anyway, it was a pleasant a way to spend the hot, sleepless nights.

All three aircraft left Kuwait on the morning of the 29th, scheduled to go home via Souda Bay in Crete. The crews were not sure the hotel was quite prepared for, or keen to see, them; but as it turned out, they proved to be exemplary guests, wasting no time in drinking the bar dry for them.

Merky's mission, for me, epitomizes the exceptional nature of the Hercules crews across almost six decades of operational service. This was a crew that, despite the considerable danger involved, chose to fly a mission into enemy-held territory with neither defence aids nor the correct equipment to facilitate a safe combat rescue should they have been shot down by enemy action. There was one confirmed episode of them being shot at along their route, but I will wager there were other engagements that happened, and they just continued on, as Mark puts it, while blissfully unaware. Some may say that they were all foolhardy and should have just said no, but that is not what military people do. It is not in our psyche – we get the job done, and when the chips are down our default is always yes. We will almost always find a way through the doubts and uncertainty, to triumph when faced with adversity.

Happily, the RAF did eventually acquire more PRC-112 radios for the crews and DIRCM sets for the aircraft. And I am glad to report that, after this mission, no 'slick' aircraft was used in enemy territory again.

19. A Life in the Day Of

I was standing in the middle of a sandy open area, having just showered using the contents of a solar-powered plastic bag of tepid water, in a cubicle fashioned from wooden pallets. I hadn't bothered to dry myself, as by the time I had brushed my teeth, the harsh desert heat would have done that for me. Just as I started squeezing the toothpaste onto my brush, the ground began to shake. But this wasn't an earthquake. It was a pair of USAF B-1 bombers in full reheat – starting their take-off roll about two miles away from where I was standing. The shaking intensified, and through the shimmering heat haze I could now see the black dots of the two aircraft barrelling towards me. The first and then the second lifted off, but they didn't seem to climb; their gear retracted and then they passed within a few hundred yards of my makeshift ablution area. The sound was deafening, the ground was shuddering beneath me, and the sight of these bringers of doom getting airborne was so awe-inspiring that I stopped brushing my teeth for all of the three minutes or so that it took them to climb away to the north and towards the Gulf of Oman. I had not long ago landed from that direction myself, but we'd had the defence of darkness. These bombers relied on speed and height to keep them safe.

My home for the last three weeks had been the airfield of Thumrait in Oman. When I called the airfield 'home', I really meant it. I was living right on the perimeter of the airfield, in a tent designed for the harsh winters of the North German Plain. (Of course it was; we had always planned, and equipped ourselves, for a cold war.) I was here, in April 2003, as a small detachment of RAF aircraft in support of our US allies, carrying out missions into Afghanistan in our Hercules.

These had been both expected – ammunition, and lots of it, plus occasional troops – and sometimes less so. Cabbages, for example, and also deckchairs. We didn't question this. Mostly because when we did, we already knew the answer: 'You don't know the bigger picture.' And that was true.

In fact, we never really thought about the bigger picture. Our Afghanistan experience so far had been all about eating and flying, and getting enough sleep in our specially provided military-issue canvas sauna. We flew at night, always, because darkness was our friend. And also because Afghan insurgents tended to indulge themselves with khat then – a local green plant, the leaves of which they chewed. As with Central and South Americans, and the coca leaf, it was a cultural norm here – even though now classified as a class C hallucinogenic drug in the UK. It made them less inclined to fight during the small hours.

I finished brushing my teeth, and with a towel wrapped around my waist moved towards my tent. It was a large green affair and there were two crews currently billeted in it, which made ten of us. We each had our own little space with a camp bed, but there was no real privacy, so you really did get to know each other very well. I was the co-pilot on a crew with another Mark as the captain, and we had just finished another resupply mission to Bagram Air-base, just to the north of Kabul. It had been a long night: we had been so heavy we flew much lower than normal, which used up more fuel, so on the way back to Oman we'd needed to make a fuel stop in Karachi. That said, when we were outside the tactical area, we all managed to get some sleep on the aircraft. But it was now time to bask in our air-conditioned 'luxury' accommodation and get some real shut eye. The air-conditioner had stopped again, however, having run out of fuel. So I decided that I'd put some shorts on and go and have some breakfast.

The chefs were amazing. And I don't say that lightly. The military life gives you a keen nose for the rare treat of decent grub. They cooked outdoors and we ate in a small tent, laid out like a school dining hall, complete with one of those drinks dispensers that always have red- and orange-coloured squash in them. I got myself some scrambled eggs and sat down to tuck in. To my surprise, sitting at the table was an old friend from my childhood, Sue, who was also an RAF officer. We caught up, and marvelled that we had to come to a war zone to see each other again. I was beginning to flag now, however, so made my apologies and headed back to the tent. Apparently a bonus, the air-conditioner was once again working, pushing cool air down a single pipe stuck into the side of the canvas. I say 'a bonus' because the outside temperature was now up in the high thirties, but 'apparently' because, seemingly defying all reason, it was actually managing to make the inside hotter! I didn't care, it was 0800 and I badly needed sleep. I flopped down and was blotto in an instant.

The plan was to sleep until 1600, have some dinner and

then prepare for the night's sortie. And I assumed that was what the time was when I heard someone whispering close by. I was really sweaty by now, dripping, and the lack of noise in the background told me the air-conditioning had packed up again. I rolled over – perhaps the whisperer was trying to get it going – but it was my skipper, Mark, lying in his bed and talking in whispers with Stu, the detachment commander, who knelt beside him. I picked up 'We need you to go as soon as possible. I wouldn't ask if it wasn't life or death.'

I checked my watch. It was still only 1400. Mark looked over. 'Get washed and dressed. We're going flying,' he said.

In the military, we don't tend to use 'life or death' meta-phorically. With adrenaline seeing off the last vestiges of sleepiness, I headed out of the tent and straight into a nice cooling wind. Now that the temperature had climbed several degrees higher, the breeze was refreshing, even if accompanied by a blast of exfoliating sand.

The second ablutions of the day then commenced. It's weird trying to shave outside in such heat; you wet your face and add shaving foam, but by the time you get around to scraping a razor over it, it has blown away or evaporated, leaving small grains of sand for you to scrape off instead. That finished, a visit to the Portakabin loos was the next order of the day, and though the less said about that the better – not difficult to imagine – it was at least a place of welcome solitude.

Next, the solar shower – which, having cooled a little overnight, was just about perfect in the mornings, but which was now so scorching as to be almost unbearable. So I was quick, and soon after, dressed and ready in my

desert combats, I headed over with the team to the operations building, to find out what we were being asked to do.

Stu greeted us, then wasted no time in getting straight
down to the briefing. It seemed a UK soldier had been
critically injured and was currently at Bagram, being cared
for by US medics. It had been decided that an airlift would
be mounted to recover the individual from Bagram to
Thumrait, where a VC-10 would then fly them straight
back to the UK for treatment at a specialist hospital in
London. We were therefore to configure the freight bay of
our aircraft as a critical care unit and recover the patient on
the first leg of that journey, with the Thumrait-based RAF
aeromedical evacuation team. Due to the time-sensitive
nature of the mission, it was likely that it would still be
daylight as we approached Bagram, stealing the advantage
of darkness from us. There was, however, no discussion
whether we should do this or not. All our focus was immediately on how we could do this in the safest way possible,
and save this life without unduly risking others.

The flight engineer and loadmaster left us to go and
prep the aircraft while Mark, the navigator and I planned
the mission. The heavily defended Bagram Airbase lay
about twenty-five miles north of Kabul within a southerly-
opening horseshoe-shaped bowl of the Hindu Kush. The
mountains presented a tactical challenge as they reached
heights of more than 15,000 feet above sea level around
the airfield, increasing the effective altitude of Strela
shoulder-launched missiles – which were deemed a credible threat at the time – from about 13,000 to 28,000 feet
and putting the normal cruise altitudes of the C-130 within
range. Even more rudimentary weapons such as unguided

RPGs and small arms took on a different threat profile when you had to descend past these mountains into a natural bowl when approaching the runway. There was also the fact that the performance of any aircraft is reduced when operating in hot areas, at high altitudes. The airfield itself was at an altitude of almost 5,000 feet above sea level, which brought its own handling difficulties for aircraft. Especially when taking off, where extended take-off runs were needed. To allow for those days when it was hot and you were trying to lift a heavy load off the ground, Bagram had an 11,000-foot runway.

We decided that the least risky route would be to fly in airways (aerial roadways for commercial traffic) across the Gulf of Oman and up through Pakistan to a navigation waypoint called LAJAK on the Afghan border, near Peshawar. We would essentially be tactical from thereon, flying over the area of the Khyber Pass, the shortest route over contested territory from Pakistan to Bagram. We would fly as high as possible here, at 26,000 feet, and keep our options open whether to arrive straight into the airbase and reduce exposure if it was actually still daylight, or continue to the overhead of the airfield at 26,000 feet if it was already night-time, spiral down in the protected area and land on NVGs on an airfield in darkness. Now we had a plan with contingencies and were ready to go, it was time to get transport to the aircraft.

We threw our helmets, body armour and flight bags in the back of a Toyota pickup truck, which Stu offered to drive out to our aircraft. It would be a very long walk otherwise – especially in the heat. Everyone was by now aware that the conflict in Afghanistan was not going to be a small skirmish, so the base at Thumrait was getting busier every day. Team America was building a huge base with a social club, a Burger King and proper accommodation, possibly with air-conditioning that even worked. The outdoor section of the social club was by now almost finished (and in true US style had a massive outdoor screen for showing football games) and we vowed to try it out after we got back from this sortie.

We pulled onto the flight line and drove past some of the world's most sophisticated hardware – KC-135 tankers, those B-1 bombers, aircraft capable of psy-ops – and, of course, parked at the end, our rather dirty and dishevelled-looking C-130. As we approached, we could see a flurry of activity at the back of the aircraft around the open ramp, and as we stopped we were met by the flight engineer, who told us that all was not quite ready. Due to a change in the patient's condition there was now a need for a ventilator, and there was concern that we didn't have enough batteries for it to last the length of the sortie plus contingencies, so a call had been put in to the Americans to see if they could assist.

A short time later, while we were all busy readying the aircraft, the lead doctor on the aeromedical team came up to the flight deck for a chat about the condition of the patient – very serious – and the need for those batteries. We discussed contingencies from an aircraft, a tactical and a medical perspective, and as we were doing so we spotted a huge box-shaped ambulance speeding down the flight line, blue lights flashing. It stopped at the nose of our aircraft and a medic jumped from the rear. It appeared the medical teams from the UK and the US used slightly different versions of the same apparatus, which meant the batteries weren't interchangeable. The US doctor, however, had brought his own spare unit and, it seemed, sufficient batteries for us to fly all the way to the US and back, should we ever want to. This was international teamwork at play, and at its best; no egos, no barriers. Just a common will to save a life. We could only hope we would.

With the thumbs up from our doc, we started the engines. The loadie climbed on board and closed the front door, and the enormous noise dropped to a more comfortable dull hum. We asked for taxi clearance, and were asked to allow the two B-1 bombers to pass us (they were mostly involved in psy-ops, which will, I'm sure, surprise absolutely no one who has been up close to one when it's flying at low level). They were already taxiing and, as they passed, I was struck for the first time by their size; those multi-record-breaking beasts are truly massive, certainly as big as the 767 that had taken me out to Cyprus a few months earlier. (For comparison, the Herc's maximum take-off weight during wartime was 175,000 pounds; the B-1's was 477,000 pounds. Wow.)

Although their flight crew were wearing oxygen masks, we discerned that the lead B-1 had a female pilot. This was something of a rarity, and prompted some comments from our flight engineer about our fragile pilot egos. 'Size isn't everything,' he quipped.

With that, we taxied off and followed the jets to the runway. Although I had seen, heard and felt these jets take off on most days, from our salubrious runway-side accommodation, I was now about to witness and feel the sheer might of these behemoths at full military power from only fifty feet away. We pulled up just short of the runway as the B-1s received their take-off clearance. The noise of their jets reached a crescendo, then the afterburners came in, and the flames that appeared from the back of the jets were astonishing – about twice the length of the aircraft!

Even from inside our noisy C-130, the outside world became subsumed beneath the power of these magnificent aircraft. The noise was immense; up in our own cockpit, we could feel the ground vibrating as they began to pick up speed. They moved slowly at first, then began to gather momentum, before disappearing into the heat haze, still at ground level. We didn't actually see them take off; the next we saw of them, they were already airborne, the four bright lights of their reheat still busy defying physics to get them up there. 'It's like *Battlestar Galactica*!' someone said. Doesn't matter how many times you see something like this, you never, ever lose your sense of awe.

We got clearance, but decided to give it a few minutes before taking off. As every aviator knows, a heavy aircraft leaves some wake turbulence, and if you fly into it, it can be an unseen and deadly killer. And then we were off; Mark pushed the power up, and we accelerated along the runway reaching our take-off speed about two thirds of the way down. (While we had little payload, we had fuelled to the max, to be sure of getting home without needing a refuel.) Once airborne and the gear tucked away, we climbed out over the Gulf of Oman and towards Pakistan. The loadie announced, 'Anyone for a brew?' and we all settled in for phase one of the trip.

It isn't just armies who march on their stomachs. It has

long been a tradition for operational aircrews to eat before going on a mission; even in World War II, the bomber crews would have bacon and eggs immediately prior to a sortie. This meal served a couple of purposes. It kept the crews' blood sugar and alertness up at a good level, and it also gave them some sustenance to keep them going should they get shot down and have to evade capture behind enemy lines. Tea brewed, the loadie reeled off a list of the inflight meals we had for the trip. Forget any notions you might have of what a commercial airline crew are served (the first-class menu, since you ask). This was, of necessity, a very different offering as the galley in the aircraft was rudimentary. Still, loadies always make an effort to do their very best with what they have, the small fan oven on our Herc having produced everything from fluffy omelettes and sausage rolls to brownies and even birthday cakes.

This afternoon, however, the choices were limited. Either chicken or lamb curry, with rice. While my bulk meant I wasn't going to waste away any time soon, I'd missed both lunch and dinner, so lamb curry it was.

As we prepared to enter Afghanistan, it felt weird to be donning body armour and helmets while slotting into the commercial air traffic flying around. Some would probably be tucking into those first-class meals I mentioned earlier, oblivious to what we were doing, and I had a powerful sense of two worlds existing in parallel. We took turns getting kitted up, which helped concentrate the mind on the nature of the world where we were headed; the body armour would hopefully protect us from ground fire, and our flying helmets would hold our NVGs, should we need them for the approach.

The general tone of frivolity on the intercom was more muted now, as we knew we were getting near the business end of the mission. It was becoming apparent that the battery delay had been a godsend. The sun was beginning to set, which meant our initial plan of a straight-in landing in daylight could be swapped for the night landing with NVG spiral descent. Unsurprisingly, everyone seemed happy with this switch.

I contacted the AWACS which was circling over Afghanistan and told them of our intention, which they approved, coming back with the phrase 'Picture clear', which was reassuring: there were no air threats they were aware of. We had fifty miles to run to the LAJAK navigation point when the Pakistani air traffic controller radioed us.

'Radar service terminates at LAJAK. You are cleared to proceed tactical. Good luck, and good night.'

With that, we were on our own in hostile territory.

Conversation during the transit to the Bagram overhead was muted, with only operationally focused, clipped exchanges. There was a significant cloud layer over the airfield, which was a plus: it would help hide our descending racetrack approach. The navigator had already picked a point in space where we should start our descent, and by the time our checklists had been completed by the engineer, we were only ten miles away from it. Time to don our game faces and prepare to bring our collective A game as well; although this approach had become routine over the last couple of weeks, every sortie had its own unique threats and potential pitfalls waiting to catch us out.

Mark and I started configuring the aircraft for the

steep approach. The first stage of flap down – deploying 50 per cent of the available flap – was immediately followed by lowering the gear, with the last stage of flap coming immediately before the descent point; it produces significant drag and, to counter this in level flight, would need more power than we probably had available at 26,000 feet.

We were now at idle power, fully configured and descending in our planned racetrack. I spoke to Bagram using the day's code words for this type of approach and aircraft, which meant they knew our intentions. 'Proceed as requested, call finals,' was the answer.

Worried about the cloud we'd just travelled through, the flight engineer put on the engine anti-icing, but the initial part of the descent was uneventful. Though not for long; as we broke cloud, it was immediately obvious that there was a firefight occurring on the ground just ahead of us, with frequent muzzle flashes and tracer rounds sparking across the landscape – a significant battle was clearly being waged just at the perimeter of the airport where we were about to land. While not an imminent threat to us, because it was mostly small arms fire and was happening far below, it was hugely distracting. It was the first real ground fighting we'd seen.

Thankfully, the firefight area was soon behind us, and the navigator called the turn that would see us line up with the runway and land. Mark had flown us a little higher than normal to keep as far away from the gunfire as reasonably possible. As we spiralled downwards, the navigator called out the track miles, while I called out the optimum altitudes and our difference; we were still a little high as we came around the corner but that was fine – Mark could easily lose that.

Mark now had the runway in sight but, as was routine, we maintained the height and distance commentary (it's difficult to get depth and height and distance in the dark). I called finals to the tower, and as there was construction work on the right, we were cleared to land on the left side of the runaway. This would be a captain's landing as only they are allowed to land on NVGs. Once we were lined up, the navigator called out the transition point from the six-degree descent to the three-degree at about 1.5 miles from the runway landing point and 500 feet above the ground. Mark advanced the throttles, and, as he did so, something in the No. 4 engine instruments caught my eye: the engine power wasn't coming up at the same pace as the others. Just as I was about to communicate that, the engines failed.

Shit.

Muscle memory kicked in and the new words formed automatically. 'Engine 4 failure,' I announced.

Mark was calm. 'Feather it,' he said, 'then ignore.'

I duly did so, which reduced the drag from the failed engine's propeller to almost zero, and lifted my focus back to the outside world, as instructed. We were now passing through 100 feet.

In the periphery of my vision, however, more engine instruments were flashing, indicating that they too were out of their normal parameters.

Holy shit, I thought, as our No. 2 engine failed as well.

Then, a heartbeat later, so did No. 3.

It took zero seconds to sink in that we were now without 75 per cent of our normally available power. I had absolutely no idea what was going on with the engines; neither, it seemed, did the flight engineer, who was suddenly unnaturally quiet, in that 'what the fuck is going on here?' kind of way. We were seconds from either touchdown or becoming an impromptu seventy-ton glider. Big aeroplanes don't glide well, especially when they have little height to recover any speed lost from a sudden drop in power. That little bit of extra height we'd held on to was now going to come in very useful, to put it mildly. Without it, as pilots would say with their tendency to understatement, we would be 'very poorly placed' – i.e. dead.

Mark, taking it in his stride, and making good use of that little extra height and speed, powered up the remaining engine a little, and touched down precisely, if firmly. And, I noted, exactly where we had planned to. He then used the brakes and the reverse on the one remaining engine to slow us (thankfully, Bagram's runway is *very* long), passing another C-130 which was waiting to depart. With one engine running, one engine feathered and the other two windmilling to a stop, we must, I thought, have looked somewhat odd.

We clearly did. 'That's impressive,' came the banter over the radio.

As we came to a halt, Mark and I looked at one another. We had absolutely no idea what had just happened.

'I didn't touch anything,' I said. And in that weird release of tension that comes after a shock, we both laughed; the kind of nervous laugh that can be provoked by an event that has the power to be life-ending.

The flight engineer leaned forward and looked at both of us in turn.

'I know what happened,' he said, contrition in his voice. 'Gents,' he continued, 'I may have fucked up.'

Mark steered us back to the matter in hand. We were sitting in the middle of a runway at an airport with a fire-fight raging to the north and we needed to get back in the game. We were way too heavy to taxi anywhere on one engine, particularly at Bagram's altitude, so given that the flight engineer seemed to have identified the problem, Mark asked us to get another engine going so that we could taxi off the runway.

We started it without any trouble, then taxied to the apron and parked, and the loadie jumped out of the crew door and placed the chocks on the nose wheel. Before we shut down the two engines that were now running, Mark needed to know in more detail what had just occurred. And, most importantly, if it meant we were now grounded.

We were just discussing this when a squadron colleague, Adam, bounded onto the flight deck, desperate to know if we could lift the casualty back to Thumrait. He was acting as a ground liaison in Bagram and was holding the other C-130 just in case; it was here on a separate mission (also classified), which they'd obviously cancel if needed. Mark politely asked him to hang on a minute as we wouldn't know if we could fly anywhere any time soon till we were sure that whatever had happened wasn't going to repeat itself.

The flight engineer explained that he had made some switching errors, which would essentially have starved *all* the engines of fuel were it not for the fact that, unbeknown to us, when we took off for Bagram the fuel control unit for No. 1 engine had an undiagnosed fault. Plus, distracted by the firefight, he had left on the anti-icing, placing an additional bleed load on the engines. So, just when we'd needed lots of power – at 5,000 feet above sea level, as Bagram was – the required elements weren't there to provide it.

Happily, he assured us, we would have no further issues; and Mark told Adam that we could take the casualty all the way to Thumrait.

Despite the flight engineer's assurances, we were understandably still cautious, and so although it would be noisy, we decided to keep operating at ground idle power the engines that we now had running, while we loaded the patient.

It took about thirty minutes for the aeromedical team to transfer the patient to the stretcher; suspended at waist height in the middle of the freight bay, it would give all-round access to the mobile intensive-care bed. The doctor then came up onto the flight deck and knelt down beside Mark to update him. The patient's condition had deteriorated and we now needed to keep the pressurized cabin at sea level.

This wouldn't be a technical problem – in fact, it was easily achievable – but it would mean flying much lower and, with rather a lot of large bits of granite in the vicinity, there were now terrain issues to discuss, as well as tactical. Colliding with the Hindu Kush would hurt.

The navigator quickly worked out a minor dog-leg tweak to keep us safe and we started the other two engines. Then, with a thumbs up from the medical team, we were good to go. Well, goodish. Mark suggested we do a standing start rather than a rolling one, as the crew could set the take-off power against the brakes, and allow the engines to stabilize at that level before releasing them. Although this would cause a more dramatic initial acceleration, it would afford us precious confidence in the engines and the veracity of the flight engineer's admission.

As the power came up, the flight engineer and I kept a close eye on the engine instruments for any anomalies, while Mark focused on the outside, to catch any movement or adverse swing caused by power mismatch. With nothing obvious, we all agreed to go, and Mark let off the brakes.

We lifted off without any issues and climbed away towards the lights of Kabul. We turned left, just before the city and started a long but slow climb to the east down the wide valley and towards Pakistan. We were still in dangerous territory and our lower altitude made us all on edge, not just because of the terrain but also because of the threat from missiles.

Once we neared Pakistani airspace, I tried to contact them on their air traffic frequency, but without any success. We obviously couldn't enter their skies without permission – it would also potentially put us into conflict with other aircraft we weren't able to see – and I was just trying for the umpteenth time when a perky British voice from above pitched in.

'Rodent 15, this is Speedbird 9. Can we be of any assistance?'

It was a commercial airliner – a Jumbo – and I gratefully passed them our estimate for LAJAK and the flight level at which we would be entering Pakistani airspace. Being much higher than we were, they were able to relay our message to the air traffic control, who in turn asked for our present position and gave us a normal transponder code to transmit. We thanked the airliner's crew for their help and let them know we were tactical and would turn on the code at the border so that ATC could see us. The Jumbo pilot, I realized, must be ex-military, because he immediately understood that we didn't want to give our position away just yet, and relayed back to ATC that we would call at the boundary. He then wished us safe flying and was on his way, and I made a note that, should we ever meet in person, I owed him a beer or two.

Finally, we crossed into Pakistani airspace, and relative safety. We could at last declare that we were a medical flight, and request as direct a route as possible back to Thumrait. The controllers, after some vectors, cleared us direct to ALPOR, a waypoint on the boundary of their airspace with Oman. Time to put the foot down.

While we were planning and executing this mission to save a life, there had been an army of people working on the next stage of the patient's journey to the UK. An RAF VC-10 (one of the fastest airliners at this time, only beaten by Concorde) had left the UK with a similar critical care facility on board and was scheduled to land at Thumrait about an hour before our arrival, with a fresh team of medics into whose care the patient would be transferred. It was now just a straightforward matter of delivering them; once we were established on the airways towards Oman we could all thankfully disrobe, remove our armour and helmets and, in my case, change my T-shirt. I was, I can't think why, a sweaty mess.

We landed at Thumrait pre-dawn and were met by literally dozens of people, all with the singular focus of getting
this patient safely back to the UK for life-saving treatment. Like any big organization, the RAF does its fair
share of things inefficiently, but I think most would agree
that one thing we lead the world in is looking after our
injured, and those in desperate need; the evidence was
now in front of us – every stop had been pulled out. I
stood on the apron with Mark, and we watched the
stretcher being unloaded and put into an ambulance for its
short journey across to the VC-10. The aircraft looked the
business; with its auxiliary power unit running, and its
cabin and external lights spilling across the dark tarmac, it
was lit up like the proverbial Christmas tree.

Our nav came out to join us. 'Time for a beer?' he
suggested.

Mark turned to him. 'Perhaps after we've finished the
paperwork for our little, ahem, mishap . . .'

A few nights later, while enjoying the distractions of the
US-built social facility, our flight engineer introduced us to
the B-1 pilot whom we'd heard at the start of our epic mission. She was sharp. And also highly amused.

'What's this I heard about you guys having a complex
about a small one?' she asked us.

Bloody flight engineers.

I never did find out what happened to the patient because
obviously that was confidential, but I am proud to have
been a small part in a massive team that worked to give
them the best chance of survival. The entire organization
that night had one single focus, and that was giving that

soldier the best care available and getting them home. (This was years before the establishment of Camp Bastion, its hospital, and the Medical Emergency Response Teams that were famous for taking critical care to the battlefield in Afghanistan.)

That night, we had a mission, not unlike many others in this book, where we saw lots of people coming together to work through several layers of ambiguity – and sometimes mortal danger – to solve problems and deliver their cargoes. Whether that be parachutists to an ocean liner, mail to a warship, relief supplies to those in need, or a critical patient to intensive care, we have always been relied on to get the job done, and we have.[3]

This is in no small part due to the amazing durability and utility of the aircraft itself, and we always had complete faith that, in that moment of need, Albert would forgive us our sins, and get us out of the shit. Always.

Stanley Beltz, the Lockheed C-130 test pilot, once famously claimed that the C-130 Hercules could be flown and landed on one engine. Many scoffed at that claim, and, though I didn't share their scepticism, neither did I think I would ever personally put it to the test. Thankfully, the claim turned out to be correct.

Sins forgiven, we got to fly another day.

20. Absent Friends

It's often said that bad news travels fast, and it does. Modern communications ensure that any kind of news can be broadcast extremely rapidly; today, with nothing more than a smart phone and an internet connection, it can be disseminated in as little as nanoseconds. But even a couple of decades ago, it didn't take much longer. All that was needed was a reporter to bear witness, and for that reporter to have half-decent comms.

It was no surprise, then, that the first I heard of a plane being shot down in Iraq, it was via a news bulletin on the radio. It was 30 January 2005 and I was on a day off at home, enjoying a brief rest from work when I heard it, my ears pricking up at the words 'transport aircraft'. I immediately phoned the squadron and, after many, many attempts, finally got through to Lyneham, only to be told that, just like me, they had only heard what had been on the news.

Though any crash, any death, is, of course, terrible, I consoled myself that there were many US assets in theatre in the Gulf, and only a small number of RAF ones. Chances were, it wasn't one of our own involved. That consolation, however, was to be very short-lived, as the reports became increasingly specific; it was a confirmed shooting down of an RAF Hercules. This time, I didn't even bother picking up the phone. I climbed into the car and made my way into the squadron.

I walked into the squadron building and looked at the face of the ops corporal. I had only one word in my head. *Fuck*. Any last hope that it was a news reporting error now evaporated. His face said it all. It was our lads. And, given that we only had one in theatre at that time, there was only one crew it could be.

I entered the crew room, where many of the squadron had assembled, some two dozen people. Most were huddled round the television, watching and listening for any nugget of information they could glean. Faces were ashen, concern and fear writ large in their expressions, as everyone tried to cling on to any small hope that the crew had survived. And there *was* hope – at least a small sliver to hang on to. After all, the Hercules was such a robust old beast. Despite the Hercules having completed thousands of missions since arriving at the RAF back in 1967, none had ever been lost in theatre. If any aircraft could take a beating before giving up, our trusty Hercs could.

'Any news?' I asked the squadron warrant officer.

He took a sip of his tea. It looked like everyone was drinking it. Always tea – the universal panacea. He shook his head. 'Nothing concrete,' he answered.

I went behind the crew room bar and poured hot water onto a teabag in my usual mug. There was surely *some* hope. A news report was never the whole story. Until such time as it was confirmed by someone who *did* know the whole story, I was as committed as the next person to practising denial. It was too awful a thing to contemplate otherwise.

An hour disappeared in the blink of eye. I'd had no sense of time passing when I found myself being tapped on the shoulder. It was one of the flight commanders. He pulled me aside, and beckoned me to the locker room, quietly, and without fuss.

'Would you be happy to be the support officer for Sheila Gibson?' he asked me.

Mark Gibson's wife. Mark. As in Mark 'Gibbo' Gibson, air loadmaster aboard XV179.

'Yes,' I replied instantly. 'Of course. Yes, of course.'

It was in that moment that it suddenly became real for me. The very worst that could have happened to the squadron *had* happened. No more hope to be clung to. They were all gone.

Back in the crew room, we were told that an announcement would be made shortly, in both the officers' and sergeants' messes, at 1800 hours, timed to be completed before a press statement went out on the evening news.

Mike Neville, the squadron commander and acting station commander, entered at just after 1800. He was wearing his No. 1 uniform, and the look on his face showed the stress of a man who had gone through hell in the past few hours. I heard him start to speak but, already knowing what was coming, became lost in an anger that hit me so forcefully that I barely heard a word of what he said. Just the cadence of his voice. The thick, eerie silence into which he spoke. The sheer numbers of our squadron family that had been slaughtered.

Once the boss was done, it was as if a collective breath had been exhaled and, seeking solace in kinship on this day of the unthinkable, almost everyone headed back to their respective messes and bars.

Having decided that what I didn't need was beer, I

walked back to the car park and, once in the car, sat for a long time, and cried. I didn't know any of the crew as well as others might have, but thinking about the families who were about to hear the worst news imaginable, the strength of my emotions – uncharacteristic for me – was over-whelming. *That could be Sharon*, I thought. *That could be my own wife and children*. What those families were now going to have to bear was beyond contemplation.

The crew of XV179 were experienced, professional and skilled. Under the captaincy of Flight Lieutenant David Stead ('Steady'), they comprised co-pilot Flight Lieutenant Andrew 'Smudge' Smith; 'Pards', the navigator; Gary Nic, the flight engineer; 'Gibbo', the loadie; Steve, the signaller; and Bob and Richie, the ground engineers. All were old hands, with dozens of detachments under their belts, and had spent many weeks training together.

On 30 January, they had started the day normally, sup-porting their customers by moving them between airfields in Iraq, providing radio rebroadcast for them, and resup-plying them while in the field. Like most of the days that had preceded it, the 30th had been busy. Sunni insurgents had been active in targeting coalition forces over the past few weeks, and the operational tempo in Iraq was relentless.

XV179, callsign Hilton 22, departed Baghdad for the final leg home at 1324 GMT, then climbed to its intended altitude of about 100 feet above the ground. The crew had been joined by two passengers, Squadron Leader Patrick Marshall and Corporal Dave Williams, one of the survival equipment fitters, and it's almost certain that, given the long day they'd had, all would have been looking forward to a cold beer.

A mere six minutes into winding its way northwards across the flat sandy desert of the Sabaa Al Bour to the crew's temporary home at Balad Airbase, Hilton 22 was engaged by a swarm of insurgents with a barrage of small arms fire and rocket-propelled grenades. An RPG struck the right wing. This ignited the fuel vapours in the tanks, which blew off the outer twenty-three feet of the wing, and, the aircraft now being uncontrollable, its fate was sealed.

The last radio call transmitted by the aircraft came at 1330 GMT, from Steve Jones.

'No duff, no duff, we are on fire, we are on fire,' he transmitted.

Hilton 22 impacted the ground shortly after, killing everyone on board.[4]

The first that Mike Neville heard of the loss of XV179 was via a telephone call from his father-in-law, who had seen a newsflash that the UK had lost a C-130 on operations in Iraq. Mike didn't immediately jump to conclusions as he knew from previous roles that press reporting was not always accurate. But he switched on his television and radio to find out as much as he could while picking up the phone to call RAF Lyneham Operations. Notwithstanding the lack of corroboration, he quickly changed into his No. 1 uniform – just in case it had been one of the RAF's C-130s, for he would be leading the response, no matter the squadron. He then drove the longest nine miles of his life, from his family home to RAF Lyneham.

By the time Mike walked into Station Operations his worst fears were realized. Though still unconfirmed, it was clear that the aircraft which had been shot down by Iraqi insurgents was likely to have been a 47 Squadron C-130. A commander's worst day had begun.

There was a fair degree of noise and, understandably, a little bit of shock as Mike arrived in Station Ops that afternoon. Telephones were ringing off the hook and the staff were keen to answer every one of them. That they had little information or indeed sense of how to answer the inquiries was clear, so his immediate task was to reassure the team and set out some parameters. They already had a tried and tested contingency plan in place, so he guided the team to implement it in a calm and measured way. Very quickly, it became more business-like, calmer and more coherent. They put in place a comms embargo until they had more certain information, and agreed lines to take with their operational headquarters at Northwood.

They then went about their business divorced from as much of the emotion as they possibly could be, though it was impossible not to feel emotion at this time as Mike, along with his team, knew the men very well indeed.

Back in Station Operations, details began to emerge from Iraq, Northwood and HQ Air Command. It was clear that it was highly unlikely that there would be any survivors. However, they were still not certain at this time, and Mike decided to wait to announce anything or make any statements to either internal or external audiences until they were as certain as they could be. Informing a relative that their partner, son or brother was dead only for him to be alive, or vice versa, was not something Mike wished to be a party to. He sensed his team agreed.

In the meantime, he gathered his wing commander cohort and asked them to come in also dressed in their No. 1 uniforms, as they had the unenviable task of officially informing the next of kin. At the same time, his flight commanders, 'Cabes' and 'PT', had appointed friend officers, and were in the process of appointing support officers to each family – not a straightforward task. Care had to be taken over getting the right match.

By 1730 or so, they had as definite information as they were ever going to receive, and Mike gave the order to inform the next of kin. He then attended to his own task of informing Steady's wife, Michelle, that her beloved husband had been killed.

The following day, Mike was at the squadron HQ by 0800, where the entire available squadron complement had once again assembled. Now back in his flying suit, he briefed them all on the events of the preceding day. They didn't fly that day, but they did fly the rest of the week, Mike being keen to get the crews back in the air to normalize their lives as much as possible. The squadron did not wallow in loss, or in grief. But celebrating the lives of the lost men was obviously essential, and so they did – with an epic get-together in the officers' mess, where all warrant officers and senior NCOs were invited, along with selected junior NCOs from across the station.

But the job didn't finish with the 'beer call'. Mike had to ensure that the bereaved families had all the support they needed. His responsibility now, as leader, was to help the squadron pull through – dealing with the immediate after-math, overseeing the repatriation of the bodies, the fly-pasts and the funerals, and supporting the bereaved families through everything from press intrusion to eviction notices (controversially, to my mind, on the death of service personnel, surviving spouses who are living on base receive a letter informing them that they have ninety days to leave their married accommodation); and, after a secret visit from the defence minister, rebuilding his wounded squadron, so that the vital work they performed could continue.

Being asked to support Mark 'Gibbo' Gibson's family after his death was an important landmark in my own life. No duty has given me more purpose or pride than doing my (very) modest bit for Sheila, and for her and Mark's daughter, Poppy.

It also caused me to reflect on the sometimes unseen aspects of service life, particularly for families. Marrying into the military brings with it the understanding that you are, of necessity, going to have to 'share' your nearest and dearest with the RAF, and often at very short notice. This was particularly so when you were working on a Hercules squadron, because there was always a significant amount of instability in the schedule – the sign of a busy squadron with competing demands. We would spend long periods away on detachments and devote the time between these keeping our multitude of flying and dropping skills honed. Also, the Herc was largely the first in and last out of any international crisis that the UK decided to support – which, by its very nature, meant we were always on call at short notice and that life was very reactive.

This was tough on all the squadron families, with many personnel having partners who themselves worked, and children at home too. It was rarely easy and often meant missing important life events, which placed an ever-present strain on relationships. Being the partner of a person serving in the military has always been difficult, and many spouses who are at home bringing up children mostly solo describe themselves as operating as single parents, with a partner who comes to visit occasionally. I have always been that 'occasional visitor', rather than the stable family rock, so I cannot comprehend what the partners and families went through during this period. (I would also like to take a moment to thank all of those who stay at home while their partners serve in the UK and overseas. It is not easy, and I do not think that we ever really give them the credit they deserve for this tough job.)

To marry into the military is one thing, however. To lose a partner to their job quite another. While our squadron family could be rebuilt by our exceptional leader following the destruction of XV179, the dead crew members' blood families – their loss so absolute – would have to rebuild themselves.

Mark's wife, Sheila, had already heard about the crash by the afternoon of the day it happened. But just as anyone else might, as she hadn't heard anything officially, she believed that her beloved husband must be okay.

At least till that knock on the door came.

Sheila had been tidying up tea when the doorbell rang,

and as she walked to the front door she could see the sil-houette of a hat. 'Immediately my heart began to thump,' she remembered. 'There was a group on the doorstep, but I focused on Teri.' Teri and her husband Gareth Evans, both of whom served in the RAF, were Mark's best friends. '"Can we come in?" Teri asked. And I remember my response clearly. "I don't think I want to hear this," I replied.'

While Teri took Poppy, Sheila was led into the lounge, and was given as much information as they knew. 'Though I literally do not recall what was said to me, apart from the words "presumed dead". Then everything seemed to plummet around me. I felt cold. I felt sick. I felt numb. There was just one brief moment of clarity when I recog-nized the man kneeling beside me was Eif, one of the 47 Squadron pilots. He was holding both my hands in his. "I didn't realize it was you," I said, and he replied, "I'm so sorry." I remember he had tears in his eyes.'

Hours seemed to pass then, with Sheila having no clear memory of what she did, much less what was happening around her, though she knew Teri must have made that grim phone call to her parents, as her mother and father arrived late that night, her mum's eyes swollen and red from crying. 'And dear Dad wearing his stoical face, the one that always made him look cross. I knew it meant that inside he was hurting.'

Over the next few days, while the necessary processes were taken care of, Sheila existed in a state of suspended animation. 'I couldn't sleep – I would just lie there crying, for hours on end, so much so that my eyes were almost swollen shut, so an appointment was made for me to see my GP for some light sedation. So many flowers arrived. The whole house smelt sweet and fragrant. Though after a while it became almost suffocating. I could barely eat; most of the time I felt nauseous, and my head was swimming constantly – I think I probably zoned out a lot when people spoke to me. I was literally going through the motions.'

But Sheila's daughter was the reason she could carry on. Poppy always went into her parents' bedroom in the mornings, and a few days later she went in and sat on top of Sheila. She held her face. 'Mummy,' she said, 'shall we pretend that Daddy is just away for a long time?'

It was a moment that Sheila would never forget. As they wiped each other's tears, she marvelled at the resilience of children. A few days later, when Mike Neville came to visit, Poppy had been out on her bike with Sheila's mum. The chain had come off, and Poppy's hands were dirty and oily from trying to put it back on again. 'When she came in, she went straight across to Mike to say hello, and used those same hands to pat his cheeks while she did so.' Sheila went from feeling mortified to laughing, which lightened the atmosphere. He took it all in good grace.

The repatriation back to Lyneham was immensely difficult for Sheila. 'Watching those ten coffins coming off the plane was heartbreaking, and later, seeing them lined up in the hangar was one of my lowest moments. My heart broke – it was real – I was in a place I never imagined I would be in. You can't think, you just exist; the pain is indescribable.'

Mark had always loved music. With characteristic thoughtfulness and attention to detail, he'd always ensured the passengers on board during their various missions had something fun to jump out of the plane to. For his funeral, therefore, Sheila decided on two of them – 'Leaving on a Jet Plane' and 'Is This the Way to Amarillo' – to be played while leaving the church and the crematorium.

Sheila chose a small, secluded grave site for Mark's ashes to be buried, and after the vicar had said a few words he left her and her sister Nell, by then her rock, for some private time together. They were both standing there, trying to deal with the tumult of their emotions, when two gunshots rang out, causing them to scream in alarm and fear. The heads of two men then appeared over the hedge which separated them from the adjacent field.

'Sorry,' one said apologetically. 'We're just shooting them rabbits!'

Sheila thought of Mark immediately, and turned to her sister. 'Oh my gosh,' she said. 'Mark will be looking down at this and laughing his head off!'

It was Mark's sense of humour, above all, that would continue to comfort Sheila as, little by little, she pulled the broken threads of her life back together, through the agonies of the funeral, the press intrusion and the conversations with the coroner. Though those days and weeks and months were a blur of pain and wretchedness, it was memories of Mark's laughter, and of the happiness he'd brought her, that would help give her clarity and therefore a modicum of calm. And in the long, laborious process of trying to heal herself, she managed to find the strength to properly honour Mark's memory, by helping their beloved daughter Poppy come to terms with their terrible loss.

'Mark was clever,' Sheila told me. 'Very handsome, so kind to everyone, and generous to a fault. And unfailingly loyal to both his family and his friends. He had such presence too. He could keep a whole roomful of people in raptures telling a story. It really was a sight to behold. Poppy has his mannerisms and his humour, and the same look in her face, the same twinkle in her eye, when something amuses her. She's also inherited Mark's tenacity, in whatever she puts her mind to. She loves travelling too, and always follows Mark's example of packing meticulously. He would be so proud of the young woman she has become.'

The sense of loss, of precious times missed, of aching to have Mark beside her, will always be a part of Sheila's life now. But there is also acceptance. And, despite the pain, the knowledge that she was very fortunate: to have met him, to have married him, to have been the recipient of his love. She also feels blessed that her beloved husband lives on in their daughter, and though she would give anything to have him back with her, that he at least died in service to others, doing a job he truly loved.

For Mike Neville, the loss of men under his command was a defining moment in his military career and an event that would bring new perspective and clarity. From that day on, his definition of a 'bad day' would be a great deal more specific, only applying to one where someone had died. If something had gone wrong but no one had died, then he would think of it as a good day that just contained a few issues – nothing that couldn't be sorted.

Of lessons learned more widely following the loss of XV179, there remains a lack of clarity to this day. Ullage, the vulnerability that the USAF had identified back in the 1970s, can be mitigated by the use of ESF, or explosion suppressant foam. Though the USAF chose to use it on their C-130s, the RAF in 2005 still did not, and it would be easy to blame this loss of life on that factor alone. Many did, and the conversation has rumbled on for many years; though, as is so frequently the case with tragedies like this, there is more often a chain of errors and/or incidents that lead to the critical event – the 'Swiss cheese' effect I mentioned in Chapter 12.

The inquest into the deaths during the crash of XV179 was held by the Wiltshire County Coroner, and the evidence heard was quite telling. It was disclosed that two Black Hawk helicopters had been engaged two hours before the crash at the spot where it later occurred. This intelligence was never passed to the crew of Hilton 22, because it had not been known that the Hercules would be operating in that area. Perhaps if this critical communications failure had not occurred, the fatal engagement could have been prevented. Yes, the final link in the chain may well be that the use of ESF could have prevented the loss of the aircraft's wing and the lack of controllability that followed. But, frankly, we will never know.

What I do know for a fact is that we lost some good men that day. Their sacrifice will never be forgotten.

Flight Lieutenant David Stead – Captain
Flight Lieutenant Andy Smith – Co-Pilot
Flight Lieutenant Paul Pardoel – Navigator
Master Engineer Gary Nicholson – Flight Engineer
Flight Sergeant Mark Gibson – Air Loadmaster
Chief Technician Richard Brown – Ground
  Engineer (Crew Chief)

Sergeant Robert O'Connor – Ground Engineer
(Crew Chief)

Lance Corporal Steven Jones – Communications
Support

Corporal David Williams (RAF) – Survival
Equipment

Squadron Leader Patrick Marshall – (HQ Strike
Command) Passenger

RIP

Postscript. The loss of XV179 was not only a tragedy for 47 Squadron. It was also a tragedy for G Squadron, 22 SAS Regiment, who felt the loss of their SF colleagues keenly. They immediately began hunting down the insurgents responsible. Later that year, after a long intelligence operation supported by the US, the SAS captured some of those to blame. (See Mark Urban, *Task Force Black: The Explosive True Story of the SAS and the Secret War in Iraq* (London: Little, Brown, 2010, p. 73.)

21. Gaddafi

When we think of Libya, our first thoughts are often the links to state-sponsored terrorism and the tragedy that took place on 21 December 1988: the destruction of Pan Am Flight 103 over the Scottish town of Lockerbie. This criminal act placed Libya in the global spotlight, and its leader, Muammar Gaddafi, was implicated in the facilitation of this heinous crime – something that was later independently confirmed.

There is no doubt in anyone's mind that Gaddafi was a ruthless leader, and one who, since achieving power back in 1969, had imposed an authoritarian regime on his country. Oppressed both politically and physically, his people were never happy, yet unable to speak out against his rule. The Arab Spring, however, was about to change everything.

The Arab Spring, which began in 2010, was a peoples' uprising against oppression and corruption across much of the Arab world. It all began in Libya's neighbour Tunisia, in response to widespread government corruption and economic stagnation in that country. Zine El Abidine Ben Ali, the ruler of Tunisia, was deposed, and this emboldened others to protest, causing the movement to quickly spread across Libya, Egypt, Yemen, Syria and Bahrain, with major uprisings and riots taking place.

In almost every country touched by these protests, the

governments countered with robust military action. In some cases, these uprisings ignited large-scale civil wars, and facilitated the rise of Islamic State (Daesh) in Syria and Iraq. In Libya, Gaddafi brought the full might of his military down on the protesters, which led to civil war and what is now known as the 17 February Revolution.

The indiscriminate bombing and shelling of civilians across Libya, but particularly in Benghazi, was described by the UN Security Council as constituting 'crimes against humanity'. It imposed sanctions, and authorized a NATO coalition to enforce a no-fly-zone over the country. The Gaddafi regime was at last beginning to topple, and to play its part in the rescue and protection of civilians, the RAF launched Operation Deference.

By March 2011, the situation in Libya had deteriorated further. The UK government, having followed events from afar, decided its first priority would be to protect its nationals by evacuating oil workers from sites scattered across Libya back to Malta. Three 47 Squadron crews were deployed to achieve this, one of them led by Hercules captain Flight Lieutenant Luke Flemington.

With the media covering the unfolding of these events, Luke was already expecting to be deployed. A couple of days before he and his crew got the call to action, the squadron had sent a couple of aircraft out to Malta and flown into Tripoli to pick up civilians who were being evacuated from the main international airport. This had been authorized by Gaddafi, allowing it to be done in a fairly orderly and safe fashion.

The following day, however, the call suddenly came in, saying there were some British people stuck deep in the southern desert with no support or means of getting out. And with the situation rapidly turning nasty, Luke and his crew were asked to go and rescue them. They were told to get their stuff together, then to go home and wait for the call.

At around 2300 it came. They were back in work at half past four the next morning. Their remit, however, was unclear. They couldn't even pinpoint where the people who needed to be evacuated were, let alone have any idea about the best ways and means to get the job done.

When Luke arrived, he met with the major in charge of the evacuation, a stocky man, who was the archetypal British officer, right down to the requisite moustache. He looked like he had the world on his shoulders. The discussion that then took place wasn't terribly enlightening, it being pretty much left up to the crew to decide what they would do, as it was all 'a bit like the Wild West'.

After sending the co-pilot to go and collect all their personal weapons, Luke had a quick briefing with the intelligence officer. How, given the Libyans' quite sophisticated surface-to-air defence, Luke asked, were they actually going to get into Libyan airspace and, more importantly, safely back out again?

The officer's response wasn't exactly encouraging. In fact, he left Luke with the clear impression that it was probably foolhardy to go at all. However, these people needed to be evacuated, so that wasn't an option, and he had a couple of ideas he thought might work.

Meanwhile, two more aircraft were being readied – both with weapons on board – to support the mission. Yet even by the time Luke's Hercules was on the apron ready to depart, at 0600, they still didn't have any idea where they were going. Everything still felt ad hoc, even shambolic, with various people trying to contact them, both via phone and over the radio, until eventually the station commander called them and told them to communicate with no one but him. He would take charge of coordinating this perilous mission, as Luke already had quite enough to deal with. Luke asked where they were going, but he still couldn't tell them. 'Just get airborne,' he said, 'and head towards Europe.'

They first assumed they'd be flying to Gibraltar, but that soon turned out to be incorrect. Just as they left British airspace they were told to head instead for the NATO airbase at Gioia del Colle, but halfway across France the destination was changed again – they were now to divert to Malta, where they would offload all the non-essential personnel and as much equipment as possible, fill up with fuel, and then make for Libya. By now, they at least had a couple of ideas where the stranded oil workers might be located, so everyone started preparing as they flew, the Major kindly loading Luke's rifle while he sat behind him.

They duly landed in Malta, whereupon everything ground to a halt again, a typical case of hurry up and wait. With patchy and conflicting intelligence about where the people actually were and what was currently happening on the ground, it was decided to allocate the crew some accommodation and wait for a clearer picture to emerge. As a relatively new captain on the squadron, Luke was then swapped onto a later wave of the operation. But even though the task at hand had been allocated to someone more experienced, it was still deemed too risky to fly for now, because it was based on such vague intelligence. Then, at 0500, just over twenty-four hours after the first call, came another. They'd be off – with Luke's the only crew sufficiently rested.

Luke and his crew still had no idea what their immediate orders were – nor, apparently, did anyone else. Every question they asked seemed not to have an answer, until they were finally given a yellow Post-it note, on which were written some coordinates. Luke naturally asked how they were getting there, what they would be doing, and what kind of tactics would have to be used; all perfectly normal questions before such an op. The answer was unequivocal – since no one really seemed to know, their best course of action would be to work it out for themselves. 'Though don't be too aggressive,' the detachment commander advised. 'Try to establish some form of communication with the Libyan authorities.'

Which of course they would. All they could do was their best, after all. Though as they walked out to their Hercules, the last order they were given was, 'From Number 10 – don't come back without them!'

They crewed in, had a brief with the support team, then got hold of Maltese air traffic control. The ATC asked where they were going, to which Luke replied that he wanted to depart VFR (visual flight rules) to the south. They repeated the question, and Luke restated, 'VFR to the south.' There was a bit of a pause while the ATC disappeared for five minutes. When they returned, they had obviously spoken to someone with authority, because they then confirmed that they were cleared to depart VFR to the south – a fairly unusual and vague clearance from a major international airport.

They got airborne again, with Luke's the lead Hercules of three, spaced about thirty minutes apart. The team on board was small now, to allow space for the maximum number of evacuees, while limiting the risk of death to as few of their own side as possible, should they be engaged and shot down by the sophisticated air defences in Libya. The support team did at least include a couple of medics – a reassuring presence amid all the uncertainty. There was also a lot of weaponry on board, just in case they ended up on the ground somewhere and had to fight their way out or protect the passengers, the aircraft or crews. They also had some airborne cover in the shape of an AWACS over the Med, which would stay north of Libya's airspace boundary, and try to give them some sort of real-time picture of what was happening over the country. Although as they neared the border, there was nothing to report. 'Picture clear' to the south was the word from the AWACS controller – a reassuring start.

The intention was to proceed into Libyan airspace at medium altitude, try to contact the Libyan authorities and declare their hand under the terms of Article 51 of the United Nations Charter, which authorized the UN Security Council 'to take at any time action that it deems necessary in order to maintain or restore international peace and security'. That, and Security Council Resolution 1970, which empowered them specifically to protect civilians in Libya, and would allow them to rescue people with disregard for the country's international boundaries. At least, in theory.

Unable to get hold of the Libyan authorities on any frequency, and without any challenge, they just floated in across the border as if it didn't exist – it felt almost a letdown that there hadn't been any challenge. And with the AWACS still calling the picture clear, they headed to the coordinates on the yellow Post-it note.

On arrival overhead of the location there was nothing; just miles and miles of sand. Luke had an old paper chart, however, which showed an old airfield a couple of miles away, so they flew there. As they made a low pass of the strip to check it out, they saw what looked like a few dozen people milling about.

The strip itself was obscured by sand, and it obviously hadn't been used in a long time, but it seemed to have no major debris on it; although, with no one on the ground to assist, it was hard to be sure. They needed more information about the length and condition – there was no point in getting there safely, only to crash off the end of the strip.

Luke flew down the strip at constant speed and at about 100 feet, timing how long it took to overfly the entire usable length, in order to get an indication of how long it was. Satisfied that landing was doable, they touched down at the beginning of the strip, managed to avoid the worst of the sand, and came to a stop with space to spare.

They taxied in, opened the door, and the major jumped out. There were in fact far more than a few dozen people – far too many for them to evacuate – but at least the situation seemed largely benign. The support team then had to process all the guys individually – it wasn't just Brits, but anyone with a foreign passport that wanted to leave Libya, none of whom, of course, they could take. The situation was getting more complicated by the minute; they were sitting on a strip in the middle of Libya, with a state apparatus that would be less than impressed if they knew they were there.

With so many people to process, Luke decided to shut down to conserve fuel. By now, they'd heard from one of the Hercs flying behind them that they'd made contact with Libyan air traffic control, and had been told not to come in. They had pushed on anyway and were now en route to their own set of coordinates. Given the numbers to evacuate, Luke then requested another aircraft to set off. But, soon after, news came in that the third Hercules also met with resistance (and possibly had something launched at it as well), and so the plane he'd just requested turned around and headed back to Malta.

They were now alone, deep in the desert, and needed to get away as quickly as they could. A perimeter was set up, to protect both the aircraft and crews, and they started processing people and loading them. With so many to carry, the evacuees were told to leave all their belongings behind; suitcases, bags, laptops, everything. Fortunately, most complied without complaint, but just like those who try to exit burning airliners with their carry-on baggage, some did not want to leave anything. Fortunately, the solution was easy: people either entered the aircraft minus their personal baggage, or stayed behind and kept their bags company as the aircraft flew off into the sunset. The stack of abandoned baggage quickly grew.

Luke had left the co-pilot up on the flight deck to stay in communication with the AWACS and was now out of the aircraft, trying to maintain a picture of what was going on in the air around them as well as on the ground. Having found out that the third aircraft wasn't coming, he decided to overload their Hercules in order to try and fit more people on, consulting with one of the loadmasters to come up with an estimate of how many they could carry without damaging the aircraft – or, vitally, being able to get airborne at all, and ending up in a smoking hole at the end of the desert strip.

They were just loading the last few British evacuees when a loadmaster became aware of a group of angry-looking men running towards the aircraft. They were clearly not interested in boarding the Herc, and when they got closer, he could see that one of them was brandishing a knife. It soon became clear that his intention was to ground the aircraft, as he began trying to slash the tyres with his blade.

A couple of the ground troops that the major had brought along with them immediately overpowered him. Though they hurt his pride, as they wrestled him unceremoniously to the ground, they didn't injure him physically, and as soon as they let him go, he went off in disgust to get his mates. The benign situation had, at a stroke, turned very ugly.

The Libyans were quick to regroup, and though Luke and the crew had no idea of their motivation, the very large gang of men now approaching in the distance were brandishing all sorts of weapons. With the Herc crew's limited resources, they were going to prove challenging to deal with. It was clear they needed to get out of there as soon as possible, taking as many people as they could.

It was at that point that the AWACS called. There were apparently two unidentified aircraft inbound towards them.

They could well be two Libyan fighters coming to destroy the Herc and all on board, so Luke was forced to decide if they should evacuate the plane and take cover in the desert, despite the threat posed by the mob on the ground.

Based on the reported groundspeed of the aircraft, however, which more closely matched transports than fighters, he decided to stay with the Herc. Fortunately, the strangers turned out to be two German Air Force Transalls, engaged in much the same sort of mission as they were.

One of them had landed and was taxiing in as the 'militia' group were coming down the road, so Luke started his engines and took off with as many people as his aircraft could carry: 156 in all – quite a lot for a Herc. Rolling down the runway at full power, he could only hope that the loadmaster's estimates of the aircraft weight had been correct; it was going to be tight. Still, they managed to get airborne with about 100 feet to spare, and left the Germans to deal with the other evacuees and the baying mob.

The AWACS warned that radar surface-to-air missile systems were active on their way out. The journey home looked like being more complicated than the one they'd made to get there; they had poked the metaphorical bear and it was now wide awake. In order to avoid the threat, Luke decided to go out at ultra-low level, which was obviously riskier in many ways, but safer against the radar and infra-red guided missiles. Using assistance from the AWACS to thread their way between the systems' footprints, they made it out, arriving back in Malta without incident. Shattered, they headed back to their hotel. They had done their bit, or so they thought.

They hadn't. The phone went at around 0530 the next

morning. Could they do the same again today and evacuate more people? So they all got up, washed, pulled on
their combat flying gear and hailed a taxi to go to the airport. It occurred to Luke that they must have looked odd
as they got into their taxi that morning, coming out of a
holiday hotel dressed to go to war, but just as they got to
the airport, the driver said, very seriously, 'Drop a bomb
on Gaddafi for me!'

Given their experiences on the previous day's sortie, they
had more of a discussion around how best to approach
the mission. They eventually decided to fly in formation
this time, and, due to one of the aircraft having been
denied entry the day before, to not even attempt to ask
permission – just press on regardless. The intelligence had
also kicked into high gear. There were exact locations for
those who still needed to be evacuated, which was good
news. Perhaps today would be simpler.

Even the airport was now getting the hang of the mission, and without even having to ask, the aircraft were
cleared to depart VFR to the south, and the controller
wished the crews luck as they got to the edge of the ATC's
radio coverage. Having made contact with the AWACS
on their secure radios, and been assured the picture was
clear, they pushed into Libya and split the formation
south of the border, to head to their individual destin-
ations. Luke and his crew were now on their own again.

Unlike the previous day, the weather was atrocious, with
big dust storms causing greatly reduced visibility – though
by now they were more concerned about the radar threat.
The aircraft they were flying had no means of detecting if
a missile radar was tracking them – or had potentially

locked onto their 'jet' – so the only warning would be via the AWACS.

Having flown to the predetermined location without incident, they found that seemingly no one was there. Not only that, but the rudimentary airstrip had been deliberately obscured by locals, who obviously thought it was a way to try and stop pro-Gaddafi forces from landing and using the facility.

They flew around for a while, until eventually they found a place clear enough to land their Herc, together with some relieved people, very keen to escape. After the previous day's flare-up of violence, they didn't shut down the engines; Luke had taken the maximum amount of fuel possible, in order to allow this. Loading in the desert with engines running is hot, noisy, sandy – essentially bloody awful – but still far better than being engaged by an armed mob of angry Libyans who had no idea whose side you were on. After picking up and processing seventy-six people, they quickly got airborne again.

They headed to another location, but being unable to land safely, Luke was just on the radio to AWACS arranging the northbound transit to exit Libya on the way back to Malta, when the satphone started ringing. Information had been received that people were stuck at another place, further south. Official permission to fly to that location was pending, but Luke quickly realized that waiting for it could mean burning so much fuel that the new mission wouldn't be viable. He therefore decided to set off anyway.

As it was, the permission came when they were almost at the location. But, upon reaching it, they found that it too had been blocked off, with a large truck positioned

across the runway to stop anyone landing. Another communication from the satphone, however, told them that
the obstruction was going to be removed, so when they
saw movement below them, they figured it was people
coming to shift the truck. Unfortunately, they weren't.

Luke wasn't sure whether they were pro-Gaddafi, or
rebels that didn't want pro-Gaddafi people to land. Either
way, as the Hercules came in low over the threshold, the
men decided to raise their weapons and fire at it.

They didn't miss. The Herc took three rounds into the
airframe: one near the main landing gear, which frag-
mented but didn't actually rupture it; one into the right
auxiliary fuel tank; and a third, which went in through the
front windscreen, the head up display, and took a chunk
out of the co-pilot's flying helmet.

The bang was loud, debris from the impact showering
all over Luke's face, while the ground engineer, who'd been
standing behind the apparently hit co-pilot, fell to the
deck, having presumably been shot as well.

Training and experience immediately kicked in. Luke's
first instinct was to get away from the ground and the continuing small arms fire, to secure the aircraft, and to get
medical aid for his stricken crewmates.

They climbed up and out over an empty part of the
desert, where they tried to work out what had happened and
assess the damage. Thankfully, it seemed that neither the
engineer nor the co-pilot had taken the round after all; it had
entered the front of the co-pilot's helmet, missed his head,
and blown part of the back off; it had been the fragments of
that, catapulted into the engineer's face, that had felled him.
They had dodged a bullet, literally, and only by millimetres.

Luke called one of the medics up to the flight deck, but it seemed the engineer was just in shock. Though he didn't have any big cuts, his face had taken the full force of the blast of helmet fragments, so he was understandably very shaken. Luke then got the loadmasters to check everyone on board, and the engineers to check the aircraft as best they could, while he assessed the fuel situation and tried to come up with a plan.

With Egypt to the east, Chad to the south and Tunisia to the west, they didn't have many safe landing options, so they decided to push back towards Malta. Meanwhile, the engineers plugged the hole in the windscreen with some wet paper roll and, with the noise level on the flight deck back to something more bearable, everyone calmed down. Yes, they were losing a little fuel from the right auxiliary tank, but otherwise all indications appeared okay.

Everything was quiet in terms of the radar threat too – unlike the previous day, nothing had been turned on. So they elected to fly at medium altitude and so try to conserve some fuel. Malta was a long way off, and getting there was now not necessarily assured.

Luke had two plans running around in his head: what to do to prepare the aircraft for a possible crash landing in Malta with damaged gear; or, if they couldn't make it that far, what to do to best prepare them for a ditching in the Mediterranean. Neither scenario was ideal. All they could do was fly in as fuel-efficient a way as possible, in a slow climb out of Libya and over the sea in order to gain as much altitude as they could, in the event of the engines becoming starved of fuel and shutting down.

The AWACS shadowed them, flying near once they

were north of the border, so that if the worst happened they could coordinate a rescue. Luke also decided to get rid of all the flares; he was concerned about the state of the main gear and knew a collapse during landing might produce a jolt that would set them all off, causing a sub-optimal situation for anyone inside the aircraft.

Malta finally appeared in the window of the Herc and, as the speck of an island started growing in size, Luke's confidence in making it down safely grew also.

At last they touched terra firma, and once they'd taxied and rolled safely to the apron, Luke patted the aircraft instrument panel. As ever, Albert hadn't let them down.

That night, they got quite drunk in Valletta.

During the siege of Malta in World War II, the island was protected by three RAF Gloster Gladiator aircraft, which were nicknamed Faith, Hope and Charity. Hope and Charity were sadly lost in the fighting, but the one that remained, Faith, can still be found there today. Though sadly minus her wings, she still sits in pride of place in the National War Museum in Fort St Elmo, in Valletta.

All Hercules pilots have complete faith in their aircraft, but during Luke's sortie perhaps the spirit of Faith was also flying alongside them, helping ensure their safe passage back to Malta. What will never be forgotten, though, was their expertise and bravery. In recognition, honours and awards were bestowed on several crew members, including their captain. For his valour and courage, Flight Lieutenant Luke Flemington was presented with the Distinguished Flying Cross.

22. First In, Last Out

Khartoum, 1923

The sun is beginning to fall below the horizon, filling the sky with a red and orange glow. It's a hue unique to Africa, a molten meteorological marvel, and Flying Officer Horace Slater thinks he might just have to pinch himself. Here he is, flying an Airco DH-9A, a tried and tested biplane, and, even better, he is en route to his new home in Sudan, to join the much talked-about 47 Squadron. Could life for a young pilot get any finer? The noise from the 400 horsepower Liberty engine is deafening, it's true, but it would take a lot more than that to spoil the moment.

He flies on northwards, the Blue Nile 500 feet below him now a river of fire, and the dunes of the Jebel Awlia just becoming visible, their long shadows casting wave patterns across the desert. In the shimmering distance, he can see the fabled city of Khartoum, and beyond that, somewhere out there in the drifting haze, lies Wadi Seidna Airfield, his destination.

Something catches Horace's eye on the banks of the river up ahead. It is a train, also heading towards Khartoum. Full of reckless derring-do — this is, after all, a career highlight for young Horace — he comes up with an idea. He's been flying for hours now and is in the mood for a little fun. Perhaps a practice bombing run on the train is in order? And after that, maybe a covert low-level approach to the airfield at Khartoum to surprise his chums, doubtless already knee-deep in a gin and tonic or two.

The infernal noise abates as Horace pulls back the throttle and pitches the aircraft towards the train, and with it firmly in his sights now, he presses ahead with his 'attack', getting closer and closer to the steam-powered caterpillar that is snaking its way through the desert. 100 feet. Horace smiles to himself as he continues to descend, knowing the terrified train driver is going to cack himself when he roars over the train, just a few feet above the engine, at full power.

Fifty feet. Horace is just a hundred yards from the rear of the train now. A bit of juice, perhaps. He pushes the throttle. Nothing. Just a cough and a splutter as the engine tries desperately to produce power. It has been at idle for a while now, and in his eagerness to 'splash' the train, Horace realizes he may just have royally screwed himself.

He certainly kicks himself. The Airco's spark plugs are renowned for getting oily. Not a problem at 200 feet, but now he's down at fifty . . . Uh-oh. He veers away from the rear of the train, now becoming very large in his front view.

'Come on . . .' he mutters. 'Come on, old girl. You can do it!'

But can she? He can hear the Airco's engine trying very, very hard. More fuel. More power. More everything. More faith. *Then, just as he's sure he's going to be landing ignominiously in the desert, the engine catches just in time to sail gloriously alongside the carriages, at no more than ten feet from the ground.*

A cry goes up, and both passengers and train crew shake their fists furiously. Horace's heart is now thumping wildly in his chest. Far from scare them, all he's actually achieved is to terrify himself.

But has he? No, of course not. He's with 47 Squadron, isn't he? He mentally recalibrates, and reminds himself of their motto: Sans Peur. *Without Fear.*

Though when he joins his colleagues, all of them oblivious to his embarrassing near-debacle, it's the best bloody gin and tonic he's ever tasted.

*

Horace could never have imagined that, in the summer of 2023, almost exactly 100 years later, his squadron colleagues would also be approaching Khartoum. But this time, rather than risking humiliation from some reckless buffoonery, they would be facing mortal danger.

Sudan, by any standards, is a dangerous place to visit. Since gaining its independence over sixty years ago, it has been no stranger to conflict; it has seen foreign invasions and resistance, ethnic tensions, and religious and resources disputes, as well as no less than fifteen military coups. This is a country that, though it has seen periods of parliamentary democracy, has largely been under military rule, which has led to the violent deaths of almost two million people, and the displacement of many millions of others, particularly in the Darfur region.

The situation in early 2023 was that even the army was split into two main factions, with the official Sudanese Armed Forces (SAF) and the paramilitary Rapid Support Forces (RSF) having divergent visions for the country. Or, more accurately, their leaders did. The former friends General Abdel Fattah al-Burhan and General Hemedti, who had jointly led a previous military coup in 2019, were now fighting each other.

In early April, RSF forces deployed to key sites across the country, and especially Khartoum, a precursor to a full-scale attack on SAF bases and Khartoum Airport. And so the cycle that had blighted this beleaguered nation for decades began again, as the SAF fought back with everything they had, resulting in Khartoum becoming the front line for the war. From the off, it was incredibly bloody. And by the summer, the UK was prompted to evacuate the embassy staff and British nationals.

The stage was set for 'International Rescue' to enter the fray, and for 'Thunderbird 2', due to be imminently sun-setted, to make a last, heroic, *Sans Peur* appearance.

There was just one small complication. They didn't have permission.

'Ascot 9909, your current track will see you enter Sudan airspace in fifty miles,' boomed the voice of the Egyptian ATC in Dai's headset. 'You are advised not to enter this airspace.'

'We are a military aircraft operating with due regard,' his co-pilot calmly responded, 'and will be continuing on our current track.'

Dai knew that the Egyptians knew exactly who they were. Only a few hours earlier, they had departed RAF Akrotiri and crossed over Cairo on their mission towards Khartoum. The ATC was just making the point that they were on their own now. And as they crossed into Sudan airspace, the controller's closing 'good luck' said it all. They had entered hostile territory without an invitation. It was probably going to be a long night.

Despite knowing the airport had already been secured by French troops – or so intelligence had told them – the 47 Squadron C-130J crew were under no illusions about their welcome from the locals. They had been tasked to be the first aircraft to land in Sudan and set up a secure pro-cessing facility for the evacuation of entitled personnel. To achieve that, their Herc was fully laden. It carried the RAF Regiment for security, RAF Police for passenger processing, and parachute and commando engineers for the airfield repairs that it was envisaged would almost certainly be needed, since the runway appeared from imagery to be in very poor condition.

It was, at least on paper, a pretty simple mission. Still, it always paid to be cautious, so the loadie, Kit, fired up all the self-protection systems, and Dai told the team to put on their body armour and to get the troops down the back to do the same.

As they neared the airport, he looked out of the window towards Khartoum. He could see very little, though, not only because it was dark, but because there was also a total absence of any cultural lighting; there was obviously no power in the capital. Still, donning NVGs as they began their descent at least confirmed they were in the right place. Though only barely visible, the Nile was snaking its familiar way through the landscape towards the blighted city.

Dai's co-pilot was also wearing his NVGs now. 'Tracer in the distance,' he reported – the first tangible sign of the ongoing hostilities. But it was a long way off and no immediate threat.

'Get the airfield on the radio,' Dai told him.

He duly did so. 'Wadi Seidna. This is Ascot 9909, a British C-130 . . . thirty-five miles to the north, requesting airfield information.'

Silence.

He tried again, then again, on a couple of different frequencies. The ominous silence continued.

'Leave it,' Dai said, after five minutes of fruitless effort. 'Let's just get this thing on the ground, and then sort it out.'

Out of the window, the area of the airfield was now

visible, the moon casting long shadows over the dunes as they descended and Dai positioned the Herc for the final run-in to Runway 23, settling at 500 feet. Ordering 100 flap, he felt the drag and pitch change, the former countered by the fistful of extra thrust he applied. The aircraft was heavy. In fact, very heavy. They had taken off from Akrotiri a mere twenty-eight kilograms below the maximum military operating weight, a new personal best for all the crew. But the aircraft felt just as it always did, solid and stable.

'Welcome to Sudan,' Dai quipped on the intercom as he pulled the throttles back into reverse and slowed the aircraft to a taxi speed.

They had planned to do a 180 turn at the other end of the runway, ground the ramp, allow all the troops to offload, then power up again and disappear back into the night sky, leaving them to process the passengers for the Airbus A400M that was scheduled to arrive four hours later. They duly began to execute the plan, the aircraft drifting across to the right-hand side of the runway, and slowing to a walking pace as they approached the end.

'Ground the ramp,' he told Josh, the other loadie, feeling the familiar dip as it touched the tarmac, and while the troops and equipment were offloaded onto the grass beside the runway, the three crew on the flight deck were once again heads down, programming the computers for the planned weights and routing on departure.

Ten minutes passed, and Dai was still engrossed when he noticed a car pulling up out of the corner of his eye, right at the front of the aircraft. The man who emerged from it was wearing a flying suit, and gesticulating in a manner that suggested he was less than pleased by the C-130's unannounced presence. Also, he didn't look very French.

'We need to get him to move his car,' Dai said on intercom, to nobody in particular.

'Leave it with me,' came Kit's answer. 'I'll go out and have a word with him.'

'Ramp is clear of the ground. We are closing up at the back,' added Josh.

In his combat flight gear, with helmet, body armour and NVGs, Kit looked a little like someone from a Tom Clancy movie as he approached the still-gesticulating driver and, in a mark of respect, showed due deference before offering his hand.

It was at this point that, from the flight deck, Dai spotted a couple of technicals approaching at speed on both sides.

This had now escalated significantly beyond a single irate man with a car. They, whoever *they* were, now had the upper hand, as angry people with big machine guns generally tended to.

'He wants us to shut down,' said Kit over the intercom.

'Tell him we're leaving,' Dai said. 'See if that placates him.'

He watched as Kit relayed this to the man and one of the soldiers from the technicals, who was now standing glowering beside him, holding his AK-47 rather menacingly. And looking enthusiastic about the possibility of using it. These were tense times, and Dai didn't need to wait for the answer from Kit. It was obvious from the shaking of heads and furious pointing that they really, really wanted them to shut down.

'Offer him some cash to get his car out of the way,' Dai suggested. But not only did the offer not improve the dynamic, the man began to angrily gesticulate even more. Worse still, an airport fire truck had now driven up as well, and parked across the front of the aircraft.

Which kind of sealed the deal. The mood was growing ever more dangerous, and there was no point in flogging a dead horse. Perhaps shutting down was a good plan after all.

Though not shutting down completely. 'Tell him we'll shut down the engines but not the GTC,' Dai asked Kit to relay. 'Say we need to keep that running to start up again.' *And I don't care what the answer is*, he thought. *That's definitely all that's going to happen.*

They duly did so, and their short, ten-minute, engines-running offload visit to Sudan had just been extended.

Happily, this seemed to placate the angry airman; Dai could see from the flight deck that he looked much less red, shouty and pointy. Kit had also established the reason for his anger; it appeared that, despite the 'intelligence' they'd been given, the French had not yet taken control of anything.

So Dai could, at least, see the man's point; that it was not okay that a huge, foreign military transport plane had just landed and disgorged lots of armed soldiers at *his* airport. It wouldn't have gone down well at Heathrow either. It also perhaps explained why none of the French-supplied communications frequencies had worked.

Dai unstrapped and went down the stairs and out of the crew door to speak to Kit and the man in the flying suit.

'*Assalaam alaikum,*' he greeted the man.

'*Wa 'alaikum assalaam,*' the man replied.

With his schoolboy Arabic now exhausted, Dai had no choice but to switch to English to explain that he was the captain, and ask the man what he wanted them to do. He was relieved to notice that shutting down the engines had indeed greatly changed the man's demeanour, and, as a result, the menacing-looking troops on the back of the technicals, though still potentially very hostile, didn't look quite as trigger-happy as they had five minutes previously.

It was quickly established that nobody at the airfield had known they were coming, so the reaction to their arrival now made a bit more sense. And though the plan was ideally still to leave as soon as possible, it didn't seem to be a vibe the Sudanese would be keen on. In fact, what they wanted – and they didn't look much like they were up for dissent – was for the aircraft to taxi to the apron, and to sort everything out from over there.

Dai headed back to the flight deck. It was clearly time to phone a friend.

'Hey, boss, it's Dai in Khartoum,' he told his squadron commander back in London. 'You're not going to believe this . . .'

He then explained what had happened and that he felt it would probably be best if they stayed put for the time being, clearing the runway for the approaching A400M and acting as a temporary on-site base for the evacuation. It was hardly as if they had any choice, after all.

The man in the flying suit now seemed a little happier. At least, he called off his technicals, and they duly backed up a bit, allowing them to start on the long, slow taxi to the apron. The man in the car led the way out front, and the technicals trailed behind, presumably to ensure that the crew on the flight deck didn't have a sudden change of heart.

As they came onto the apron, they were faced with three big hangars. The car drove towards the front of the one on the left, and Dai followed, taking care not to hit anything as they squeezed carefully through the almost too tight gates – something that would definitely be an issue for the even wider A400. He made a mental note of this to pass on to the A400 crew. He stopped and applied the brake.

'Josh, get the ramp on the ground,' Dai ordered. 'Kit, get the chocks in. Then we'll shut it down.'

Once that was all done, there was silence.

Kit returned to the flight deck, and having been given the actual tower frequencies from the man in the flying suit, Dai jumped on the satphone to London and passed them on, along with the state of the runway and the fact that the Sudanese would like to park the A400M on the apron too. He then decided to go and see how he could help with the evacuation.

The RAF Regiment had already set up a security perimeter around the aircraft and the RAF Police were negotiating with the Sudanese military to get temporary use of some hangar space in which to carry out their screening of the evacuees. Back outside now, Dai noticed Kit was chatting to some troops sitting on the ground at the edge of the parking area.

'I've found the French,' Kit told him as he wandered across to them. 'They're awaiting orders and certainly didn't have any interest in the airfield. Or anything that we're doing,' he added, shrugging.

A pretty *laissez faire* approach, Dai mused. But *c'est la guerre* . . .

They were both walking back to the aircraft when they heard the unmistakable growl of the 'Grizzly': the A400 was nearby. They watched it land and were relieved to see it not get quite the same robust, gun-toting reception that they had; it simply turned right off the runway and taxied to the ramp. There was no hiding it now: the Brits had arrived.

The sun was coming up too. The heat became oppressive really quickly, making it tough for all the teams to function, especially the parachute and commando engineers they'd brought in, since they were the ones grafting out in the sun. The runway was austere at best, and they immediately started repairing the worst of the surface to prevent aircraft damage for the inevitable follow-on operations.

By early evening, things had started to have more structure, and the team had already completed processing the first evacuees for their flight back to Cyprus. To help the evacuation effort, they took thirty on board the Herc, then followed the Airbus down to the runway and departed over the Nile, flying northwards into the blood-red sky just as the sun was setting.

During the flight, a couple of the passengers visited the flight deck, one of whom was the Norwegian ambassador. His face was ashen, he was in shock, and he had the look of a man tested to his limits – one who had survived the toils of a long and dangerous journey, and, having phoned home from the aircraft to let his loved ones know he was safe, was now almost too emotional to speak. Looking at his expression brought home to Dai how important this mission was and the impact that it had on the lives of those they had rescued from such a desperate and bloody conflict. He didn't need to speak. Nothing more needed to be said.

All that was needed, once they were safely back at Akrotiri, was, just like Horace Slater before him, a nice, cold, post-mission G&T.

The evacuation of Sudan continued after the first night's 'excitements'. Over a period of days, a total of 2,467 entitled personnel from twenty nations were flown out in some forty-seven sorties, thirty-four of which were at Wadi Seidna. While the focus of the mission was always to save lives, it also saw the first operational battle-damage repair of any runway since the Falklands campaign in 1982. The parachute and commando engineers poured 7 tons of asphalt and 1.25 tons of concrete and applied 790 litres of bitumen paint to keep the airfield open. A real feat in the relentlessly searing temperatures.

On the last night of the evacuation, Dai returned to Wadi Seidna, as the captain of a C-130, with Kit also on the crew, flying the very last aircraft to leave. He witnessed the Royal Engineers hand the airfield back to the Sudanese military, proud that they had left it in a better state than they had found it. Friends now, they all shook hands with their Sudanese counterparts, boarded Albert and departed Khartoum for the final time.

As Dai climbed away from the airfield, he was acutely aware that he and his crew had the privilege of flying the last operational sortie of an RAF Hercules ever. It also seemed fitting that it had been a 47 Squadron crew who'd flown the last aircraft to leave Khartoum, bringing to a close, at least for the time being, a distinguished squadron history, and a long one. It had spanned an entire century, and had come to an end where their predecessors had first set down roots, at the confluence of the White and Blue Niles. Even at the eleventh hour before the aircraft's retirement, and just like all those who had gone before them, they were First In, Last Out. *Sans Peur.*

Epilogue

The year 2023 saw the end of two amazing chapters in the history of the RAF: the cessation of Hercules C-130 operations, and the laying up of 47 Squadron as an operational entity. These events were marked on 30 June 2023 by a formal dinner at the RAF Museum in Hendon attended by over 500 aircrew and guests. A more restrained celebration of the C-130 and those who have made it all work from 1967, this formal black-tie function better matched my current vintage than the raucous parties of 47 Squadron legend . . .

Many of the contributors to this book were at the dinner and we took time to reflect on the spirit and expeditionary nature of the fleet, from the first day that it entered RAF service to the last. The old girl went out with a bang, flying operationally up to the line and taking centre stage on an evacuation from Sudan. We also pondered which of the exuberant youth at this event would be outside the boss's office in the morning with a formal letter of apology. Age may have got us, but nothing much changes on the squadron.

The C-130 will be replaced in operational service by the Airbus A400M, another large turboprop transporter. This aircraft started out as an idea in 1982 when the Future Military Airlifter joint venture between the French, Germans, Brits and Lockheed Martin was established with the purpose of finding a replacement for the C-130 Hercules and C-160 Transall.

As with many collaborative projects with many user-requirements, the complexity and politics meant that Lockheed Martin dropped out and went on to develop the C-130J. The remaining partners in the consortium were joined by further countries, and in 2013, after failing to meet many national requirements, and being hugely over budget, the aircraft finally entered service, with the RAF receiving its first in late 2014.

The RAF has received twenty-one of these aircraft to date, but its entry into service has been dogged with several operational and engineering challenges. That aside, the aircraft is hugely capable and is a great addition to the RAF airlift capability, and those who fly her really love the aircraft. I was very lucky to have an opportunity to fly the A400M simulator and it is a joy to fly at low level; it feels a little like a caged lion, just waiting to leap out and bound around like a fighter. The fly-by-wire flight controls are similar to those employed on airliners such as the A380 and A350 which are from the same stable. Indeed, those who fly either of those aircraft will feel at home on the A400's flight deck, as it is based on the architecture of the A380 systems. During our simulator sortie, we flew at low level and then pulled up to rendez-vous with a tanker, an Airbus A330 MRTT, of course. Tanking was a relatively easy skill to master with the A400; not having the pressures of needing the fuel to get home did help. Being able to do this in the high-fidelity simulator was amazing.

The A400M is, in my opinion, yet to come of age.

Though not a direct replacement for the C-130, it is what it was originally designed to be: a tactical airlifter that bridges the gap between C-130 and C-17. It will serve the RAF and the nation well, but it will never be adored with quite the same passion that those who flew the C-130 felt for their aircraft. Just as so many of the airliners that have recently replaced the Boeing 747 will never reach the legendary status as the Jumbo (nor be held in such public affection), the same applies to the C-130 and the A400M.

The last flight of Hercules was a little more moving than I thought it would be. I watched the aircraft fly over the Wiltshire countryside from afar, as that oh-so-familiar noise droned across the landscape. I had wondered if I should go – my C-130 days all seem very long ago now – but I am so glad that I did. As the familiar sound reverberated along the valley, I reflected on having had the privilege of officially operating in three of the five crew positions on the aircraft, and of having a reasonable, yet unofficial, go at the other two – although Loran-C navigation was beyond me.

Seeing my old ride brought up a kaleidoscope of emotions, and lots of smiles, as I remembered the fun times, and some of the ludicrously silly things we used to get up to, thinking we were largely invincible. Ah, the naivety of youth . . . This was mixed with a few tears, I'll admit, of both joy and sadness, as I remembered the last time I had seen friends and colleagues who had made the ultimate sacrifice doing what they loved so much. They, the aircraft and those legendary nights out will all live on in our collective hearts.

*

This book has been about the C-130 Hercules in RAF service, but none of these great stories about amazing people doing extraordinary things (often with little more than their grey and green four-engined love machine) would have been possible without the camaraderie and spirit of those who flew in it. For at least the last thirty-five years, the C-130 has been continuously involved in operations, and this high-tempo, high-risk flying, which relies on absolute trust, forms relationships and bonds with colleagues that you will not find in any other work environment. Although I have been away from this family for almost fifteen years, and now feel a little like the awkward uncle who stands in the corner, being a small part of the C-130 story in the RAF is something I am very proud of.

Though both the C-130 and 47 Squadron have retired from RAF service, a very rich legacy remains. Just as the squadron standard is laid up in the rotunda of the RAF College for safekeeping, so the badge and all the history will lie dormant, until another opportunity to serve emerges. It seems fitting that the journey ended where it had come of age, in Khartoum. The C-130 Hercules may have been sunsetted, but memories of 47 Squadron will live on in those who have had the privilege to be part of this band of vagabonds and pirates, until it is time to rise again in a new guise.

I am sure those who will write new stories in the future will do so with the same vigour and spirit as those who preceded them.

Afterword

By Wing Commander Simon Footer
MBE RAF (Retired)

It has given me immense pleasure to be involved with this book of memorable stories about the RAF Hercules and its crews. I know I share this view with all the other contributors to its chapters. At the heart of all these stories are the iconic aircraft and the many people involved with its operation. The Hercules has been an incredible workhorse, the backbone of tactical air transport for over half the life of the RAF, involved in virtually every operation over the past fifty-seven years. 'First In, Last Out' was always the mantra, but it really is true. Hercules flown by crews of 47 Squadron operated in and out of Sudan at the eleventh hour of the aircraft's professional life; they deployed the UK protection force for the airfields and airlifted hundreds of entitled British nationals to safety in Cyprus and back to the UK. Within hours, the Hercules was there, ready and waiting for clearance to get on with its job. I heard one of the evacuees comment on what a relief and comfort it was to hear the familiar sound of Hercules engines humming away as he got to the airfield to load up. This was the very last operation the Hercules ever undertook – the last of dozens and dozens of operations over its illustrious RAF service.

I feel a strong bond with the Hercules, having been

involved with the aircraft for over twenty years of my career (1982–2003). It played a significant part in my life and that of thousands of others. The RAF Hercules has not just been an airframe, it has been a way of life for all those involved. RAF Lyneham was the home of the Hercules for almost five decades, and every single person there supported the Herc fleet in every respect. These included all the aircrews, engineers, movers, RAF Police, medics, air traffic controllers, mess staff, gym staff, educators, MT drivers, padres, civil service staff and our amazing 47 Air Despatch friends from the Army – all focused on keeping the Herc airborne and doing its job. I'm sure this was the same at RAF Brize Norton, after the closure of Lyneham meant the Hercules moved there. Of course, our families played a huge part in supporting the Herc force and its servicemen and women. Judging by the attendance we always got at station and squadron families' days, and membership of Hercules squadron associations, our families enjoyed life in the Herc community as much as we did – it was palpable. I remember my wife, Jane, commenting that, whenever I was away, she drew comfort from hearing the Hercules on the airfield four miles from our house in Compton Bassett doing engine-runs in the middle of the night. The feeling that all was well and the Herc and its people were always there. In fact, I would extend this feeling of family to the local towns, villages and communities such as Royal Wootton Bassett, Lyneham, Calne, Carterton next to Brize, and many more. All the locals have been proud to see and hear on the news what 'their' Hercs have been up to. As a result, the Hercules force always had great spirit and morale, which probably accounts for all the fun we had at home and overseas over all those years. What a story – what a legacy.

I won't list a bunch of statistics and achievements of the great workhorse, as you can read these elsewhere. All I will say is that the stats are hugely impressive and surely cannot be matched by any other aircraft the RAF has operated in its history. The Herc was superb to fly, reliable, relatively simple to engineer and always felt safe – climbing on board was like putting on a warm glove, a comforting place. Albert would look after you. Considering the hundreds of thousands of hours of risky low flying, and flying in dark, inhospitable and dangerous places, and in hazardous and dodgy weather at times, it's a tribute to the rugged beast and its crews that we had so very few accidents and crashes over the years. Sadly, when those rare tragic incidents have occurred, we have lost whole crews of friends and colleagues, which is hard to deal with and has always had a huge impact on the families and Herc community. We of course salute every one of those brave individuals. We will always remember them.

So there we have it – what a story – what an aircraft – what a great bunch of people. I don't think we could have had more fun if we'd tried – a sentiment echoed by so many Herc people.

Yes, it is the end of an era – no new stories – but the people live on and will continue to tell the incredible and often very funny tales and hopefully write some of them down.

Goodbye, Albert – you lived up to your heroic name and now deserve a good rest!

Si Footer
May 2024

The C-130 HYMN

Standing midst the cargo, got no place to
  sit,
Watching the hydraulics dripping oil upon
  your kit,
T'was there that you whispered tenderly
Why did we leave the Beverley,
To fly the C-130, to try to work the Herc.

Some of us wear khaki, some of us wear blue,
All of us have ulcers from the rations from
  the 'Q',
There must be a way with much less strain
To get the troops to Salisbury plain,
Why don't they go by taxi, it's cheaper
  than the Herc.

Orders came for action from the Air Support
  Command,
Ops have lost the signal, but the matter's
  well in hand,
We've all been issued with K.D.,
So Norway must surely be,
So fly with Forty Seven, and lurk around
  the Herc.

Bahrain or Bermuda, all the same to me,
No matter where we wander we wind up A.O.G.,
Just give that cowling one more shove
Then we can hack it in much gov
The Charlie leaves one dirty, there's murk
  upon our Herc.

Roaring down the runway, throttles open
  wide,
Co-Pilot's sleeping, he came just for the
  ride,
Engineer can't find the nosewheel pin,
We think he's gone and left it in,
The gear just simply will not, fold up into
  our Herc.

Circling the airfield, coming in to land,
Navigator's screaming, he can't tell sea
  from sand,
Quartermaster's fiddling the declaration
  form,
The Captain wishes he'd not been born,
A bottle and two hundred, our perk upon the
  Herc.

GERRYATT & WALLEN

Publisher's Notes

6. Long Way South: The Birth of the Flying Petrol Station

1 MoD rules prevent the author from sharing details of a plan
during the Falklands War to use the Hercules to launch an
SAS raid against Rio Grande, the air base in Tierra del Fuego
from which Argentine Navy Super Étendard jets flew deadly
Exocet missions against the British Task Force. However, Sir
Lawrence Freedman's book *The Official History of the Falklands
Campaign*, commissioned by the British government and
published in 2005, records that, on 13 May, Britain's Chief of
the Defence Staff proposed 'offensive action' that would
involve 'getting around 55 men close to Rio Grande in Hercules aircraft and, after they had destroyed the Super
Étendards, getting them out again'. The following day Margaret Thatcher's War Cabinet approved the plan, and a signal
was sent from Northwood HQ to Admiral Sandy Woodward
aboard HMS *Hermes*, telling him that this 'bold move could
significantly tilt the balance in our favour'. Harry Burgoyne
was one of the pilots who trained for the mission. On 20
May the Hercules crews received orders to launch their two
aircraft assault against Rio Grande from Ascension Island.
They were, as one of the pilots said later, 'all loaded up and
ready to go' when the planned operation was cancelled.

15. Parachutes

2 On 13 January 2021 the three RAF Hercules flew from
Ascension Island to West Africa to conduct its first British
mass-parachute airborne operation for over sixty years. Again,
MoD rules prevent the author from sharing the details in
Hercules; the RAF website records that Operation SILK-
MAN was 'the last phase of the British military action to
support the Government of Sierra Leone [in] the successful
campaign against the Rebel United Front' and was intended
to send a clear message to the Rebel United Front and their
Liberian backers, who were threatening the stability of the
country, that 'British Forces could arrive at any time and
place and conduct aggressive military operations if required'.

19. A Life in the Day Of

3 The MoD was unwilling to allow the author to acknowledge
the role played by the Hercules during Operation PITTING,
the dramatic evacuation of Kabul in 2021. The then Chief
of the Air Staff, Air Chief Marshal Sir Mike Wigston, was
more eager to celebrate their achievement in a speech delivered in September of the same year. It was, he said, 'the
largest Royal Air Force airlift since Berlin in 1948. Up to five
C-17s, three Voyagers, two A400Ms and two C-130Js were
involved on any day, and we flew eighty-four sorties out of
Kabul, we supported people from thirty-eight countries. We
saw bravery, immense good judgement, professionalism and
overwhelming compassion. As an Air Chief, I could not have
been more proud of our Service and I am sure I speak for

everyone in this room in saying that. We rightly celebrate the role of our people on that mission, but the operation [. . .] demonstrated yet again why Hercules has been our workhorse for over fifty years.' But not for much longer.

20. *Absent Friends*

4 XV179 was not the only RAF Hercules lost during the long wars in Afghanistan and Iraq. These include ZH876, a Hercules C-130J lost in Iraq in 2007, and XV206, a Hercules C1 lost the previous year. MoD rules prevent the author from writing about either, but Bob Ainsworth, the Minister of State for Defence, told Parliament in 2008 that the official Board of Inquiry had established that:

On 12 February 2007, Hercules C-130J ZH876 was on a routine operational passenger flight to conduct a roulement of troops, landing at a tactical landing zone (TLZ) in Maysan Province, south-eastern Iraq. As the aircraft was about to touch down, it was subjected to an improvised explosive device (IED) attack which damaged the aircraft. The captain brought the aircraft to a stop and ordered the aircraft's evacuation. All passengers and crew evacuated successfully; only slight injuries having been sustained. A second RAF Hercules aircraft was in the vicinity of the TLZ on another task and offered to provide assistance. It subsequently landed to recover the crew and passengers who were due to depart on ZH876. This second aircraft sustained minor damage on landing as a result of running through some debris from ZH876.

This damage was later repaired at its detachment base and the aircraft was quickly returned to service the next day. Due to operational considerations, ZH876 was judged to be unrecoverable. Consequently, it was destroyed by coalition forces on 13 February 2007 in order to deny enemy forces any exploitation opportunities. Following extensive investigation, the board concluded that the cause of the accident was the detonation of two arrays of improvised explosive devices (IEDs) buried along the edge of the landing strip at the TLZ. The board of inquiry commended the crew on its handling of the immediate aftermath of the explosion and the successful evacuation of the aircraft. Further, the board stated that, even if the aircraft had been fitted with explosion suppressant foam, it would not have reduced the damage sustained by the aircraft in the IED attack.

The Board of Inquiry's report, said Ainsworth, would be placed on the MoD's public website. The previous year, XV206, a 47 Squadron Hercules C1 was lost in Afghanistan. The MoD press release from July 2007 records that:

The Board of Inquiry concluded that the aircraft was destroyed by fire after detonating an anti-tank mine on the Tactical Landing Zone. The explosion caused significant damage to the aircraft's landing gear, resulting in debris puncturing the left-wing fuel tanks. In turn this caused an uncontrollable fire leading to the loss of the aircraft. The Board of Inquiry concluded that, even if the aircraft had been fitted with Explosion Suppressant Foam (ESF), it would not have prevented its loss. This is because ESF does not prevent leaks when the fuel tanks are punctured. Three passengers suffered minor injuries in the incident. The Board of Inquiry commended the crew on how they managed the situation, and for ensuring that all on board were evacuated quickly.

Some measure of the seriousness of the incident can be gauged from the MoD's recommendation that all C-130 crews operating in Iraq and Afghanistan be issued with 'Fire Retardant Combat Soldier 95 clothing' and leg holsters for personal weapons. Rifle racks were also to be fitted in the aircraft flight deck for the aircrew 'to expedite emergency egress'. Work on this was expected to be complete by the end of the year.

Acknowledgements

The nature of this book, covering over five decades of Hercules service in the RAF, has meant that I have relied on the good nature and collaboration of many veterans from the RAF and British Army (47 Air Despatch Squadron, Royal Logistics Corps) to bring these stories to life. It is not possible to thank everyone individually here, but I am eternally grateful to you all.

That aside, the project would not have been possible in the first place without the support of a couple of key people, legends in the Hercules world: Wing Commander Simon Footer RAF (retd) and Squadron Leader Harry Burgoyne RAF (retd). Si has been a supporter of the book from the outset, and without his advocacy it would never have – forgive me – taken off. Si, I am truly grateful for your time and facilitated access to the 'Wakey Wake' club of ex-Hercules operators; I couldn't have done this without you. Harry, your storytelling, experience and eye for detail have also made a major contribution to the book, and for this I will be eternally grateful. I am also happy to acknowledge the compelling source material that is Ewen Southby-Tailyour's excellent *Exocet Falklands: The Untold Story of Special Forces Operations* (Barnsley: Pen & Sword, 2014).

I would also like to thank:

Group Captain Mike Neville RAF (retd) and Sheila Gibson for sharing their very personal experiences in the wake of the loss of Hilton 22 (XV179) in Iraq. The words here will never truly be able to do justice to the loss and grief that were felt by you during this time, but thank you both for opening up and sharing your innermost thoughts.

Although, due to security restrictions, they were unable to collaborate directly in the book, Air Commodore Martin Cunningham, in his past role as President of the 47 Squadron Association, and Wing Commander James Sjoberg, as the last Officer Commanding 47 Squadron (for the time being), for their wise counsel at the beginning of the project, without which I would have gone down so many more rabbit holes than I did.

The amazing media team at Lockheed Martin, in particular, John Neilson and Stephanie Stinn, who provided access to their archive, photographs and diagrams, as well as facilitating an interview with Joshua Shani, the hero of Entebbe. The latter was a true privilege, and I am in your debt.

Brigadier General Joshua Shani IAF (retd) for taking the time out of his busy corporate schedule to talk to me in London. It was truly humbling to meet you and hear about the exploits of the first pilot in the IAF to fly the C-130 and, of course, about the Entebbe mission.

Clifford Oliver for sharing his exploits during the mission to 'save' that famous liner from a terrorist threat. It is rare to get insight into this clandestine world, and Clifford was able to share his insightful first-hand account.

My wonderful wife, Sharon, and the kids, who are always there with love and support and, obviously, to keep my feet on the ground when I start getting distracted by other projects.

The expert team at Penguin, for their faith in me and

their advice throughout the project, particularly the commissioning editor, Rowland White. Also Kit Shepherd, for his meticulous copy-editing – a details man par excellence!

A book wouldn't be the same without some great pictures and Sergeant Lee Matthews is a master in capturing aircraft at their best. Thank you for allowing me to use some of your photographs. I am also grateful to Alan Pettigrew, for sharing his personal images of the crash of Star Trek 3 (XV193).

Talking of pictures: Sir John Major for agreeing to allow the use of the photograph of him having a Guinness with the team after his mission out of Sarajevo.

This book has been a collaboration between me and my co-writer, Lynne Barrett-Lee. I would like to thank Lynne for her patience and her magic ability to translate my Scottish ramblings into something that is readable, and we would both like to express our gratitude to all the contributors.

So a huge thank you to all those 'Ascoteers' who have worn blue and brown uniforms and who have given their time and their stories so generously. Your inputs, large and small, have brought the book to life in ways we just couldn't otherwise have achieved. Thank you, Mark Baines, Garry Brown, Dave Cranstoun, Mick Crosby, Pete Edgington, Tony Evans, Luke Flemington, Dave Fry, Doug Marsh, Chris Mead, Max Roberts and Tony Webb. To those who didn't wish to be mentioned by their full names or who wanted to remain anonymous, your contribution is no less important, and I will still buy some beers. (A first, I know!)

Picture Permissions

p.1, top, Lockheed Martin; middle, US Navy / Public Domain; bottom, US Army / Public Domain

p.2, top & bottom, Crown Copyright; middle, Godfrey Mangion

p.3, top, Crown Copyright; middle, bottom left & bottom right, Squadron Leader Dougie Marsh RAF (Retd)

p.4, top left, author's own; middle, IDF Spokesperson's Unit (via Wikimedia); bottom, Public Domain

p.5, top & bottom, Collection of Squadron Leader Harry Burgoyne RAF (Retd); middle, Lockheed Martin

p.6, all, Collection of Squadron Leader Harry Burgoyne RAF (Retd)

p.7, top, Collection of Squadron Leader Harry Burgoyne RAF (Retd); middle left, Simon Footer; middle right (Crest), Crown Copyright; bottom, unknown

p.8, all, author's own

p.9, top left, Dave Cranstoun with the kind permission of Sir John Major; middle right, middle left & bottom, author's own

p.10, top, Crown Copyright; middle left, middle right & bottom, author's own

p.11, all, author's own

p.12, top, RAF; middle & bottom, Master Aircrew Lee Rogers